Debussy's Paris

Debussy's Paris

Piano Portraits of the Belle Époque

Catherine Kautsky

ROWMAN & LITTLEFIELD
Lanham · Boulder · New York · London

Published by Rowman & Littlefield
A wholly owned subsidiary of The Rowman & Littlefield Publishing Group, Inc.
4501 Forbes Boulevard, Suite 200, Lanham, Maryland 20706
www.rowman.com

Unit A, Whitacre Mews, 26-34 Stannary Street, London SE11 4AB

British Library Cataloguing in Publication Information Available

Library of Congress Cataloging-in-Publication Data

Names: Kautsky, Catherine.
Title: Debussy's Paris : piano portraits of the belle époque / Catherine Kautsky.
Description: Lanham, Maryland : Rowman & Littlefield, 2017. | Includes bibliographical references and index.
Identifiers: LCCN 2017007048 (print) | LCCN 2017009195 (ebook) | ISBN 9781442269828 (cloth : alk. paper) | ISBN 9781442269835 (electronic)
Subjects: LCSH: Debussy, Claude, 1862–1918. Piano music. | Debussy, Claude, 1862–1918—Homes and haunts—France—Paris. | Paris (France)—Description and travel. | Piano music—20th century—History and criticism. | Piano music—19th century—History and criticism.
Classification: LCC ML410.D28 K2 2017 (print) | LCC ML410.D28 (ebook) | DDC 786.2092—dc23 LC record available at https://lccn.loc.gov/2017007048

∞™ The paper used in this publication meets the minimum requirements of American National Standard for Information Sciences—Permanence of Paper for Printed Library Materials, ANSI/NISO Z39.48-1992.

Printed in the United States of America

To my husband, Dan, with love and thanks.

Contents

Figures

Preface

As a pianist and piano professor I spend most of my days playing the piano, or—so much more easily—telling other people how to play. Writing this book is an aberration, and it feels a bit foreign; I'm accustomed to hearing rather than seeing my thoughts take shape. As it happens, not only the writing, but also the music itself lies out of my comfort zone. The music I first knew and loved is the music of Vienna—Mozart, Haydn, Beethoven, and Schubert. Perhaps something is genetically transmitted about geographical origins, for both my parents grew up in Vienna, and though I am very American, that music feels like home. Or it did until a splendid sabbatical year spent in Paris in the midnineties, when all of a sudden that city became a lasting and treasured part of my life. We lived in the beautiful sixth arrondissement, surrounded by stores whose wares we could never afford, but also next door to the famous Poilâne bakery and near the incomparable Debauve & Gallais chocolate shop. I needed nothing more to fall in love with France, but as it happens the people were as special as the chocolate. Their generosity was astounding, and the value they placed on friendship was transformative. I was hooked, and I have returned to France almost every year for the twenty-some years since that sabbatical.

And so, little by little, this book was born. It emerged out of a fascination with the intimate interactions between music and social history, and nowhere, it seems to me, is that more evident than in the music of Debussy and the city of Paris. Though Debussy himself was avowedly apolitical, his compositions, or at least their titles, are so consistently referential that one can glean from a simple glossary a whole array of social issues confronting Paris at the turn of the century. And ditto for literature. Debussy is known for his sensitivity to images, and in fact we all, mistakenly or not, have happily labeled him an "impressionist," thus placing him perpetually in the company of painters. But he was at least as attuned to words, and not only his use of text and his references to stories and poems but also his thoughts and concerns themselves place him smack in the middle of the literary traditions of his time. Baudelaire, Proust, Colette, Verlaine—these are his colleagues in every sense of the word.

For me, this combination of words, music, political inference, and a wonderful city has been irresistible, and the necessity of returning to Paris again and again in order to complete research for this book has been a glorious by-product of the decision to write. For those trips, and in a larger sense, for the support of almost every project I have undertaken in the last thirty years, I have Lawrence University to thank, and in particular its very wonderful provost emeritus, Dave Burrows, who somehow, miraculously, managed to treat every faculty member as if their interests were not only his own but also absolutely critical to the world-at-large.

I also have two people, in particular, to thank for the inspiration they provided in undertaking this project. Shortly following my first sabbatical in Paris, I spent a year in London, directing the Lawrence University London Center. I was lucky enough that year to meet both Roy Howat and Paul Roberts. Both are first-rate Debussy scholars as well as superb pianists, and both have remained friends to this day, proving invaluable as I pursued this project. Roy, one of the editors of the new complete Durand edition of Debussy and the recent author of the all-encompassing book *The Art of French Piano Music*, has provided not only vital knowledge but also much personal assistance at crucial moments in my research. And to Paul, I owe the entire idea, and much of the working out, of this project. His magnificent book *Images: The Piano Music of Claude Debussy*, provided me with my first inkling of all the many strands—artistic, literary, and historical—that relate to Debussy's compositions. I returned to it several times over the years but refrained from reading it recently as I worked on this manuscript, preferring to rely as much as possible on primary sources. When I glanced at it again in preparing my final draft, I was struck (and somewhat taken aback!) by how many similarities there were between his thoughts and mine. My interests veer toward social history where his veer toward visual art, but we have used many of the same sources, and there is no question that his book, for good reason, lodged permanently in my subconscious and influenced much of my thinking as I planned the topics I'd address. I continue to find his insights brilliant and can only hope to have added a very little bit to his splendid descriptions of Debussy's larger world.

Since most of the topics in my book are well outside my area of expertise as a performer, I am beholden to any number of sources on a large variety of topics. Two spring particularly to mind: Rae Beth Gordon's extraordinary book *Dances with Darwin*, 1875–1910, which introduced me to so many of the ideas regarding the intersections of dance, race, and mental health that are mentioned in chapter 4, and Mary McAuliffe's impeccably researched books entitled *Dawn of the Belle Epoque* and *Twilight of the Belle Epoque*, which provided not only countless stimulating facts but also models of readability and lively prose.

My list of more personal helpers to acknowledge is long, and my thanks to them heartfelt. I'll start with my editor, Natalie Mandziuk, whose unflagging enthusiasm for the project, thoughtful criticisms, and constant availability has quite literally made the difference between success and failure. I have never stopped feeling grateful for her engagement, clarity of mind, and commitment. She has always been there when I needed her, and her advice is unfailingly sensible and helpful. The librarians at Lawrence University, especially Antoinette Powell and Colette Lunday Brautigam, have made my work infinitely easier, assisting with both research and the mechanics of permissions and scanning. Kim Kroeger has worked with me on logging artworks and on constructing a website; her patience and expertise have saved me many an hour of organizational work for which I'm both ill suited and ill disposed.

Next come my friends. Three wonderful friends read the manuscript in its entirety: Lisa Leizman, my dancer/philosopher friend, was the first. She read it long before it was ever even submitted for publication, and, despite being neither a musician nor a historian, she could not have engaged more fully with the subject at hand—as indeed she seems to engage with every subject (and person and creature) put before her. Betsy Blackmar, whose splendid mind and dear friendship mean more to me than I can ever say, read the entire book in a weekend when I called her desperate for advice; she subsequently spent hours providing precisely the advice I needed. And Lora Deahl has provided not only specific suggestions but also an ongoing stream of encouragement over months and even years; as another pianist/writer exactly my age, she often feels to me like an alter ego, and indeed, not only our children, but also our books have been born simultaneously. Lastly, my intrepid younger son, David Hausman, himself an erstwhile musician, read the book more than once, assuring me that all was not lost many times over when I was certain of the contrary, and fighting a valiant, though losing, battle to rid me of excess verbiage. Other lovely friends such as Marna Sternbach, Robert McDonald, and Richard Goode read portions, gave much-needed feedback, and offered support at many a crucial juncture.

Last, but so far from least that he deserves an entire acknowledgment to himself, is my husband, Daniel Hausman, who has been involved every step of the way. Indeed, he no doubt feels as if he helped to place every comma. And even had I managed the placement of punctuation without him, I certainly would never have managed the ins and outs (mostly outs) of Microsoft Word, Preview, Track Changes, and a perceived computer-takeover-of-my-world without him. When I have found it unbearable to face my computer screen for one more moment, I have turned my wayward margins over to him and returned to the joys of Debussy at a different kind of keyboard. I cannot believe my good fortune that I'm married to a man who understands *both* Microsoft Word and me.

Claude Debussy (1862–1918)

A Biographical Note

Figure B.1. Claude Debussy, 1908. Photo by Félix Nadar (1820–1910). Wikimedia Commons, https://commons.wikimedia.org/.

It's not the purpose of this volume to provide a lengthy biography of Claude Debussy but rather to view him through the lens of his piano music and the city he so fully embraced. Nevertheless, a few facts about Debussy, the man, can't help but better situate him as a mirror for the social and artistic concerns of the Belle Époque.

Achille-Claude Debussy was born in Saint-Germain-en-Laye, a suburb of Paris, on August 22, 1862, the first of five children born to Manuel-Achille Debussy and Victorine Manoury. His parents were remarkable only for their lack of remarkability. His father moved from job to job, with intimations of unreliability and dishonesty along the way. His mother was a disengaged parent who left the nurture of her children to her husband's sister, Debussy's aunt. Neither parent was educated, none of Debussy's siblings showed any notable talents, and only the father's service in the Paris Commune and subsequent jail term provide a flash of interest in the famous composer's background, though even that service would appear to have been rendered for financial, rather than ideological, reasons.

Debussy's early life was marked by embarrassment over the bony protuberances on his forehead (a form of benign tumors, which he later connived to hide with his hairstyle); frequent moves from one address to the next; and no organized education until his admission to the Paris Conservatoire in 1872, at the age of ten. One year earlier he had begun piano lessons in Cannes, at the instigation of his aunt, and later that year, on moving back to Paris, he had piano lessons with a Mme. Mauté, whose purported claims to be a pupil of Chopin's are dubious but who, nonetheless, seems to have admirably recognized and nurtured the unexpected talents of her pupil.

Upon entering the Conservatoire in 1872, Debussy began his formal education, one marked by a certain degree of success in piano, harmony, and ear training, but just as notable were his clashes with the conservative bent of this august French institution. He began composing by the late 1870s and in late 1880 entered the composition class of Ernest Guiraud, who was, by luck, an unusually open-minded member of the Conservatoire faculty willing to tolerate his pupil's unruly ways. Debussy's first publication, the song "Nuit d'étoiles," appeared in 1882, and by that time he had also written a number of other songs, a piano trio, and other smaller works. From 1880 to 1882, he joined the household of Nadezhda von Meck, the patroness of Tchaikovsky, for summer employment, and it was his travels to Russia, Italy, Austria, and Switzerland with this well-educated, upper-class family that gave him the confidence to finally declare himself a composer.

Not only Mme. von Meck but also another madame that he met shortly thereafter inspired his early compositional efforts. In 1881, Debussy found himself accompanying singing classes back in Paris, and among the pupils was a Marie-Blanche Vasnier, with whose voice and beautiful eyes he was inordinately smitten. He proceeded to compose songs for the fair lady and quite possibly to engage with her in nonmusical ways as well, despite her married state. Their supposed affair, though never confirmed, endured for several years, but her more lasting effect was to reinforce Debussy's love affair with song, a genre that happily combined his highly honed pianistic abilities, his preference for short forms, and his lifelong sympathy for the work of symbolist poets.

Songs for a beloved, however, were not enough to launch a career, and despite his reluctance to identity with the official musical establishment, Debussy twice entered its prestigious arts competition, the Prix de Rome. The competition has a dubious history of judging artistic merit, rejecting such luminaries as Ernest Chausson and Maurice Ravel along the way, but Debussy was selected on his second attempt, and in early 1885 he set off for the requisite two years at the Villa Medici in Rome. Most would hardly characterize subsidized travel to Rome as punitive or "requisite," but for Debussy it turned out to be a required torment. An unhappy traveler for much of his life, Debussy was particularly distressed to be away from Paris for such a long term and at such a sensitive juncture in his personal and professional life. His discomfiture in Rome was reciprocated, and his first "envoi," or submitted composition, sent from the villa to his eminent judges, was proclaimed "bizarre, incomprehensible, and unperformable";[1] his second, hardly better in its "highly pronounced tendency to seek out what is strange."[2]

Debussy had shown himself capable of writing conventional music or he would never have won the Prix with *L'enfant prodigue* in the first place. But clearly now, in his early twenties, he was determined to set his own path, without regard to the opinion of self-proclaimed authorities. That path proved tortuous; he was never one to compose easily or to judge his own progress with optimism. Indeed, his letters are filled with self-doubt and deprecation. The deprecation extends generously to others as well, and throughout his career he heaped scathing criticism on both himself and his peers, frequently worrying about the fate of French music in the hands of those unable to carry on the noble traditions of the eighteenth-century French masters, Jean-Philippe Rameau and François Couperin.

Thus, merciless in his assessments, frequently depressed, and self-professedly grumpy in his demeanor, Debussy did not have an easy time of it. He was perennially short of money, and had it not been for loans and allowances from beneficent friends and publishers, he would have careened from the verge of bankruptcy right over the edge. In fact, at his death he owed his publisher, Jacques Durand, 66,235 francs,[3] or approximately $189,000, a not inconsiderable sum. Never in his adult life was he able to happily reconcile his income with his expenditures.

His romantic affairs were equally studded with catastrophe. Certain of his affairs with women remain shrouded in mystery; others, such as his precipitous engagement and just as precipitous disengagement to the soprano, Thérèse Roger, in 1894, were infamous among his Paris acquaintances. Both the joining and the unjoining took place most indecorously while he was cohabiting with Gabrielle (Gaby) Dupont. Three years later, poor Gaby attempted suicide in response to her partner's infidelities, and at that point a number of Debussy's closest friends jumped ship. Debussy found himself quite alone but was undeterred from yet another romantic fiasco with his marriage to Lilly Texier in 1899. In both Gaby and Lilly, he chose long-term partners of lower class, education, and intellect than his own, and when the relationships failed, Debussy, and only Debussy, appeared relatively unscathed. Both the deserted women responded by shooting themselves. Fortunately they survived, but the same cannot be said for Debussy's remaining friendships; only a benevolent few remained loyal to their companion of the roaming eye.

The rupture with Lilly was precipitated by Debussy's 1903 meeting with Emma Bardac, the mother of one of his piano students and former mistress to the great French composer Gabriel Fauré. Emma was an excellent amateur singer and a woman accustomed to high living. By 1904, Debussy had chosen her permanently over the more modestly endowed Lilly, and Emma had left her husband as well. They didn't formally marry until 1908, but in 1905, their daughter, Claude-Emma, known as Chouchou, was born, and their union was firmly established. The union was never an easy one, and Emma is known to have seriously contemplated separation, but the marriage endured until Debussy's death in 1918, and if the marriage itself was not a source of unmitigated pleasure, their daughter, Chouchou, was the light of Debussy's life.

Meanwhile, despite the distractions of his affairs with women, Debussy needed to make his way in Parisian musical life. His tastes were expensive ones, and Emma's demands added yet more sous to the package. Debussy's income came from a combination of teaching (he taught the piano, apparently very poorly), conducting engagements (again, both his interest and his gifts were limited), annual retainer fees from publishers, and commissions for various compositions. He refused to consider any permanent full-time positions, but he did also undertake the role of journalist, earning extra income through his music criticism for *La Revue Blanche*, *Gil Blas*, and *La Revue Musical S.I.M.* He often used an alter ego, M. Croche, as a stand-in, and M. Croche spoke in diabolically uncompromising terms, condemning fashionable "music [written] to soothe convalescents in well-to-do neighborhoods" and looking doggedly for ways to save French music from inferior talents.[4]

Debussy's compositional path, like his music criticism, was divisive, and not surprisingly, it earned him plenty of enemies. Early on, he alienated the musical establishment with his new approaches to form and harmony, and throughout his life he was derided by the likes of Camille Saint-Saëns for his "absence of logic and common sense."[5] He found his identity through eschewing accepted tonal and melodic procedures and the traditional sonata forms of generations of composers. Despite his disavowal of much of the Austro-Germanic legacy, he found it hard to free himself of Richard Wagner, and the German behemoth, who was the current darling of the operatic world, was a thorn in his side. Debussy wished desperately to declare total independence, but like most other composers of the day, he couldn't quite crawl out from under those grandiose and daring ideas that linked all the arts and revolutionized harmony.

Ever searching for new ways to hear music and bring it closer to nature, he eagerly explored the exotic scales and colors he encountered at the Paris World Exposition of 1889. He found new methods of approximating speech in his great opera *Pelléas et Mélisande* and incorporated the work of the symbolist poets in both songs and his early, famous orchestral tone poem, *Prelude to the Afternoon of a Faun* (1892–1894), based on Stéphane Mallarmé's poem of the same name. It was *Pelléas*, first produced in 1902, that firmly established his fame and reputation, but he was, by that time, already on his own path, and a great deal of the piano and vocal music by which we know him today was already published. Seminal orchestral works included the *Nocturnes* (1892–1899), which imaginatively incorporated a wordless female chorus of "Sirènes" and was based loosely on poems by Debussy's friend Henri de Régnier, and *La mer* (1903–1905), a colorful three-movement evocation of the sea. Debussy was, in fact, never to write something so humdrum as a simple symphony, and the range of his allusions is striking. The later *Images* (1905–1912) for orchestra includes a movement, "Ibéria," paying special homage to Spain; another, "Gigue," is based on a poem by Paul Verlaine; and a third, "Ronde de Printemps," draws on French folk tunes. *Jeux*, written later yet (1912–1913), is a ballet score written for choreography by Vaslav Nijinsky of the Ballets Russes, its oblique plot overlaid with eroticism.

The references to images, poetry, and dance in these, his most famous works, are far from anomalous, and in fact, the Debussy oeuvre is replete not only with works completed but also with works only begun or contemplated that are based on literary themes. Throughout his life Debussy was in close contact with writers, painters, and dancers, and the list of his acquaintances reads like a *Who's Who* of the Parisian artistic scene: Degas, Bonnard, Gauguin, Toulouse-Lautrec, Redon, Rodin, Colette, Louÿs, Gide, Verlaine, Mallarmé, Proust, Diaghilev, Nijinsky, and Loie Fuller constitute only the beginnings of the catalog. In addition, Debussy himself dabbled in both art and literature; he's reported to have designed the cover of a novel by his friend, René Peter, and he toyed with playwriting himself, both writing and teaching at one point. In fact, it's the "absolute music," the music without reference to a nonmusical idea, that is rare in his oeuvre. Compositions of special note in that rubric include the early *String Quartet* (1893); the piano *Etudes*, of which we'll hear more later; and three late instrumental sonatas, for Cello and Piano (1915), for Flute, Viola, and Harp (1915), and for Violin and Piano (1916–1917). These last three mark Debussy's only overt reference to the "sonata," a form that had dominated musical history for well over a century. The sonatas signal a fascinating adieu for this revolutionary composer, who in his final years made peace with the past by reshaping a conventional form to fit his own radical ends. In so doing, he dispensed with the verbal and pictorial descriptions that had heretofore inspired his imagination, or perhaps more likely, he simply declined to share them with the listener.

Either way, those images remain firmly embedded in our experience of this composer, and they irresistibly inspire the coming discussion. With or without overt descriptions, through all his works Debussy strove to capture not just abstract musical ideas but also "the murmuring of the breeze . . . mystically mingled with the rustling of the leaves and the scent of the flowers." He believed that "music can unite all of them in a harmony so completely natural that it seems to become one with them," and it is indeed the sheer inevitability of his harmonies and colors, chosen without reference to a system, that still astounds us today.[6] He was exquisitely sensitive to nature, to words, and to images, and all three determine not only his vocal and instrumental works but also his piano music, with a force rarely encountered before or since.

Debussy died on March 25, 1918, of the rectal cancer that had been diagnosed in 1909 when he was forty-seven years old. He suffered greatly from the disease in his later years, and his illness, along with the trauma of World War I, no doubt accounts for the difficulty he reports in trying to compose at the end of his life. Despite that struggle, the works composed in that grim time—the late instrumental sonatas, the piano *Etudes*, and *En blanc et noir* for two pianos—number among his greatest compositions. Taken in toto, the range of his lifetime exploits, from cabaret to tragic opera, from cakewalk to ballet, from mere hints to coloristic swells, and, even outside of music, from drawing to creative writing, was nothing short of staggering.

Debussy's beloved daughter, Chouchou, died in 1919 of diphtheria, but the composer was no longer alive to experience that loss.

Introduction

Debussy's Paris was a city filled with contradictions, energy, and a fanatical desire to be entertained. The photo of the Cabaret de l'Enfer (literally the Cabaret of Hell) in figure Intro.1 by the famous French turn-of-the-century photographer Eugène Atget, captures the grotesque appeal of one particular nightspot, but its unabashed excess tells us about more than a single address.

Debussy, the dreamy French composer par excellence, was hardly the man one would expect to identify with such intemperance, but this is the tale of his interactions with a Paris that was confronting and deposing tradition at every turn. His lifetime, spanning the years 1862–1918, covers the entire Belle Époque, from 1871 to 1914. Those were the years of Paris's ascendance in the world of art and entertainment, as well as its infatuation with race cars, morgues, and electric lights. Though Debussy's music avoids reference to the Grand Prix or to the dead bodies on proud Parisian display,[1] it is nevertheless unashamedly referential, with descriptive titles that allow us access to his own remarkably disparate inspirations. Debussy evidenced an astonishing ability to convert social reality into musical paraphrase, and despite a persistent inclination toward self-disparagement and distrust of those around him, he absorbed Parisian trends in art, literature, politics, and popular culture with a specificity and eloquence that no other composer can begin to rival. Eighty-eight keys have never before brought to life so varied a progeny: dolls, clowns, mermaids, goldfish, and elephants; poems, essays, myths, fairy tales, postcards, and newspaper articles; paintings, illustrations, sculptures, and wall hangings; ballerinas, modern dancers, ballroom dancers, and cakewalkers; orientalism, colonialism, nationalism, and racism. The list goes on and on. Personal biography was in fact a paltry resource next to the city whose every artistic and cultural gesture took on fantastical proportions

Figure Intro.1. Cabaret de l'Enfer, 53 Boulevard de Clichy, Eugène Atget, 2nd series, 1910–1912. Cliché, Bibliothèque nationale de France.

in Debussy's imagination. So a close look at that city and its ever-evolving identities is essential to understanding this image-laden music.

In fact, Debussy's early biography seems to have impacted his future primarily through its sheer lack of joie de vivre. The so-called Belle Époque seems far removed from that poor family, the father unable to hold a steady job, the mother disconsolate at harboring a brood of five, and neither parent remotely capable of educating a musical genius. Surely these facts pushed Debussy outward and into the arms of a great and enticing city. And if the limited attractions of his parents hadn't been enough, there was the Paris Conservatoire, which he later described as "the same gloomy, dirty place we remember, where the dust of unhealthy traditions still sticks to the fingers."[2] Despite winning its top honor, the prestigious Prix de Rome, at the age of twenty-two, he wanted nothing more than to flee from both the school and the Roman villa where his prize later imprisoned him. And once he abandoned Rome for Paris in 1887, he remained in his city of birth, with only brief sojourns abroad, for the rest of his life. The city's influence on him was incalculable, and he, in turn, ensured French music a permanent position in the epicenter of twentieth-century music history.

Debussy was anything but a firebrand. He was introspective, ill at ease, and full of self-doubt. But he hated rules, and he lived by the musical dictum, "There is no theory. You have merely to listen. Pleasure is the law."[3] When he came back to Paris, he found himself in a city caught between old and new, highly ambivalent about tradition versus revolution, and committed on all sides to sensuality and entertainment. Opera, theater, and ballet flourished. The Commedia dell'arte found its home there. The circus was a nightly occurrence. Not a day passed without masked balls, both privately and publicly sponsored. The city took inordinate pleasure in theatrical disguises, and a composer such as Debussy, groping for a new and original language, not to mention a personal identity, could happily hide and thrive amid all those masks.

Cabaret de l'Enfer exhibited only one mask among many in the city, but its swagger highlighted a central aspect of this daring city. Where does a man such as Debussy fit into such overt flamboyance? Despite the fact that Debussy's music is dotted with soft pianissimos rather than booming fortissimos, he nevertheless loved the cabaret and the circus and the novelties of newfangled dance. Reticent though he may have been, his romantic entanglements provide a good deal of risqué titillation: Those two romantic affairs (one, a marriage) that ended with revolvers and rejected lovers attempting suicide were an undeniable moral question mark in an otherwise proper biography. And Debussy's early limited financial means and burgeoning literary interests allied him easily with avant-garde bohemian elements in the city—he hung out with practitioners of Theosophy and the occult, and he regularly attended events on Montmartre, where music halls featured not only accordions and French popular music but also scantily clad women and provocative dance. He wrote piano music filled with cutting-edge ragtime rhythms, and he portrayed minstrel shows that were all the vogue in hip Paris cabarets. And yet, not long before, his *Suite Bergamasque* had fêted the French clavecinistes, the keyboard composers of the ancient regime, in traditional dances and straight-laced rhythms, and his most famous early pieces were minuets, waltzes, and other dances of the French aristocracy. Impoverished early on, this was a man who later enjoyed luxury, who habitually lived beyond his means, and who eventually married a woman of wealth. Debussy inhabited multiple classes and wore as many masks as did Paris itself.

This Paris he loved was filled with blazing oppositions. While the modern connotation of Belle Époque Paris may be unmitigated beauty, peace, and carefree delight, his city was nothing if not complicated. As Debussy came of age, it was just emerging from a wrenching turn toward the modern with the Baron Haussmann's broad avenues and grandiose monuments, constructed from 1853 to 1870. At the same time, however, the Latin Quarter retained its dark and narrow byways dating from the middle ages. The city was a doppelgänger, flaunting the new and secreting itself in the old. Crowds were everywhere, flowing through the newly built shopping arcades and the glamorous department stores while poets sequestered themselves in elite salons. The city was, in Walter Benjamin's famous phrase, "The Capital of the Nineteenth Century";[4] within that city, the casual "flaneur" or stroller, whom Charles Baudelaire described as "a prince who everywhere rejoices in his incognito"[5] wandered, secure in his masked anonymity, while dancers and entertainers displayed themselves and brought fame to the city.

Paris came alive at night. Music halls thrived, stores were open until 10:00 p.m., and gas lights and then electric ones illuminated and cast shadows. Within the darkness and the shadows, courtesans such as Émile Zola's Nana and Marcel Proust's Odette held court. Men whose respectability went unchallenged by the light of day took on illicit lovers by the cover of night, losing their fortunes and their everyday "selves" as they acquiesced in love's demands. Women, such as Gustave Flaubert's Madame Bovary and Madame Arnoux, were likewise duplicitous. With or without a material mask, Parisians led a divided existence.

Those with particular government connections or artistic passions often took off for exotic locations in the new French colonies or in the Far East. The wildly successful World Expositions of 1889 and 1900 fueled those desires, and writers such as André Gide were only too happy to leave behind a straight-laced French Catholicism for a libertine existence in northern Africa. Everywhere, ambiguity reigned and identities were challenged.

As technology soared, livelihoods, class structure, and government were transformed, but there was always a residue. The aristocracy lost all privilege, although titles and attendant prestige remained. The last emperor, Louis-Napoleon, was deposed in 1870, yet monarchist parties retained popular support. Automobiles and trains belched fumes across the capital, but horse-drawn carriages traversed the city as they had for centuries.

And across the arts, modernity also collided with tradition. Designs of the Eiffel Tower were derided, but the tower then prevailed, proving perhaps that "construction plays the role of the subconscious."[6] Its designers had access to a subterranean spirit that trampled older values predominating elsewhere in the city. Manet, Whistler, and others had works refused by the Paris Salon; they thrived in the Salon des Refusés. The artificial was prominently touted as more beautiful than nature by Baudelaire and Huysmans; meanwhile, the city built massive shrines to nature along its periphery. And courtly dance schools obstinately espoused the minuet while the cakewalk and the cancan took the capital by storm. Nobody captured these paradoxes more fully than Debussy, who adored nature while showing a collector's passion for the artificial and composed wicked cakewalks side by side with proper minuets.

In a nice symbolic rendering of this hyped and ambivalent society, the famous music-hall performer, Jane Avril, moved directly from a mental hospital to the stage of the Moulin Rouge, launched into prominence by Paris's most famous insane asylum, Salpêtrière Hospital. The treatments of its psychiatrist-in-chief, Dr. Jean-Martin Charcot, were of dubious value, but the hospital's annual "bal des folles" (ball of the crazy women) transformed her twitching from an illness into an art. Agony was reinterpreted as ecstasy, and her mind was simultaneously celebrated and scorned.

The city where such contradiction was not only possible but also laudable was infinitely seductive. Anything could happen there, and its magical powers were burgeoning. The extravagant World Expositions in 1889 and 1900 ensured that "Rome is no longer in Rome, Cairo no longer in Egypt, and Java no longer in the East Indies. All that has come to the Champ de Mars."[7] Its painters, including the impressionists, the symbolists, the Nabis, the primativists, the Dadaists, and the cubists, were unequalled across the Western world, and they embraced dreams and subconscious desires, discarding the heavy rationality of the Realists. This Paris hovered consistently between the old and the new, its new architecture emboldened while an ancient city lay alongside, its politics careening from anarchism to monarchism, and its modern arts daringly reckless in the face of a population's self-righteous decorum.

And so, how can it be surprising that Debussy too embraced contradiction and found disguise an irresistible allure? Debussy's music, in turn flamboyant and mysterious, embraces both the bustle of the contemporary Parisian music hall and the stillness of classical antiquity, the clatter of a city newly replete with motorcars and subways and the meditation of artists deeply in search of mystery and symbol. More bluntly, Debussy is a chameleon. At one moment, he seems pleasantly dreamy, perhaps even innocuous, and at another, his vision of the world is godless, dark, and ominous, "an exploration of anguish," as he himself said.[8]

Like most—no, all—of us, he delights in masks. In fact, when writing music criticism, he had frequently ditched Monsieur Debussy entirely in favor of the fictional Monsieur Croche, who could register his renegade opinions without fear of retribution. More than any other composer except Robert Schumann, with whom he has intriguing similarities, Debussy makes masks and alternate personas central to his every undertaking. As I've surveyed the chapters of this book in retrospect and wondered what possible thread might unite such disparate subjects, it has seemed to me that those masks, which are indeed "a way of leaving the self, breaking connections imposed by morals, intelligence and customs,"[9] encapsulate the aspects of Paris that most appealed to Debussy. The word "masques" in French and "masks" in English is derived from Latin "masca," meaning masks, witches, ghosts, and demons. What a vast and splendid vocabulary for Debussy to draw on.

And so, as you read on, you'll encounter the Commedia dell'arte, with its famous masked characters and the balls that emerged from that tradition. You'll read about the circus and reconsider clowns who cover their faces in makeup and are by definition unknown. You'll discover minstrel shows, where whites apply blackface and pretend to have been born a different color. And then you'll reencounter the fairy tales of your childhood, where frogs emerge as princes and witches as saviors. You can cavort among mermaids and satyrs—the hybrid creatures that dominate mythology—and in a more adult universe, you can be entranced by the infinite seduction of women's hair as it covers or falsifies an image, and by the allure of the Orient, where naked bodies and illicit sex create an alternative universe. Edgar Allan Poe presides in the background, beloved by Baudelaire and Debussy alike, and reminding us that within each man, no matter where he lives, resides another man, an "Imp of the Perverse," as Poe tellingly titled one of his stories. In the world of psychoanalysis, the outer man is simply a mask for that inner imp, our irrepressible "id."

How can one resist the infinite variety of these doubles? Debussy could not, and neither could Baudelaire, Satie, Redon, Picasso, and many others. While masks sometimes enable falsehood, at other times they simply reveal that truth is complex and irreducible, ambiguous in its very essence, and it is no doubt this essential enigma that Debussy found most appealing. It jibed perfectly with his fascination with the East, whose unfamiliarity and mystery left him hypnotized. As one author reports about embracing Islam, "In the West anything that must be hidden is suspect; availability and honesty are interlinked. This clashes irreconcilably with Islam . . . where the things that are most precious, most perfect and most holy are always hidden: the Kaaba, the faces of prophets and angels, a woman's body, Heaven."[10] Debussy, in his turn, said, "Art is the most beautiful deception of all! . . . Let us not disillusion anyone by bringing too much reality into the dream" and "But music, don't you know, is a dream from which the veils have been lifted. It's not even the expression of a feeling, it's the feeling itself."[11]

The veils that Debussy lifted, generally with infinite delicacy and reluctance, were ubiquitous, and the "feeling" thus revealed was far more genuine than the "reality" he disavowed. He would have agreed that "the mask hides the face with its doubles. . . . Giving form to mystery, it is a pretense that unveils the fundamental";[12] art's deception thus exposed the deepest of truths.

To explore his music and its origins is to explore the many masks of Paris and, through them, the many ways in which humans have always chosen to disguise themselves, often revealing more in their disguise than in their unadorned state. Much of this book strays from musical analysis and meanders through historical and social phenomena, wondering often not only what possessed Debussy to go in certain, apparently bizarre, directions but what possessed his countrymen as well. For genius though Debussy may have been, neither mermaids nor blonde hair, clowns, nor cakewalks were peculiar to his individual mindset. Like every other human being in the world, he was the product of his age and nation. Though we can move to the exuberant syncopations of the ragtime *Golliwogg* while knowing nothing of the history of the cakewalk and can enjoy the serene reverberations of distant lands in *La terrasse des audiences du clair de lune* without knowing the colonial history of India, Debussy would have known both, and we enter into his world with infinitely more subtlety and comprehension if we place ourselves in his universe.

If there were a prize for artist/place symbiosis in the world of classical music, Debussy/Paris would be the winning team. They stride through the Belle Époque in tandem, and to our everlasting good fortune, Debussy's titles provide a key to their partnership.

• *1* •

Pierrot Conquers Paris

I first encountered the Pierrot in figure 1.1 in a Paris café and, a few weeks later, discovered a duplicate in a French-style bistro on Cape Cod. Pierrot, the age-old hero of Commedia dell'arte, is apparently still thriving internationally and seems happy to have bonbons emerging from every orifice.

Debussy might well have encountered a similar, if more elegant, version in his French arrondissement. Pierrot and the Commedia dell'arte were in their heyday in nineteenth-century France, despite having originated three hundred years earlier as an itinerant troupe of improvising actors across the border in Italy. Twenty-first-century Americans, and even the Commedia's closer countrymen in Europe, are hard-pressed to comprehend why Pierrot, Harlequin, Columbine, and their friends inspired such adulation, but the French poets, novelists, and painters of the Belle Époque were obsessed with these stock figures of the Commedia. Hundreds of important paintings, poems, and events explored their mysteries, and Debussy shared fervently in the general enthusiasm. Apparently he and his cohort were all reassured to find their own insecurities and instabilities so perfectly mirrored on stage by Pierrot's troubled clan, and they were mightily pleased, in addition, that the Commedia was untethered by written plots and capable of unbidden shifts without a moment's preparation. How enviable to be freed from the pesky demands of consistency, predictability, and rational explanation!

It must have been precisely that predilection for caprice and improvisation that ensnared Debussy. The ceaseless physical action, the acrobatic exploits of the players, and the bawdy humor helped as well. The Commedia was a veritable indoor street fair, and many of Debussy's piano pieces feature a similar exuberance. Pieces such as *"General Lavine"—excentric—*, the portrait of a juggler-clown, and *Minstrels*, a song-and-dance routine in blackface, are

Figure 1.1. Pierrot in the window of a Paris café. Photo by Catherine Kautsky.

heavily indebted to the Commedia and its boisterous mindset. One piano piece, *La boîte à joujoux* (The Toy Box), intended as a children's marionette show, even incorporates specific Commedia characters such as Harlequin, Punchinello, and Pierrot into the action, but whether named or incognito, the spirit of these people is everywhere. Their character is present, morphing, and ever fickle, even in the very late and relatively abstract, post-Belle Époque *Etudes*. In fact those *Etudes*, composed, paradoxically, during the most painful years of war and illness at the end of Debussy's life, seesaw more delightedly than any others between Pierrot's wit and his melancholy, Harlequin's duplicity and Columbine's naïveté, and the Commedia as both slapstick entertainment and profound commentary.

The earlier and more sedate *Suite Bergamasque*, whose very title refers to Bergamo, known as home of the Commedia, is also an obvious heir, though in a far less flamboyant vein. The *Suite*, first sketched in 1890 when Debussy was only twenty-eight and then later revised, draws its title not only from the Italian town but also from the name of a renaissance dance, the "bergamasque," which the poet Paul Verlaine (1844–1896), another Commedia aficionado, made famous. Debussy's piece is a polite compendium of dances, modeled after the dance suites of his eighteenth-century compatriots, François Couperin (1668–1733) and Jean-Philippe Rameau (1683–1764), and in another bow to those composers, Debussy includes a movement with a descriptive title, in this case, the celebrated *Clair de lune*. That was the title of a famous poem by Verlaine, and Debussy set it to music twice as a song but must have felt that a solo piano could explore new aspects. Thus was born Debussy's most well-known work of all time. The piano became the vehicle for his imagining, and the moon and its fluctuations entered into the midst of this dance suite, an otherwise cool, rather stern, classically constructed composition, most of which remains a rarity on the concert stage. Verlaine's poem is replete with contradictory images: "triumphant love" gets sung "in a minor key," fountains "sob with ecstasy," and "happiness" is something the dancers "seem not to believe in." Disguises hold sway in the deceptive light of the moon, and the world, as the soul of an unidentified loved one, is an unknown and unknowable "landscape."[1] Debussy's music likewise sways in misty harmonies and ambiguous rhythms; this poem is obviously close to the composer's own soul. Unlike most tonal pieces, *Clair de lune* avoids announcing what key it's in. Instead of beginning with its home-base pitch, it delays the arrival of that tonic for a hefty eight bars; it's just as reluctant to commit itself as is the Commedia. It undulates between groups of three notes and groups of two notes, its oscillating triplets and duplets refusing to settle on any preferred subdivision of the beat. The music exists in a land of pleasurable indecision, where major is tinged with minor, tempos take hold only briefly, and a pervasive yearning infuses Debussy's unusually long and songful melodies.

Debussy planned a later *Suite Bergamasque* as well, and though it never materialized in toto, its first movement bears the title, *Masques*, or *Masks*; a perfect ode to the Commedia's power of disguise. It's joined in the set by *L'isle joyeuse* (Joyous Island), a tribute to a painting by Jean-Antoine Watteau (1684–1721), who was yet another, much earlier, ardent fan of the Commedia. By now Debussy was in his forties, so it's clear that his obsession with the Commedia was no mere product of youthful excess or conformity, and this piece hones in on the very heart of the Commedia as it explores the subject of masks. In fact, its raison d'être appears to be an examination of six/eight meter from every possible angle. Six/eight is a veritable doppelgänger of a time signature; it does indeed consist of regular measures containing six eighth notes each, as its title claims, but that regularity is a mirage. Those six eighths can be heard grouped in either twos or threes, so the listener is consequently left perpetually (and delightfully) confused about whether there are two or three large beats per measure. Debussy was hardly the first composer to grasp the quixotic possibilities of this rhythmic trick, known as *hemiola*; Bach already enjoyed it two centuries earlier, and Brahms, in particular, was obsessed with its possibilities. But, unlike Debussy, these more absolutist German composers didn't tie their rhythmic experiments to extramusical metaphors. There's an inherent instability built into *Masques*, and the listener never knows what to expect: The music's relentless, propulsive rhythm, combined with the incessant shift from two to three beats in the measure, creates an identity crisis for Pierrot and his cronies, who lurk behind the gaunt and edgy masks. The music is nervous with its disguises, and even the middle section, potentially a moment of respite, never succeeds in banishing the percussive rhythmic figure from the opening segment; its competing melody, drawn from a pentatonic scale built exclusively on the five black notes, is far too lonely and quiet to take control of a very volatile situation. To a Western listener, ensconced for centuries in the familiarity of major and minor, those pentatonic intervals inhabit precisely the contradictory worlds to which Verlaine alludes with his "charming masqueraders" of "Clair de lune."[2] Their splashes of sound from the very tip of the piano's high registers lead a shadowy existence indeed.

But centuries separate the piano and its exotic scales, dissonance, and hard-hammering hemiolas from the Commedia dell'arte. What made these Commedia masks, entrenched in so old-fashioned a spectacle and one imported to boot, so dear to the French *espirit*? And more to the point, why would the soul of a French musical genius such as Debussy resonate so strongly to these mute shenanigans? Was it the disguises, the improvisation, the loneliness, the buried sexuality, or the renunciation of language that made the Commedia take root? Who is this lead character, Pierrot? Why does he become the idol here, and why does an earthly idol appear so often in tandem with the extraterrestrial moon? How does the French flaneur, that freshly named urban citizen who roams the streets and enjoys the anonymity of crowds, provide the audience for a passion so far afield from his own more worldly concerns? And how, on a more titillating front, do we relate the mania for Commedia costume balls, with their scantily clad women and delight in provocation, to Pierrot, who rarely succeeds in love and is himself so utterly devoid of sex appeal? What a cornucopia of contradictions and uncertainties we see. Where does Debussy fit?

We'll start with Pierrot, who, sexy or not, is the star of the show. Interestingly enough, the first Commedia plays did not include him. He seems to have made his first appearances in Molière's 1665 play *Don Juan*, and the Commedia, which played alongside Molière's comedies, gleefully usurped him. Musicians will happily recognize Molière's original Pierre as Masseto, the jilted suitor in Mozart's *Don Giovanni*, and will be glad to know that Mozart himself adored the Commedia. In fact, Mozart wrote an entire scenario for Commedia dell'arte characters for carnival season in Vienna, and he himself, in full Harlequin regalia, performed in it.[3] The crossover from high art to low art is delightfully apparent here, with the Commedia both giving to and receiving from more erudite forms of entertainment. Indeed, this convenient class mobility probably contributed mightily to the Commedia's longevity and, most especially, its triumph in nineteenth-century France. Debussy, with his lower-class family roots and longtime love for the music hall, was no doubt particularly susceptible.

Debussy's piano pieces are about Pierrot more in spirit than in name, but the songs display their heritage openly. One of Debussy's early songs, for instance, is simply entitled "Pierrot," and it's laced with references to the French folk song "Au clair de la lune," which itself is all about Pierrot and provides a nice link to the common people. Debussy's chanson fairly bristles with playful dissonance and athleticism; both piano and voice leap across great distances as if to imitate Pierrot's lithe gestures, and by the final bars only gestures remain. Words have been banished, and the singer cavorts on "ah," joining Pierrot in his mute pantomime.

At the end of the text, before "ah" wins the day, Jean-Gaspard Deburau makes a cameo appearance, so a bit of history is in order. It was in 1825, at the Théâtre des Funambules in the Montmartre entertainment district of Paris, that the most famous Pierrot of all time appeared on the scene. His name was Jean-Gaspard Deburau, and he began his career as an acrobat, emerging shortly as the enigmatic mime in floured face and billowing white blouse who was later immortalized in Marcel Carné's 1945 film *Children of Paradise*. Though perhaps most familiar to twentieth-century cinephiles in that guise, this is only one of Pierrot's many celebrated appearances. In his literary and theatrical life, Pierrot was a chameleon; he appears in countless roles, ranging from silly to desperate, and thus fills the need of legions of imaginative artists. In a dramatic scene imagined by the poet Théophile Gautier, for instance, he blithely kills his wife by tickling her feet.[4] Debussy is less macabre in his humor, but a comic piece such as *La sérénade interrompue* (Interrupted Serenade) certainly reminds us of Pierrot's ploys and foibles and places him on the receiving end of merciless abuse. Here the poor, rejected lover could easily be pantomiming his distress as he starts his amorous serenade in pursuit of a lovely lady and finds himself repeatedly and rudely interrupted, midsentence, by the harshest and crudest of dissonance. Comic timing and artfully placed cacophony defeat our hapless hero just as surely in music as they could on stage. This is farcical clowning, with no need of words to convey its plot; the doomed protagonist could as easily be garbed in Pierrot's pale robes and engaged in endless pursuit of the Commedia's duplicitous Columbine as perched beneath a Spanish villa importuning a coquettish Spanish señora.

Pierrot appears again, this time under his own name, in *La boîte à joujoux* (The Toy Box), the remarkable dance work for marionettes that Debussy wrote in 1913 with author and illustrator André Hellé. Debussy must have delighted in this project, for not only is the story a childlike fantasy of good triumphing over evil but also the score itself is a decorative masterwork, filled with stunning color illustrations and descriptive stage directions. Rarely have art, theater, and music been so imaginatively combined. The main story revolves around the love affair of a doll and a soldier, but lest we think the Commedia is no longer important to Debussy in his later years, a Harlequin and a Pierrot also emerge from that well-endowed toy box that gives its name to the composition. Like the characters themselves, the boxes are, as Hellé reflects at the beginning of the tale, metaphors for human existence: "The toy boxes are in effect a sort of town in which toys live like persons. Or perhaps towns are nothing but toy boxes in which people live like toys."[5] The implication here is that boxes, which can act as jails, and masks, which are so often a subterfuge, are really the bailiwick of human beings. Debussy puts far more faith in the dolls than in his fellow creatures. As he comments to his publisher in a letter on September 27, 1913, "The soul of a doll . . . doesn't easily tolerate the kind of humbug so many human souls put up with."[6]

These delightful dolls, eventually acted by children rather than marionettes, give insight into the quirks of humans but are far more successful at circumventing evil. The heroine here grows fat and content as many a stereotypical housewife; however, unlike real housewives, she also lives happily ever after. She starts out in a world as turbulent as *Masques* and ends up on a veritable "Joyous Island" with cupids in ascendance! Her companions, Harlequin and Pierrot, presumably accompany her into the eternal satisfaction of happy marriage. There's a nice inversion going on here, for the dolls, who emerge from their imprisoning boxes only under cover of darkness and are, in fact, nothing more than puppets wearing disguises, unequivocally defeat evil. And in doing so, they point out, by way of contrast with their own benign disguises and domiciles, the insidiously dangerous masks worn by humans and the inescapable prisons in which men and women reside. In this era, the year before the start of World War I, people's dishonesty went far deeper than the dolls' masks and with far graver consequences.

Debussy generally latched onto the less frightening aspects of Pierrot, but horror, shame, power, and hapless love, as well as laughter, are all well within the reach of this innocent-looking demi-clown. Pierrot was the only star of the Commedia who walked unmasked; his whitewashed face was something of a mask itself and more than sufficient to emphasize his isolation, his mutations, and his sorrows. He was the direct emissary to the audience, with whom everyone could identify—he was everything to everyone, and his absurdity, whether violent or laughable, captured the pervasive mood of alienation among artists and poets. That mute, pale face and baggy white costume conveyed the poets' ubiquitous melancholy and ennui to perfection. For Verlaine, "His gaiety, alas, is, like his candle, dead."[7] His torpor is paramount, rivaled only by that of his bards, who likewise existed in a state of perpetual regret.

The candle Verlaine refers to dates from that eighteenth-century French folk song "Au clair de la lune," which Debussy had also happily usurped in his song "Pierrot."[8] The folksong, which has successfully migrated across oceans and centuries, may mark the first time Pierrot was linked not only with a candle but also with the moon, a link he has never shed: "Au clair de la lune / Mon ami Pierrot" (Under the moonlight / My friend Pierrot). Later, Albert Giraud, who, in 1884, wrote the verses for Arnold Schoenberg's masterpiece *Pierrot Lunaire*, made the partnership unmistakable with his title *Pierrot of the Moon*. The moon these men imagine is a mystical presence. It is always mutating, it radiates a veiled light, and its cycles correspond to our calendar and to our fertility cycles. It exerts a mysterious gravitational pull on both the earth and its inhabitants. And its powers can drive one mad; "lunacy" is its well-chosen namesake.

Debussy was no lunatic, but he too was besotted with that moon, forever associated with the mysteries of Pierrot: for the piano alone, he wrote *Clair de lune*, *Et la lune descend sur le temple qui fut*, and *La terrasse des audiences du clair de lune*. In each case, the moon is still and serene; it resides primarily in the silvery, upper reaches of the instrument, and it moves only slowly, outside the imperatives of marching time. Remember the indecisiveness of *Clair de lune*, dwelling always in the undulating dreamland of indeterminate light. Debussy's songs and his opera *Pelléas et Mélisande* are drenched in moonlight as well, and there again the moon functions as a backdrop of quiet, though sometimes more ominous, light. The Internet now even features a website devoted to Debussy and the moon; note that the sun, far too bright and revealing for Debussy's tastes, rates neither composition nor website. Love, mystery, and truth, as well as madness, tend to reside in shadows and reflections.

And yet comedy apparently resides with the moon as well. For the "amour," or lover, of the unlucky lady pictured in figure 1.2, the moon's crescent shape was more evocative of breakfast than eternal love. There's a kind of friendly madness here, and that's a segue to the friendliness with which many nineteenth-century artists regarded madness in general. After all, lunacy entailed a liberating freedom from conformity, rationality, and morality.[9] For artists such as Debussy who felt estranged from society, madness could be a welcome escape, and the moon was an ally. Debussy would have enjoyed the moon's bit part cast as melon rather than aphrodisiac.

Here, two possible lunatics confer: "Tell me, sweetheart, does the moon make you dream of love?" "No, it reminds me that, this morning, I ate melon."

Figure 1.2. "Dis, mon chéri, la lune te fait rèver d'amour?" "Non . . . elle me rappelle que, ce matin, j'ai mangé du melon." ("Tell me, sweetheart, does the moon make you dream of love?" "No, it reminds me that, this morning, I ate melon.") ***Le Rire, Nouvelle Série*****, no. 28, August 15, 1903, cover.**

Sometimes the madness partakes of sadism rather than breakfast. The Pierrot of Giraud's verses thinks nothing of drilling a hole in Cassander's skull through which to smoke his pipe,[10] though his bravado deserts him when the vengeful moon threatens decapitation. He wasn't alone in his murderous impulses. A song printed in the turn-of the-century *Courrier français* was as eager to color the moon as blood red as he. It intoned, "During the night, thick and dark, / Succeeding pale day / Suddenly the red moon rose / The full moon all in blood. / I had fear of the gold, I had fear of the blood. / It was red and it was like the guillotine appearing."[11]

Debussy incorporated that same bloody moon, "full, setting, and blood-red,"[12] in his sketches for his opera *The Fall of the House of Usher*, based on Poe's gruesome tale of incest and destruction. The moon, blood, madness, and the night were indissolubly linked, and our friend Pierrot of the Moon existed in that same twilight zone between lover and murderer, beloved fool and vengeful executioner. "He would create fear if he didn't make us laugh, this mute being who emerges at night by the light of the moon," intoned the ever-observant *Courrier français*.[13]

So it was that this sexless, mute, and anonymously clad character proceeded to enthrall a city rife with illicit sex, poetry, and fashion, and the crowd scenes he engendered are both cause and effect of his epic popularity. His lonely role set him apart, yet he was, in fact, never alone; his performances about solitude provided the perfect excuse for a crowd to gather. And those crowds were newly welcomed in Paris, lauded in poetry by Charles Baudelaire and cultural commentary by Walter Benjamin. This was the age of the immortal flâneur, or stroller, immortalized in Baudelaire's *Painter of Modern Life* (1863) as "the passionate spectator," who adores life among the multitudes and simultaneously cherishes the anonymity granted him at the very center of action. "For the perfect flâneur, for the passionate spectator, it is an immense joy to set up house in the heart of the multitude, amid the ebb and flow of movement, in the midst of the fugitive and the infinite."[14] These flâneurs swelled the audiences for any street entertainment, and Debussy was the perfect case in point: a public presence who drew nourishment from every corner of Parisian life and at the same time a citizen whose inner life could scarcely have been more private.

That ambivalence toward public versus private existence occurs in music too, and Debussy's twelve *Etudes* illustrate the conundrum. Composed in 1915, toward the end of his life, they are dedicated to and inspired by Chopin's two sets of études, twelve apiece, which are unabashedly virtuosic in their conception. Debussy took a genre meant to impress the public and used it to reveal his most intimate fantasies, leapfrogging irrepressibly from one mindset to the other. The *Etudes*, his last substantial pieces for solo piano, are such a striking musical incarnation of the Commedia temperament that they sum up an entire lifetime of Debussy and Pierrot in cohabitation. Like the Commedia, they present a daring combination of physical demands and emotional extremes, and nowhere in Debussy's works are patrician sensuality and low comedy more strikingly juxtaposed. Like so much twentieth-century music, they happily dispense with connective tissue between disparate thoughts, and they move from one emotional world to another with no attention given to trail markers. This is precisely what the Commedia encouraged in Pierrot, and it's fun to watch Debussy, too, bounding from the voice of angels to the temptation of devils with never a backward glance.

Indeed, if the *Etudes* represent Debussy's piano writing at its most adventurous, we owe that daring to the Commedia. The very essence of their modernity resides precisely in the ways they resemble Commedia dell'arte—their violent contrasts, their unpredictability, and their use of farce and trickery. Their capriciousness seems to dispense with a rational universe once and for all. It's easy to listen to them and imagine "Pierrot fâché avec la lune" (Pierrot angry with the moon), the title Debussy, according to some sources, contemplated for his *Cello Sonata* of the same year. It's a nice image: Pierrot shaking his fist at the moon as the music chuckles at his hopeless, ill-starred efforts. Humor and paradox are as deeply embedded in this music as they are in the Commedia, and the sheer physicality of études as a genre brings us closer yet to Pierrot, whose every motion communicated a nuance of elemental feeling. Compare these works to Chopin's. The latter are unfalteringly dazzling, with each étude a single-minded study in a particular pianistic challenge. Debussy, like Chopin, puts the pianist through his paces, but unlike Chopin, he eschews consistency of tempo, rhythm, and texture in pursuing those goals; he chooses instability over stability—and thus marks himself a modern man.

The French poet and writer Théodore de Banville (1823–1891), one of the first writers Debussy set to music, was particularly keen to describe the Commedia as a metaphor for the ill-fated caprices of life: "[You] fill your glass so that another can empty it, [you] surrender to a barber who cuts off your nose."[15] Likewise, no sooner do you invest in one heartfelt musical phrase in the *Etudes* than you're mercilessly catapulted toward its antithesis. Best to be less trusting, a philosophy congenial to skeptical crowds, antisocial individuals such as Debussy, and music that delights in the unexpected.

Those crowds, hungry for diversion, were gathering in all corners of Paris, and masked balls were the natural outgrowth of all this pleasure in disguise, anonymity, and amorality. Masks, costumes, revelry, and decadence moved shamelessly into private salons and public settings, and Debussy was surrounded by masks at the opera, the cabarets, and the homes of friends. Across Paris, at party after party, stock characters from the Commedia mingled with lesser-known masked figures, and reports, pictures, and cartoons festooned the periodicals. Though occasionally chaste, more often the suggestive images scattered throughout the press testify to the intimate connection between masks and sexual freedom, as is evident in figure 1.3.

Figure 1.3. "Qui n'a pas son masque?" (Who does not have his mask?) *Le Courrier français* 17, no. 11, March 18, 1900, 7, BnF.

Relieved of their everyday identities, participants were free to acquire alter egos as Pierrots, Harlequins, or simply nude imposters. And more and more authors assimilated Commedia personae into their own, often happy to trade or augment their own identities for ones less fixed and more amusing. Among the smitten were Baudelaire, Verlaine, Huysmans, Flaubert, and Mallarmé, to name just a few. Many were intrigued by the same sexual innuendos as the daring couple in figure 1.3. Jules Laforgue, for instance, who was born just two years before Debussy in 1860, made an amorous Pierrot the centerpiece of his poetry, with many of the poems entitled "Complaints." His disgruntled, silly, and ever-so-human Pierrot arrives replete with a beardless face in cold-cream and the air of a hydrocephalic asparagus,[16] but despite that moist face and the bloated airs of a most unnatural asparagus, sex is very much on his nervous mind. He defines himself as "a man about the moon,"[17] and in "Complaint of the Outraged Husband,"[18] his stand-in proposes to drill a hole through his wandering wife's skull, coincidentally the same kindly approach Giraud's Pierrot undertook a year later with the unfortunate skull of Cassander.

Pierrot, no matter under whose authorship, exults in abusive behavior and complains about everything under the sun, or rather the moon. Debussy, with his own history of disgruntled lovers, must have quite enjoyed the ruffian's unpunished crimes and the permission to be defiantly noncompliant. He had, after all, complained in an 1897 letter about his first deserted lover, Gabrielle Dupont, "you can't wipe out a mouth's kisses or a body's caresses by passing an india-rubber over them. It'd be a handy invention, an india-rubber for removing adultery."[19] Pierrot was apparently well equipped with his own india rubber when it came to ungentlemanly behavior, and Debussy, whose real life as well as musical plots dealt often with infidelity, was a ready-made aficionado. This vulnerable, yet violent, timid, and insolent personage, "is all that our imagination wants him to become . . . he is our incarnation,"[20] and Debussy exults in the exoneration he offers. His blank face allows not only for deletion of past transgressions but also for instantaneous, magical, and mysterious transformation. No explanation or justification is required; only intimations are provided. Debussy loved that poetry of innuendo and felt a deep kinship with these artists of pantomime.

And he wasn't alone. With a range from shattered skulls to ticklish toes and hydrocephalic asparagus, who could resist? How fitting that when Picasso painted *Three Musicians* in 1921 (see figure 1.4), two of the three musicians, Pierrot and Harlequin, were characters from the Commedia. Music, masks, and the Commedia remained indelibly linked, and Debussy could have happily painted himself into that picture along with the thousands of other flâneurs in Paris.

Figure 1.4. *Three Musicians*, 1921, Pablo Picasso, Museum of Modern Art, New York. © 2016 Estate of Pablo Picasso / Artists Rights Society (ARS), New York.

• 2 •

Clowns, Poets, and Circus Daredevils

Pablo Picasso, Claude Debussy's contemporary in Paris, may well have encountered his Pierrots and Harlequins at the circus rather than the theater, and that's where he would have found the dog whose tail peaks out slyly from between the legs of Harlequin in *Three Musicians*.

The line between the Commedia and the circus in Paris 1900 is ill defined at best, and performances by Commedia characters often took place at circus venues. Their acts, filled with slapstick humor and daring acrobatics, were a perfect fit. Unlike the Commedia, the circus is a well-known commodity in our modern world, but its wild popularity among Belle Époque Parisian artists is still decidedly puzzling to our sensibility. It's hard to imagine recent artistic luminaries such as Leonard Bernstein, John Updike, or Georgia O'Keeffe trotting nightly to the circus! Nevertheless, Picasso literally went daily, and Debussy was equally enthusiastic, if not as diligent. They found the clowns, acrobats, wild animals, and vaudeville variety irresistibly alluring, and they were hardly alone: Degas, Toulouse-Lautrec, Renoir, and Seurat were similarly smitten. Poets too were galvanized by the spectacle. In fact, the writers, painters, clowns, and Debussy all hung out together after the shows at the Irish and American bar Reynolds, where they drank and exchanged tales of daring. It's no surprise that Debussy was enamored enough to immortalize a later clown in his prelude *"General Lavine"—excentric*—as well as provide music befitting a circus in other works with less clear subject headings.

First and foremost, the artists seemed to identify with the circus personnel, drawing a strong parallel between their own situation and that of the itinerant entertainer. They were outsiders, alone and unappreciated. Examine the painting in figure 2.1 by Fernand Pelez (1843–1913) and the misery of the circus performers becomes evident. Pelez wasn't alone in stressing deso-

Figure 2.1. ***Grimaces et misères: Les saltimbanques,*** **1888, oil on canvas, Fernand Pelez, Musée du Petit Palais, Paris. Sotheby's.**

lation; this spectacle, replete with painted smiles and spangled outfits, was deeply unsettling to many an observer. In *Le vieux saltimbanque* (The Old Showman), Baudelaire, known as the father of the symbolist poets, immortalizes an "old poet without friends, without family, without children, brought down by misery and public ingratitude, into whose booth the forgetful world does not wish to enter any longer!"[1] A contemporary account in *Le Courrier français*, accompanied by a festive drawing, meditates on the dangers clowns encounter, noting bluntly that, despite their apparent good cheer, laughs and bravos may scarcely compensate for a broken neck.[2]

And similarly disheartening paintings about the circus abound. In some paintings, acrobats hang on for dear life, in others they cavort with skeletons, and in yet others they stare with blank faces, bereft. What attracts us to these people? There's a religious element here. In fact, in a newly irreligious world, maybe the circus provides the same death-defying, shared ritual that faith provided in an earlier day. It provides not only community but also heroes. The great painter, Marc Chagall, another Parisian resident and inveterate admirer of the circus, experienced his circus figures as pseudo-Christ figures; they crossed between the human and the superhuman and were martyred in the process. And the poet Théodore de Banville, whose work Debussy had set already back in 1883–1886, sent his most famous literary acrobat flying up into the stars, fearlessly orbiting, presumably into heaven and continuing through eternity. His man goes higher, ever higher, into the stars, reaching for the unreachable in a physical act of daredevilry commensurate with the spiritual risks incurred by artists, and finally breaking through a barrier always assumed impermeable.[3]

Debussy, though not a bona fide daredevil, also stormed barriers and probably liked to imagine being propelled into the heavens as well. Unlikely to arrive there on a trapeze, he depended on music for locomotion and had to settle for the lesser accolades accorded a sedentary composer. But he wanted his rightful place in the circus world. In a famous conversation with the clown Footit, he made the bargain explicit:

> FOOTIT: Monsieur is an artist?
>
> DEBUSSY: But you, too, monsieur, I believe . . .
>
> FOOTIT: No, I am a clown.
>
> DEBUSSY: That's also art.
>
> FOOTIT: The art of getting kicked and performing pirouettes.
>
> DEBUSSY: We musicians too, we too sometimes make harmonic pirouettes, and we also get kicked.[4]

And in a later article, he caustically notes that "the attraction of the virtuoso for the public is very like that of the circus for the crowd. There is always a hope that something dangerous may happen: Mr. X may play the violin with Mr. Y on his shoulders; or Mr. Z may conclude his piece by lifting the piano with his teeth."[5]

Artists got exploited and kicked, and in a masochistic touch, they bragged about it. They clearly both celebrated and rued their isolation, and perhaps there was a certain sadistic satisfaction in going to the circus and watching others take blows. The performers and artists together could imagine themselves as a tight group of insiders outside the mainstream, both suffering and delighting in that exclusion and exclusiveness. On the one hand, they were alone, hurting, with nothing practical to show for their Herculean efforts, yet simultaneously, they whirled on tiptoe, performing pirouettes and achieving the unachievable in less worldly terms. Debussy's favored team, Footit and Chocolat, achieved both insider and outsider status within one act, for Chocolat was black, and his role consisted in receiving kicks from Footit, as is obvious in figure 2.2.

Jean Cocteau, in fact, described Chocolat as "a stupid negro in tight black silk pants . . . serving as a pretext for blows."[6] Race opened the floodgates when it came to dominance and subordination, inclusion and exclusion, and like most everyone else, artists liked to perceive themselves as both victims and perpetrators. Debussy was no different from others; he identified with the dominant side on race, but when it came to being an artist, he took some pleasure in being a victim as well.

Other aspects of the circus were equally bewitching in their ambiguity, for the circus, unlike the real world, allows for opposites to coexist. Animals are both wild and tame. Clowns are simultaneously happy and sad. Acrobats are both human and superhuman. Even sexuality is ill defined. Are these

Figure 2.2. ***Footit et Chocolat*, 1895, lithograph in black, Henri de Toulouse-Lautrec (1864–1901), National Gallery of Art, Washington, DC.**

performers even people? They have no homes but live in tents. They do not speak. They consort with beasts and communicate through bodily gesticulation. They are situated in a sexual no-man's-land: Guillaume Apollinaire identifies harlequins as "neither male nor female,"[7] and the character Jean des Esseintes recalls a circus acrobat who undergoes "an artificial change of sex . . . in short, after being a woman to begin with, then hesitating in a condition verging on the androgynous, she seemed to have made up her mind and become an integral, unmistakable man."[8] These hermaphrodites, with their wigs, masks, and makeup, are reminiscent of people far away on whom we pin our desires and from whom we stay aloof. Perhaps they remind us of our childhoods, before sexuality or even language has taken hold, when we can in some vague way still be all things, good and bad, male and female.

Artists, poets, and novelists delighted in these ambiguities. For Picasso, whose circus pictures number more than most artists' entire oeuvres, the combination of masks, loneliness, athletic skill, bodily deformity, and kinship with animals in the circus provided a cornucopia of inspiration. His circus athletes seem to defy death, courting eternal life just as artists do through their

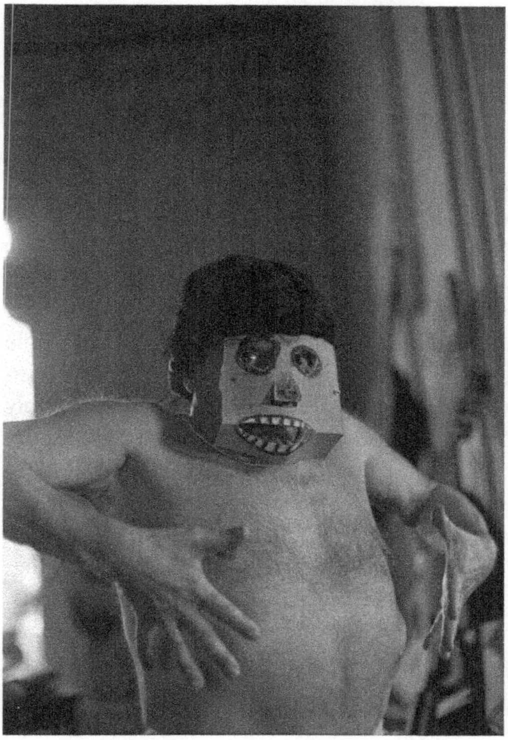

Figure 2.3. ***Picasso with a Mask,*** **1957, David Douglas Duncan (1916–). Photography Collection, Harry Ransom Center, University of Texas at Austin. © David Douglas Duncan.[10]**

undying words and etchings, and lest we miss the parallel, he paints himself into pictures as a frequent guest Harlequin. Picasso was clearly as bewitched by "l'attrait du gouffre" (the attraction of the abyss) as was Banville, who coined the phrase.[9] And he saw the human face as an abyss, a blank slate, as well, thereby moved to create countless circus masks, sometimes empty ones, sometimes with himself inside and sometimes created for his daughter. They play off the African masks that had long enthralled him, and their primitivism, evident in figure 2.3, emphasizes the lowbrow nature of the circus.

Music does well at conveying analogous masks and the lowbrow frivolity of the circus. Musicians like the idea that an identity can be slipped on and off, and doppel-, triple-, and quadruple-gängers translate well on the multivoiced piano, as Robert Schumann (1810–1856) pointed out tirelessly a century earlier. Debussy had early on arranged some of Schumann's music for two pianos and must have felt a kinship for Schumann's great piano cycle *Carnaval,* which features a veritable parade of masked friends. Pierrot makes an appearance, as do Harlequin, Pantalone, and Columbine, along with Chopin, Paganini, and Schumann's alter egos, Eusebius and Florestan. Schumann revels in similar identity switches in his piano piece *Papillons*, based on Jean-Paul Richter's book *Flegeljahre*, and the masked ball that forms the centerpiece of that novel was also right up Debussy's alley. He might not have taken the same delight Schumann did in Richter's long and convoluted Germanic descriptions, but he would have been equally smitten with the identical twins whose hopeless entanglement with one another drives the plot.

The great French circus novel, Edmond de Goncourt's *Zemganno Brothers*, similarly tells the tale of two brothers locked together in success and failure and literally dependent on one another for sheer life, but the language here is more streamlined; the descriptions, less copious. The Goncourt brothers were towering literary and social figures of the day in Paris, and Edmond's tale came out in 1879, just as Debussy was coming of age. He would have been spellbound by its story of the two brothers, Nello and Gianni, inextricably linked through their heroic acrobatic feats and doomed finally to tragic failure when one brother catapults the other to disaster. The circus is conveyed in all its glitter, replete with props galore, but the "lovely things" and "fascinating . . . tricks" were only one side of the coin.[11] The similarities between the gestures of acrobats and those indicating physical and mental illness are striking: "Every movement, however involuntary, was shot through with melancholy. . . . Nello could not keep his body still . . . he felt as if he was being magnetized by some unknown force . . . as if his nerves were forced to obey the impulses of some barbaric, leaping, electrical, natural force."[12]

For all intents and purposes, the brothers' lives were wired together, shot through with a single current, and that state of oneness when two minds become one—or its converse when one mind becomes two—partook of both magic and psychosis. Music, with its ability to convey two states simultaneously, may express the paradox better than any other art, and Debussy learned a lot from Schumann's pervasive masks and his reliance on literary sources such as E. T. A. Hoffmann (1776–1822) and Jean-Paul Richter (1763–1825) for inspiration. Both composers were fascinated by words and the piano as storyteller; both made use of quotations, fragments, and interruptions in an effort to convey multiple personalities. Both composers even took on alternate personae in their critical writings, Debussy as M. Croche and Schumann as Florestan and Eusebius. Above all, the two composers shared a fascination with shifting meters and moods whose very identity resided in their perpetual instability. *Masques*, or *Masks*, discussed in the previous chapter, is the perfect illustration. And just as *Masques* puts on and off its metric groupings, never establishing whether six is actually three times two or two times three, so artists and writers across the centuries have assiduously applied and removed their own masks. Debussy's own selfhood was brittle, though far more stable than Schumann's. He was estranged from his parents, estranged from former lovers, ill at ease with the public, and caught between love and hate for German music. Is it any wonder that he loved the circus, where he was surrounded by others in flux?

Debussy wasn't the only French composer to feel that way. Those before and after followed suit. Consider Camille Saint-Saëns's (1835–1921) *Carnival of the Animals* or Igor Stravinsky's (1882–1971) *Circus Polka* as leading examples. And in fact, the circus received its most famous musical enactment in 1916–1917 when painter Pablo Picasso (1881–1973), composer Erik Satie (1866–1925), dancer Michel Fokine (1880–1942), and writer Jean Cocteau (1889–1963) all turned their considerable talents to the collaborative creation of *Parade*. A bizarre creation it was. The year 1916 marked the beginning of the European Dadaist movement, and this show was a meditation on that very emptiness that Dada thrived upon. It features a circus bereft of spectators, an announcer touting acts that no one comes to see, a plot with no narration, random pistol shots, and shrieking sirens. This show was a testament to a futuristic world in the grip of change but change to no avail. Debussy saw it performed in Paris and was probably appalled at the crudeness of the sounds and sentiments, while sympathetic to the circus metaphor. Debussy and Satie had a long history together. They'd suffered the Conservatoire and adored the cabaret Chat Noir in tandem. Their aesthetics diverged, but they shared a fierce desire to rid French music of German domination. And it's no coincidence that they met on the common turf of the circus, the French musician's perfect retort to Valhalla, Wagner's home of overblown gods and superheroes. Unlike the painters and poets, they chose to paint it with merriment, not despair.

For Satie, the circus was a perfect setting for the absurd, the reduction of life to meaningless yet entertaining acts. Cocteau's opined that Footit, the clown, "brought into the ring the atmosphere of a diabolical nursery, where children could rediscover their sly malice,"[13] and Satie was happy to join him there. His ostensible innocence and cheery tunes may have conveyed bad news on the existential front, but there was no reason not to dance to their ragtime rhythms in the interim. For Debussy, the circus was less about ulterior motives or existential proclamations. Rather, it represented a diversion from the abyss, even a chance to redeem one's experience through daring and primitivism. The circus animals who turn up in his "Pas d'éléphants" from *The Toy Box* exude primeval innocence, and the kindly elephant who befriends Chou-Chou in "Jimbo, the Elephant" from *Children's Corner Suite* is similarly well disposed. It's no coincidence that this is the music of children. Not all nurseries were diabolical, and Debussy was living proof that, as Baudelaire grandly proposed, "genius is nothing more than *childhood recovered* at will."[14]

We can see the childlike proclivities in all Debussy's pieces about the Commedia dell'arte and the cakewalk, but our very best shot at seeing the composer/genius, clown, and child all wrapped up in one is *"General Lavine"—excentric—*, Debussy's portrait of an actual clown, from the second book of *Preludes*. Lavine is an engaging character and would clearly have slipped into total oblivion were it not for Debussy's doting attentions. General Lavine was an American clown (1879–1946), whose act Debussy witnessed in Paris. According to some sources, there had been discussions about Debussy writing music for a show with Lavine, but nothing came of it. Edward Lavine, who was born in New York and died in California, emerged from a workingman's career to appear in 1910 and 1912 at Paris's Théâtre Marigny. A multipurpose specialist, he juggled, walked on stilts, played the piano with his toes, and performed as "General Ed Lavine, the man who has soldiered all his life." He's reported to have "seemed to be at least 9 feet high," and no doubt his American pedigree and outsize stature made him all the more enticing to the French, to whom American brawn presented a decided fascination. He performed in Europe frequently from 1910 into the 1920s, but his act must have eventually fallen into oblivion, because he then settled back in the United States where he took up the very mundane manufacture of service bars, the campaign ribbons worn on military uniforms.[15]

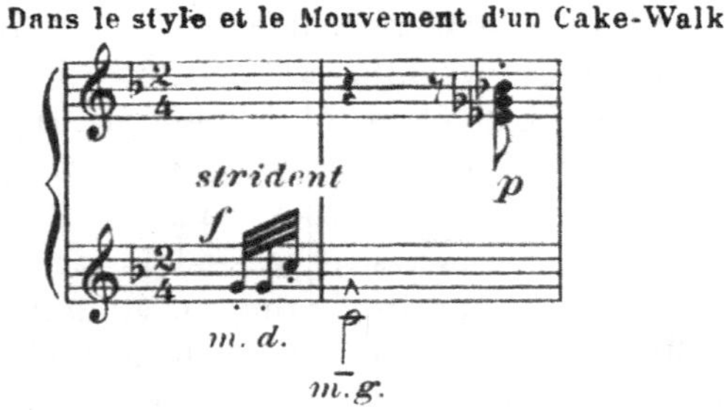

Figure 2.4. ***"General Lavine"—excentric—*, m. 1, in *Preludes, Book 2*, by Claude Debussy (Paris: Durand, 1913). Digital image from Hathi Trust Digital Library.**

Debussy's immortalization of Lavine is his only acknowledged portrait of a real person. And while he was at it, he took on the general tumult of the circus as well, clearly reveling in its bedlam. A look at the music itself, as in figure 2.4, confirms his intentions. The strident middle C in the left hand that opens the piece so incisively is immediately negated by an E♭ minor chord in the right hand, the two hands impersonating entertainers who've neglected to communicate with one another about something as basic as the key of their show! Or perhaps these are two brothers (twins?) who are not on speaking terms? After all, the key of C shares barely a note with E♭ minor.

Regardless of their relationship, these chords seem to get along only by ignoring one another. Such are the advantages of a pianist having two independent hands! What follows their opening exchange is catchy cakewalk music; General Lavine is blasé about his routine, and despite rude interruption—perhaps by that recalcitrant brother—he always sets off again, unperturbed, on his merry way, that is until the middle section, where the brisk opening chords suddenly slow down, barely recognizable in their new morose state. It's not until the determined clown alights upon yet another transformation, this one the barely recognizable riff on "Camptown Races" in figure 2.5, that his outlook improves.[16] He's probably proud, like Debussy, to show that cakewalks, like "Camptown Races," originated in the pre–Civil War era, and disguising his brilliance makes him feel all the more clever.

Figure 2.5. ***"General Lavine"—excentric*, mm. 51–52, in *Preludes, Book 2*, by Claude Debussy (Paris: Durand, 1913). Digital image from Hathi Trust Digital Library.**

When the chords come back yet again at the end, setting off a veritable explosion of offbeat accents and dissonance, we're happy to find General Lavine trotting off in a blaze of tonal glory. He has triumphantly surmounted the difficulties posed by those wayward triads with their many identity crises, and his jaunty self-esteem has remained intact despite all the obstacles he's encountered. In the end, Lavine seems to have been a clown who sets his topsy-turvy world aright; Debussy must have appreciated that confidence amid his own more tremulous world. He looks altogether jolly in the sketch in figure 2.6 by Charles Gir (1883–1941) and like a smug general indeed in the poster in figure 2.7 by Paul Colin (1892–1985).

Despite General Lavine's obvious charms, he was, of course, a relatively minor figure in the history of the circus, and aside from Debussy and a couple of minor artists, no one seems to have paid him great mind. But the circus was a phenomenon far larger than one clown, and in a bigger sense, these clowns are mirrors of our irrational, none-too-happy selves. Baudelaire, Banville, Picasso, Toulouse-Lautrec, Chagall, and countless others tell us so with far less mercy than Debussy. We may keep our distance from these performers through awe, laughter, or disdain, but as we ogle them, we are inescapably filled with envy, respect, and dread. Small wonder that clown phobias are a persistent cause of serious mental distress, even today. Debussy steered clear of terror in his portraits of Lavine, Golliwogg, and his marching elephants, but in his own life the abyss loomed large, and the tightrope he walked was far from secure despite the sure-footedness of his musical stand-ins.

Figure 2.6. ***Clown "Général Lavine,"*** **Charles Gir. Bibliothèque nationale de France, Department of Performing Art, reading room, cote: 4-O ICO-2-82.**

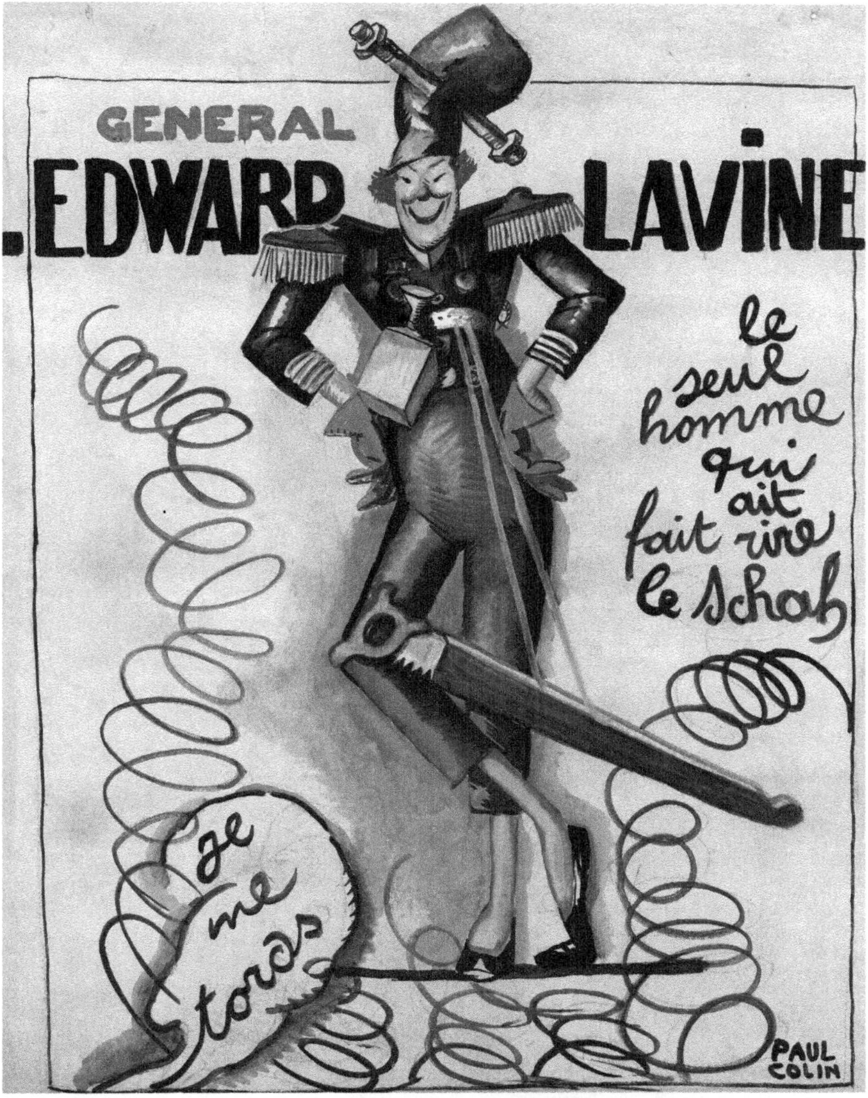

Figure 2.7. *General Lavine, le seul homme qui ait fait rire le schah*, 1925, Paul Colin, La Bibliothèque-musée de l'Opéra. © 2016 Artists Rights Society (ARS), New York / ADAGP, Paris.

• 3 •

Dance Steps out of Line

"There is but one true music . . . whether it borrows the rhythm of a waltz (even one from the café-concert) or the imposing frame of a symphony. And why not admit that of the two, good taste will often be on the side of the waltz, while the symphony will scarcely hide the pompous heap of mediocrity!"[1] Thus, in 1913, toward the end of his life, Debussy put those German symphonists in their place and inveighed in favor of more modest musical undertakings. As we shall see, he had held this opinion for a long time.

Dance, as an entertainment art, is of a piece with the Commedia and the circus; the three flourished simultaneously in the Belle Époque, sharing audiences and performance venues. But the history of dance is far more complicated politically—here we encounter a divide between high and low art and plenty of class friction as a result. Since dance is found in Debussy's music from its very beginnings, it seems wise to look at how its radically changing meanings chart real upheavals in society. Though many of his important dance pieces are treated in other chapters as well, here we'll take a glance at them as a group.

Just a quick perusal of the early works shows how strong Debussy's attraction was to dance from the very start. He was truly the son of Chopin and Fauré, and we're reminded irrefutably of the differences between nineteenth-century French and Germanic piano music when we look at his work. The Germans and Austrians were following in Beethoven's footsteps; they were writing sonatas and large-scale works that grappled heroically with form and fate. The French were writing miniatures where beauty of sound and instrumental color were paramount. Brahms and Schubert wrote exquisite waltzes, but one would hardly claim these as their major legacy; their greatest works are far more "serious" statements, and their little dances, though charming, are peripheral. And for their predecessors, Mozart and Beethoven, dances are barely in the picture. But for the Parisian Chopin, it's the mazurkas, the waltzes, and the polonaises that are irreplaceable. Likewise, in orchestral works, one is hard-pressed to discover many ballet scores by Mahler and Bruckner, but as these Austrian composers churned out gargantuan symphonies, Debussy, Ravel, and Stravinsky wrote for dance. Not only did Debussy write expressly for ballet, but also, as we shall see, works such as the *Nocturnes* were choreographed by the modern dancer Loie Fuller, and some of his most famous piano works, such as the *Petite Suite* and *Suite Bergamasque*, are compendiums of various dance forms.

The tradition of ballet in France goes way back to the court of Catherine de Medici in the 1500s and to the works of Lully and the formation of the Paris Opera Ballet in the late 1600s under Louis XIV. Louis XIV not only produced ballets at Versailles but also apparently even danced in them himself! In fact, all the venerable traditions of formal dance, including both ballet and the many forms of ballroom dance in France, are easily traced back to the monarchy, with its many rituals and its vast *richesse*. The formal steps, elegant costumes, ornate wigs, and impeccable manners of baroque dance were perfect symbols of wealth and aristocracy, and the lavish entertainments Louis XIV staged at Versailles displayed them with aplomb. For him, consummate showmanship signified consummate power; there was no better way to assert the supremacy of France.

The later French were far from tone deaf when it came to echoes of that ancient regime and time-honored tradition, and in the nineteenth century, with a society still partially awash in monarchist sentiment, the revival of such dances couldn't fail to indicate some nostalgia for the old order. The conservatives, whose most powerful monarchist proponent was General Georges Boulanger, had threatened a takeover in 1889, and meanwhile, from the other side, freewheeling anarchists were throwing bombs and publishing incendiary position papers throughout the 1880s and early 1890s. There's no indication that Debussy chose to take his place with extremists of either persuasion; in fact, throughout his life, he remained leery of politics, apparently regarding government as a necessary evil with few accomplishments to its name. Despite being the son of a Paris Communard, he seems not to have inherited his father's left-leaning political activism, and despite his fondness for courtly dances, there's no indication that he was always of right-wing political inclination either. Merely dancing a minuet—or writing one—didn't consign one to the reactionary peripheries, and the old dances were appropriated by citizens across the political spectrum.[2]

Nevertheless, old dance forms were potent cultural weapons,[3] and even in Mozart's time they could convey class allegiance or hostility. Consider "Se vuol ballare" (If You Want to Dance) from act 1 of Mozart's *Marriage of Figaro*. It's the quintessential example of class warfare musically encoded; it's art with a dagger. An aria cloaked in courtly minuet guise, it allows Figaro, an upstart servant, to usurp the count's rightful aristocratic dance and boast that the count shall step to *his* tune, rather than vice versa. The play that inspired the libretto was banned; and the opera, regarded as suspect—for good reason: Its bottom-side-up view of society proved prescient, and the arrival of the French Revolution a mere three years later proved the point.

Debussy was born only seventy-three years after that 1789 Revolution, and the intervening decades had been rough—guillotines, Napoleon, revolutions, repression, and wars lost. The French had tried it all, and it was no wonder that there were plenty of people who looked back fondly upon the monarchy, with its rules, courtesy, decadent luxury, and above all, the relative stability it bestowed on the nation. As the next chapter shows, Debussy's own struggle between the new and the old is played out vividly on the dance stage and is far from idiosyncratic; the battle between minuets and cakewalks, one proper, the other licentious, was as widespread and impassioned as the new dances themselves. Debussy wasn't given to political statements, but he was well aware of the tumult surrounding him, and dance was one way for him to code the opposing forces.

As Charles de Bussy, a minor poet and no relation to the composer, versified in 1903, "A new arrival, a negro / . . . Enters the rooms, joyously / And jumps, breaking everything, more marmoset [monkey] than human / with hat, cane in hand."[4] This quote, featuring a monkey-like newcomer dancing the "Cake-Walck," manages to touch on multiple issues of the day: racism, Darwinism, and anarchism. The imposter's jumps didn't land gently, and Debussy wasn't sure he wanted a part in all the resultant breakage. His reconstructions of historic dances are far from facsimiles of the originals—no baroque composer could have dreamt of his acidic harmonies or complex rhythms—but these early dances nevertheless have propriety at their core, and there are no monkeys on the scene.

A quick look at the piano works written between 1880 and 1900 shows, remarkably, that almost every one of them is, or contains, a dance. The trend begins already with the very early *Danse bohémienne* (1880), with its vigorous rhythms and robust charm. Then, between 1886 and 1889, as Debussy found his voice as a composer, he wrote the *Petite Suite* for four-hand piano; its movements (En bateau [In a Boat], Cortège [Procession], Menuet [a courtly dance with three beats per measure], and Ballet) are all suggestive of dance, and the minuet and ballet dance in title as well as spirit. (The other two titles, as Paul Roberts points out, are drawn from Verlaine's collection of poems, *Fêtes galantes*, and the Menuet is a rework of an early song, itself with the title "Fête galante."[5]) The piece remains infinitely popular today, particularly among students who find both the notes and the sentiments gentle and easy to navigate—like the waters that titular boat traveled in, and very much *un*like the bumpy waters where Debussy found himself trying to honor the past while also embracing a very fractious present.

Virtually on top of the *Petite Suite*, with its amiable four-hand mien, came the two *Arabesques* (1888 and 1891), equally friendly and accessible, and equally popular with posterity. In fact, few later pieces of Debussy have received as many performances as these early character pieces; no radicals are lurking here. Their title is worthy of a slight detour, though never leaving the province of dance entirely. The word *arabesque*, of course, evokes the traditional ballet position the "arabesque," where a dancer stands on one leg with the other extended behind the body. But more mysteriously, it evokes the curvaceous shape of a line, also called the "arabesque," which took on magical meaning for nineteenth-century art nouveau painters and the symbolist poets, who were happy to find mystical meanings lurking around every corner. Edgar Allan Poe led the way with his set of stories entitled *Tales of the Grotesque and Arabesque* in 1840. Then Baudelaire replaced Poe's suspense with a symbolist's awe, announcing that "the design of the arabesque is the most spiritual of designs."[6] For artists, this freely undulating line, reminiscent of plants and waves, may have been about the spiritual, but it was also about the feminine—the curve of women's bodies and the turn of their hair, and no doubt, the turn of their figure in ballet. Its influence was found everywhere, even in the Paris metro, whose graceful station stops were adorned with wrought-iron patterns designed by Hector Guimard in 1899, just in time to show off for the 1900 World Exposition.

Several years after writing the *Arabesques*, Debussy made his own comments on the role of arabesques in music, noting that "the primitives—Palestrina, Vittoria, Orlando di Lasso, etc.—had this divine sense of the arabesque . . . [and] Bach . . . imbued it with a wealth of free fantasy so limitless that it still astonishes us today."[7] It must have been that freedom, the avoidance of pedantry, that so appealed, and it is that spirit that suffuses the *Arabesques*, particularly the ever-popular No. 1, with its swirling triplets and free-floating cross-rhythms: The groups of twos and groups of threes proceed so peacefully here, untroubled by their apparent contradiction of one another.

The titles of Debussy's next piano pieces read like a compendium of dance forms, *Ballade* (first published as *Ballade Slav*), *Danse* (originally *Tarantelle styrienne*), *Mazurka*, and *Valse romantique*, all written in 1890, and the *Nocturne*, from 1892, which, though not a dance form, was descended straight from Chopin as well. It's as if Debussy had set out to prove his rightful heritage in the best of French ballroom traditions. At the same time, these pieces are also imbued with a voyager's delight in evoking distant landscapes. Though indisputably tonal, they use every manner of chord, scale, and modulation to create unusual, often Slavic, harmonies. When he wrote these early piano works, Debussy had recently discovered the Russian composers, Alexander Borodin and Mily Balakirev,[8] and as the chapter on Orientalism further emphasizes, that far-off world abroad was a magnet for him. He was still a young composer, and the pieces are derivative, combining his voice as a dreamer with the pungent harmonies he heard emanating from the East. It's already clear that musical excursions abroad were much to his liking.

What comes next, conversely, situates him squarely at home, engaged in time travel rather than geographical crossings. We encountered the *Suite Bergamasque* already in chapter 1, where *Clair de lune* made a cameo appearance in the hands of Pierrot. This *Suite* is the first of Debussy's multimovement piano works, and, with a Prelude, Menuet, and Passepied, it models itself on a long tradition of similar French dance suites. But it's the outlier third movement, *Clair de lune*, that we all remember. The title, *Suite Bergamasque*, itself favors that movement, for it's drawn from Paul Verlaine's poem "Clair de lune," where the "Bergamasquers"—dancers from Bergamo—people the "chosen landscape,"[9] and the drowsy dreaminess of its music has offered comfort for life's inevitable woes to generations of music lovers.

The entire suite is important because it straddles styles and centuries, using dance as its magic carpet. It's filled with symmetry, repetition, and sequences—all the familiar organizational devices that had made music coherent for centuries. It pays homage to the eighteenth-century French keyboard composers with its courtly ornamental lines, sparse textures, and ceremonial overture, and it salutes the Commedia dell'arte with the title honoring Bergamo. But the element of surprise is there as well, and the piece is downright impudent in its disregard of assorted hallowed conventions: Passepieds should have two beats, not three per measure; conflicting harmonies should not be merged in a single pedal; and the keys of the dance movements should relate closely to one another if not remain outright identical. This may be Debussy's tender homage to a past he loved, but it's far from a carbon copy of what older masters had done.

The very opening of the Prelude begins in textbook manner and then assaults one's expectations: two beats of the requisite tonic harmony, obediently locating the piece around its tonal center, and then a crashing dissonance on the third beat. Within a nanosecond, the stress of the measure has moved indecorously away from both the downbeat and the home pitch, throwing the listener into far more ambiguous territory than those charming dancers might have presaged. Then comes the Menuet, which, despite its penchant for good behavior, ends with a beguiling glissando, unimaginable on an eighteenth-century harpsichord and telegraphing that aristocratic dances aren't what they used to be. Even the gentle, unargumentative *Clair de lune* ends with a subtle jolt. The final return of the lovely, mild-mannered opening takes place accompanied by a totally unexpected and uninvited guest: a dissonant C♭ that appears accented in the first measure of the return, lest anyone overlook its stark presence. It disappears as speedily as it appeared, like an apparition, but the mutiny it has staged is not a solitary one.

The suite is able to have its cake and eat it too (as befits a "sweet") because its overriding mood of melancholy looks both backward and forward. Even amid the cheerful energy of the Menuet and Passepied, the promenaders are "singing in the minor key," precisely as prophesied by the poem. The ennui that dominates French poetry at the end of the nineteenth century is unmistakable, and doleful harmonies belie a surface cheer fed by brisk tempos and airy articulations. In *Clair de lune*, originally called *Promenade sentimentale*, the melancholy is yet more exposed; this moon is imbued with an ambiguous major/minor yearning throughout. The sentimentality of the music is unabashed, and Debussy is at his most romantic as the downward glide of that beloved opening idea lulls the listener into a contented trance. Even the unruliest moments in this suite never come close to total insurgency; a disturbing accent here and there, an unexpected sharp or flat, and a missing downbeat are mere hints of rebellion. Debussy broke rules but remained deferential.

Ditto for the other traditional dances, which mark Debussy's debt to the past and his stay within its orbit. Most important are the stately sarabandes in *Pour le piano* (written in 1894 and originally belonging to a set called *Images oubliées*) and in *Images, Book 1* (1905). The latter sarabande is given the title "Hommage à Rameau," but in a larger sense both are tributes to the past. Jean-Philippe Rameau, who lived at the same time as Bach, was a multitalented genius, and he, along with François Couperin, defined the French baroque. Debussy made no secret of the fact that he much preferred the purity of that bygone era to the heroic postures of the nineteenth century, and here, just as in *Suite Bergamasque*, the modern crunch of dissonant intervals is eclipsed by the elegance of the traditional baroque dance. Both pieces are "lent et grave," or "slow and grave," and both incorporate the stress a sarabande traditionally places on the second beat, thus displacing the natural accent of the triple meter and providing its own very particular gravitas. Even the ABA form here is redolent of an earlier epoch: The opening "A" material recurs following a contrasting "B" section, and the resulting symmetry telegraphs order and predictability. Though Rameau could not have conceived of Debussy's harmonic language, instrument, or dynamic palette in either piece, the sentiments of both would have been familiar to him. In the earlier piece, the sarabande is a short but needed respite from the athleticism of the outer movements. In "Hommage à Rameau," it forms a far larger sweeping narrative arc, and Debussy speaks as a mature composer across the centuries to his older compatriot. The solemnity and graciousness of the music's opening arabesque and the processional in the middle section are majestic matters that befit a king's court, and that court was greatly missed by many in Debussy's France. It did not revel in abstruse counterpoint or religious dogmas; it was neither Lutheran nor Germanic. It depended on grace, delicacy, and refinement, where both Debussy and Rameau reigned supreme.

That delicately tinted world of the past never completely disappeared from Debussy's oeuvre, but it's striking how the image of dance begins to shift, reflecting, without question, shifts in society at large. Whereas dances such as the minuet were decorative, contained, and emblematic of a bygone world of manners, the turn of the century brought a shift toward the wild and indecorous; those "déguisements," or disguises, of Verlaine's dancers were being ripped off in quick time, replaced by rougher gear. Even *La plus que lent* of 1910, an unapologetic waltz intended to slow the passage of time, is a modern product of the cabaret scene, far removed from the ballroom.

Those cabarets were hopping, both figuratively and literally, in both France and south of the border in Spain, and they take us far from Rameau and the eighteenth century. As anyone who's watched *Carmen* knows, a Spanish woman dancing can be a sultry temptress, and the French were far from impervious to her charms. Debussy, like his countryman Ravel, devotes a substantial portion of his compositional catalog to these mythical Spanish women whose sensuous surroundings fairly blaze with color and warmth. *La soirée dans Grenade* (The Evening in Granada) from *Estampes* (1903), with its guitars strumming and castanets clicking amid snappy habañera rhythms, affords the perfect example. Debussy kept coming back to these dances. They're in the two-piano piece, *Lindaraja*, named after a terrace of the Alhambra and a maiden who may have lived within its walls,[10] and also in the preludes *La sérénade interrompue* (1910) and *La puerta del vino* (1913). Like many of the dances Debussy wrote in the last fifteen years of his life, and decidedly unlike his previous minuets, these straddled the border between propriety and licentiousness—they could be suggestive without offending, a handy combination.

The same cannot be said of Debussy's ballets, which, surprisingly enough given the chaste origins of ballet, tilted heavily toward indelicacy. Though these pieces are scored for full orchestra, Debussy did not always complete the orchestration himself. And he was a pianist, who, like many composers, made a habit of playing his orchestral works at the keyboard. His ballet scores exist in two- and four-hand piano versions, often made by the composer himself, and pianists are happily rediscovering them. Even those that have disappeared or were never completed give indications of the composer's preoccupations in pure instrumental works. His first attempt at a ballet was *Masques et Bergamasques*, undertaken in 1909–1910 with Sergei Diaghilev (1872–1929) of the famous—and risqué—Ballets Russes. The title and broad outlines of the plot, obviously suggestive of masks and melancholy and Pierrot, were innocent enough, but Diaghilev and his company had recently arrived in Paris from St. Petersburg and were only too eager to create a sensation. Debussy himself wrote the scenario and began the music, but when neither seemed promising, the project was dropped, and barely a trace remains to the present day. The failed project deserves mention, however, because it indicates a continued engagement with the Commedia and also foreshadows later, more disastrous, collaborations with the Russian troupe.

The next undertaking, *Khamma*, got a little further along but still failed to see the light of day in Debussy's lifetime. A bizarre Egyptian tale of gods and virgins and human sacrifice, it was commissioned, choreographed, and danced by the Canadian dancer Maud Allan, who was already infamous for her sexually explicit portrayal of Salomé. Her collaboration with Debussy, which began in 1911, was far from cordial. By the end Debussy asked sardonically whether "an arrangement for piccolo and bass drum might please her perhaps?"[11] This was an odd denouement given that Allan was originally trained as a classical pianist and should have had reliable taste. *Khamma* wasn't performed until 1924, well after Debussy's death, and then only in concert version, the figurative piccolos and bass drums thus consigned to posterity. Debussy had, thankfully, completed a piano version in 1912, without threat of those nefarious circus instruments (he never completed the actual orchestration), and it was recently rediscovered and recorded, providing clues not only to his thoughts about dance but also to his lifelong fascination with the larger Orient. Its ritualized rhythms and pungent harmonies are remarkably potent on the piano, and he uses the instrument in a strikingly dramatic and orchestral manner. The movement entitled "It is the dawn cold and grey of the morning that slowly becomes pink" (C'est l'aube froide et grise du matin qui lentement devient rose) is a nice bookend to the colors swirling in the evening air of the piano prelude "*Les sons et les parfums tournent dans l'air du soir*," though this dawn, despite sharing some of the same stately elegance as the evening air, also assaults us with the violence of the ballet's human sacrifice.

These sundry ballet plots provide intimations not only of Debussy's interests but also of something more intangible; namely, his attitudes toward sex. He and his artistic cohort were hardly Puritans, but explicit stories were outside Debussy's comfort zone, and outright vulgarity affronted him. Immediately following *Khamma*'s unhappy gestation came *L'après-midi d'un faune*, choreographed and danced by Vaslav Nijinsky (1889–1950), again of the Ballets Russes. That effort was truly scandalous. With sets and costumes by the flamboyant Léon Bakst and a premiere at the Théâtre du Châtelet, the 1912 ballet was a major public event. The poem itself, a hallucinatory ode to phantom nymphs, was already plenty suggestive, but Nijinsky's overt portrayal of sexual arousal and orgasm was shocking to the Parisian public. To make matters worse, his explicit contortions stole all attention away from the music, which had been written twenty years earlier in 1892–1894 as a free evocation of Stéphane Mallarmé's poem. The music is famous for its curvaceous lines and exotic colors, but since it originally had no words, costumes, or gestures there was no question of indecency. Debussy would never have gone further; he found the ballet in "atrocious dissonance" with the music.[12] Diaghilev apparently planned another Debussy ballet, this one based on *Fêtes* from the *Nocturnes*, but nothing came of the project,[13] happily perhaps for all concerned. Ballet in France was no longer modeling aristocratic discretion.

One other project had already been undertaken, however, with the Diaghilev/Nijinsky team, and this one did get produced. That was the ballet *Jeux*, with a plot based on nocturnal trysts and covert homosexual innuendoes. Debussy should probably have learned from past disappointments and opted out of this particularly suggestive plot, but he was tempted by a large fee and must have enjoyed the initial working out; he happily announced in September 1912 that "passion now flows through every bar."[14] The ballet was premiered at the elegant Théâtre des Champs-Élysées on May 15, 1913, site of the scandalous premiere of Stravinsky's *Rite of Spring* in the same year. Suffice it to say that Debussy was displeased with the results; voilà his summation of Nijinsky's choreography: "The man adds up demisemiquavers with his feet, checks the result with his arms and then, suddenly struck with paralysis all down one side, glares at the music as it goes past. I gather it's called the 'stylization of gesture.' . . . It's awful!"[15] The score is now performed not only by orchestras but also on one and two pianos—sans Nijinsky and sans paralysis.

While Debussy was grappling with the Ballets Russes from the East, he was also looking westward, to American-born dancer, Loie Fuller, and with far safer results. Fuller, born, appropriately enough, in Fullersburg, Illinois, in 1862, the same year Debussy was born, moved to Paris after a successful visit in 1892. She had trained not in ballet but in vaudeville and the circus, so that the Folies Bergère, the cabaret where she frequently appeared in Paris, was her ideal milieu. She was attracted to Debussy's work, choreographing his *Petite Suite* in 1911, his *Children's Corner Suite* in 1916, and most ambitiously, two movements of his *Nocturnes* in 1913. Though Debussy apparently lost interest and refused collaborations after the *Nocturnes*,[16] his relationship with Fuller was nevertheless far less tempestuous than with either Maud Allan or Nijinsky. It probably helped that, short and chubby, she approached sexual innuendo via flying veils rather than nude body parts.

In his book *The Painter of Modern Life*, Baudelaire describes woman as "dazzling and bewitching . . . in the muslins, the gauzes, the vast, iridescent clouds of stuff in which she envelops herself."[17] Though he lived too early to know Fuller, the quote is delightfully prescient. Debussy's prelude *Voiles* ("Veils" or "Sails"), with its diaphanous whole-tone scales and pentatonic glissandos, is likely inspired by Fuller's trademark accoutrements (see figure 3.1) and is likewise an ode to Baudelaire's enigmatic woman.[18] Those whole-tone scales, which negate the normal major-minor modes by avoiding half steps entirely, and the pentatonic scales, which use only black keys, are yet another way of "dazzling and bewitching" the complacent listener accustomed to more traditional fare.

Fuller's creations were the sensation of the music hall, and Debussy, like the other spectators, was clearly captivated by these sensuous dances, filled with the curves of art nouveau. They were less wild and gyrating than the cakewalk, less explicit and offensive than Nijinsky's choreography, but far less decorous than the minuet. Consider the conflicting meaning of veils in a bridal ceremony and in striptease and you will have a good idea of her range. (Famous, like Maud Allan, for a dance of Salomé, it's clear that she cannot have been entirely chaste.)

Not only veils but also lights were Fuller's claim to fame. Electricity didn't arrive throughout Paris until the last decade of the nineteenth century, so Fuller's imaginative exploitation of electric lighting in the theater was an especially striking innovation. She used mirrors and colors to create a swirl of hazy action, and Debussy was happy to follow suit. He is, in fact, on record as seeking ballet scenery that boasts "a dreamy imprecision . . . with changing effects of lighting rather than clear-cut lines,"[19] and the piano him offered an audio-only opportunity.

The centrality of color in music was a relatively new idea in Debussy's time. Certainly, orchestral instruments had always been known for their distinctive timbres, and every great symphonist had exploited their differences. But not until Debussy and Ravel did color become so pivotal. Fuller, who had applied her ideas to the 1913 production of "Les nuages" and "Les Sirènes," two movements of Debussy's *Nocturnes*, said, "Colour so pervades everything that the whole universe is busy producing it, everywhere and in everything."[20] And, later, "I wanted to create a new form of art . . . where reality and dream, light and sound, movement and rhythm form an exciting unity."[21] She could, with these fantasies, have been Debussy's ventriloquist.

I wonder if Debussy would also have followed her toward "gentle Satanism, of a gentle and poetic demonality . . . [which] sets one on the starry and luminous path of hashishian dreams."[22] Satanism, demonality, and hashishian dreams are heavy stuff and hardly the words we associate with Debussy. But

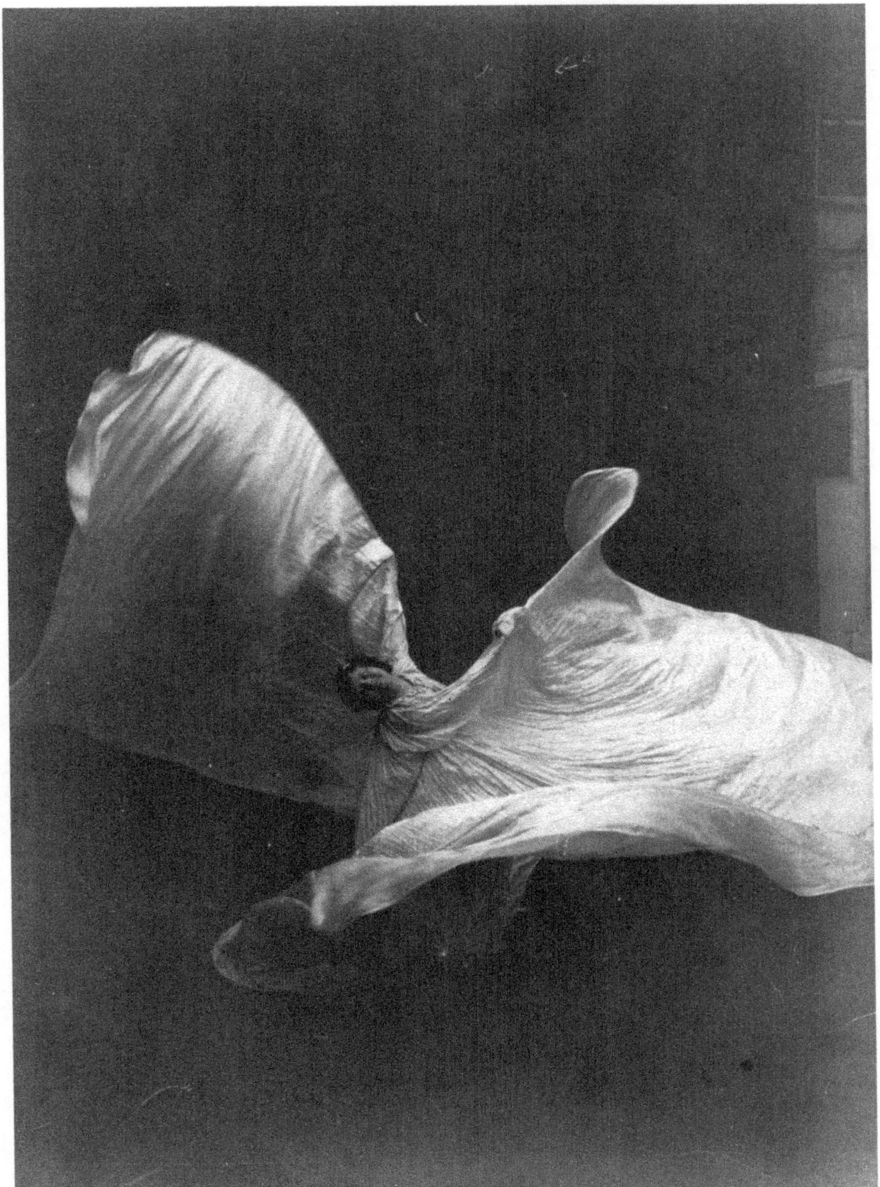

Figure 3.1. *Loïe Fuller Dancing with Her Veil*, 1897, Isaiah West Taber (1830–1912), Musée d'Orsay, Paris. © RMN-Grand Palais / Art Resource, NY.

linking color and sound could emanate from sources other than the devil—synesthesia, above all.

Actually seeing specific colors when hearing specific music requires some serendipitously crossed neurological wiring. E. T. A. Hoffmann, who lived nearly a century before both Fuller and Debussy, spoke of seeing E♭ Major in a "raiment . . . green like the dark forest."[23] He proudly boasted of having "discover[ed] a congruity of colours, sounds, and fragrances."[24] Robert Schumann loved Hoffmann, and this appropriation of colors to musical means offered yet another mask his music could wear. He wasn't alone. Alexander Scriabin (1872–1915), Debussy's contemporary in Russia, went so far as to write a piece, *Prometheus: The Poem of Fire*, with a part for color organ. The machine, never fully implemented, was intended to project the colors implicit in the harmonies and emotions of the piece during performances, but not surprisingly, engineering and conceptual difficulties left the design in its infancy. And Charles Baudelaire wrote an entire book, *Artificial Paradises* (1860), which also dissects the hallucinatory experience of light and color, but this time with the aid of drugs: "You know that hashish always invokes magnificent displays of light, the most glorious splendors, cascades of liquid gold." He then moves on to music: "Sounds are clothed in color and colors in music." Dance is clothed in both, for "you feel gifted with a marvelous lightness."[25]

Since Debussy was not synesthesiac or Satanic, demonic, or hashishian, he was harder pressed to achieve these unified sensory perceptions, but whether he actually saw green when listening to E♭ major is less important than the colors he created at the piano. His magnum opus on the subject is entitled "*Les sons et les parfums tournent dans l'air du soir*" (Sounds and Perfumes Turn in the Evening Air), and the title is drawn from Baudelaire's synesthesiac poem "Harmonie du soir." In fact, Debussy set the text as both a song (the second of the *Cinq poèmes de Baudelaire*) and as a prelude, taking the suggestive title of the prelude verbatim from the third line of the poem. The poem is a pantoum, meaning that the second and fourth lines of one verse are repeated as the first and third line of the following verse, and Debussy manages, miraculously enough, to retain this form musically in the song. In the piano piece, the repetitions are less exact, but the descending intervals, various sorts of fourths and fifths, which permeate the texture of the entire prelude, have the same incantatory effect. The poem mixes flowers, violins, and melancholy waltzes in equal parts, making it clear that color, smell, sound, and dance are inextricably linked. Baudelaire makes the link even more explicit in another poem, "Correspondences," where he says outright, "Les parfums, les couleurs et les sons se respondent" (The perfumes, the colors and the sounds correspond). Dance isn't mentioned in that last bargain, but in "Harmonie du soir" the waltz is pervasive.

Debussy's colors and sounds, and even dances, tend to be muted, but he was increasingly alone. The Fauvist's colors were savage and bestial, posters of Loie Fuller whirled by in a panoply of bright and rapid brushstrokes, and electric lights glared. Refinement was yielding to tumult, and Debussy was caught in the middle of that historical moment. The history of his dance forms shows how fraught his choices were. As he moved away from the demure flirtatiousness of *Suite Bergamasque*, he moved toward a world infused with sexuality—brazen in the case of Nijinsky; edgy, even hysterical, as we shall see in the case of the cakewalk; veiled and mysterious in the case of Loie Fuller. Though he proclaimed himself happy, as in *Jeux*, "to convey a rather *risqué* situation," that was as far as he went.[26] His preferred musical mode was understatement, and he was surrounded by excess. Authors were writing about live jewel-encrusted tortoises,[27] dancers were having orgasms onstage, and painters were twisting the human body into inconceivable contortions. We shall follow this turbulence further in the following chapter and trace Debussy's participation. The story touches on mental illness, monkeys, and the elevation of the Ugly in art. One is reminded of Keats's "Ode on a Grecian Urn" from 1819, which declared, "Beauty is Truth, truth beauty—that is all." No longer so in Paris 1900.

• 4 •

The Cakewalk Wars

The advent of ragtime and the cakewalk was cataclysmic in Paris. It was simultaneously liberating, shocking, and illicitly delightful, and Debussy was swept up in that energy. Race is inextricably tied to some of Debussy's most popular piano pieces such as *Golliwogg's Cakewalk* and *"General Lavine"—excentric—*, and these pieces, as well as those with titles like *Le petit nègre* and *Minstrels*, surely benefit from historical context.

The arrival of the minstrel show in Paris, with its white American performers made up in blackface, created a sensation. Quite aside from the simple novelty of the affair, imagine the excitement of watching another nation's degrading and titillating racial stereotypes unfold before your very eyes! Blacks themselves were a curiosity, perhaps that much more curious when the black was faux black. An appealing theatrical trick, this was, to color yourself the color of the oppressed—but how reassuring to be able to wash it off on command.

The minstrel show, a form of entertainment merging song, dance, and deeply embedded racial attitudes, was already thriving in America in the 1830s and 1840s but only arrived in Europe in the 1860s. The shows took England by storm initially, and it was actually there, in 1905, that Debussy first encountered minstrels. By the late 1870s, however, minstrels had arrived in Paris as well, and by the 1890s, blacks, as well as whites, were appearing in the shows.[1]

Paris was certainly ready. Music halls had already taken on extraordinary importance. In 1869, the famous Folies Bergère opened as a café concert; that is, a café where informal singing and vaudeville acts on stage took place amid the general hubbub of customers drinking, chatting, and singing along at their tables.[2] By 1886, this café concert was reconceived with the more elaborate entertainment and setting typical of music halls. The famous Chat Noir opened in 1881, and other similarly celebrated cabarets, such as the Nouveau Cirque and the Moulin Rouge, followed in short order. In all of these establishments, singers and entertainers wooed both upper- and lower-class Parisians, and the audiences poured in, eager to escape the grind of urban life. There was a motley sprinkling of the rich, the middle, and the working classes, a mix that was notable in a society replete with class divisions. Artists were, of course, attracted by that potpourri and the bohemian escape it afforded from propriety. Debussy participated as both singer and piano-player at Chat Noir, joining other luminaries such as Toulouse-Lautrec and Satie, as well as writers Verlaine, Maupassant, and Huysmans. And it would have been at the Folies Bergère that Debussy first encountered the dancer Loie Fuller, whose veils we encountered in *Voiles*. Minstrel shows, with their foreign cultural roots, provided a certain novelty amid the other singing and acrobatic acts at entertainment centers. Highly racist in origin, the first minstrel shows in the United States had featured white plantation owners who acted the part of dancing and singing plantation slaves. The genre allowed for the admiration of slave culture, with the familiar paean to black rhythm, while still assuring that blacks were subservient, well behaved, and resigned—well-nigh celebratory—regarding their fate. Blackface was hardly a new idea, but its previous associations were with evil or catastrophic misfortune: witness Shakespeare's Othello. To convey a whole generic population through the application of wax crayon, and to thereby reinforce stereotypes of submission mixed with perennial good cheer, was a far greater act of hubris.

Not surprisingly, blacks soon began forming their own minstrel troupes, and their shows, when they eventually appeared in Paris, were wildly popular. The cakewalk, as featured dance, allowed Parisians to enjoy laughter, sexuality, and exoticism in one fell swoop; it was a potent cocktail indeed and one particularly appealing to a composer such as Debussy seeking new forms and escapes from tradition. Popular at the period when the French were colonizing Africa, the dance gave safe access to native cultures that were seen as primitive, forbidden, and thereby infinitely enticing. While Picasso painted masks and Gauguin headed for Tahiti, the less gifted Frenchman could spend his evenings watching, learning, or dancing the cakewalk.[3]

The term "cakewalk" is itself quite vague. The cakewalk originated with slaves dancing a parody of plantation owners' more formal dancing and, according to some sources, is said to have received its name when an especially impressive couple was awarded a cake. Although cakewalks originated as parodies of whites, whites, never to be one-upped, took them over as a parody of blacks, and finally blacks reclaimed them. As one black man recalled about the beginnings, "Us slaves watched white folks' parties where the guests danced the minuet and then paraded in a grand march. . . . Then we do it too, but we used to mock 'em, every step."[4]

Even in America, it wasn't until the 1890s that blacks themselves performed the cakewalk publicly; before that public performances featured only the usual whites in blackface. The music of the cakewalk first appeared in France in 1900 at the Paris World Exposition in performances given by John Philip Sousa and his (all-white) band. The syncopated rhythms of ragtime were tossed in amid patriotic songs and classical favorites, providing a veritable potpourri of typical American circus music. Later, when Sousa came to town again, Debussy expounded on him in the Parisian literary periodical *Gil Blas*:

> At last . . . the king of American music is in town. By that I mean that M. J.P. Sousa and his band have come for a whole week to reveal to us the beauties of American music as it is performed in the best society. One really has to be exceedingly gifted to conduct this music. M. Sousa beats time in circles or tosses an imaginary salad or sweeps away some invisible dust. Or else he catches a butterfly that has flown out of a bass tuba.
>
> If American music is unique for its invention of the famous "cake-walk," and I must admit that for the moment that seems to be its single advantage over all other kinds of music, then of that M. Sousa is unquestionably its king.[5]

Meanwhile, American blacks were relegated to—or awarded?—their own separate pavilion at the exposition, entitled "The American Negro Experience." It was organized in part by W. E. B. DuBois and was filled with photographs and documents but no music. It was in 1902 that the French finally saw African Americans dancing: A couple, Mr. and Mrs. Elks, performed the cakewalk to wild acclaim at the Nouveau Cirque, and while they themselves were white, they performed as part of a mixed-race company.

It was exciting for the French to have this exotic race in the midst of the overwhelming whiteness of their society; unlike Americans, they had no experience of slavery or a large black population at home. Going back to the 1400s,[6] the French had righteously regarded their own land as a land of freedom for all, though they were admittedly far from totally consistent in observing the principle. Infinitely more problematic for them, however, was the role of slavery in the French colonies, where its convenience was indisputable and its geographical distance from the homeland made moral considerations less distasteful. The twists and turns of government policy on this front are dizzying: Slavery was abolished in the colonies in 1794, reinstated under Napoleon in 1802 (who successfully reimplanted it everywhere but Saint-Domingue, or present-day Haiti, where the world's first successful slave rebellion was carried out). It was then again made illegal in 1818 after the fall of Napoleon, but the ban was honored mostly in the breach until the revolution of 1848, which finally made the laws more potent, allowing only expert outlaws to profitably export African slaves.

By Debussy's era, slavery in any of the Francophone world was no longer a subject of raging debate, but France was hardly color blind. The image of blacks even before, and certainly after, the arrival of music hall entertainers is often that of something akin to a far-off circus exhibit. Consider, for example, Debussy's dismissal of Maud Allan by suggesting she's off "dancing for the negros in darkest West Africa,"[7] and the comment that "she supplies a scenario so boring a negro could have done better."[8] Then there was a French society woman's description of a costume ball in which her husband appeared "dress[ed] up as a negress dragging along a hurdy-gurdy."[9] Or, most striking yet, the author Joris-Karl Huysmans (1848–1907) reported "a funeral banquet in memory of the host's virility" where, "while a hidden orchestra played funeral marches, the guests were waited on by naked negresses wearing only slippers and stockings in cloth of silver embroidered with tears."[10] And even those "progressive" forces who set out to parody racism reveal a society beset by racial stereotypes—regard, for example, a small excerpt from an apparent attempt at humor, entitled "Nègre," in a 1901 issue of *Le Courrier français*: "The little negro, the good negro, like his white brother well, the big teeth clear and white make us remember that there are still cannibals here and there, the white brother has tender skin."[11] Another cartoon from a few months later facetiously proposes a "white slave trade" and pictures a rape scene in the guise of dance, with the muscular black male carrying away his nude, ravaged, and very white victim.[12] The artistry and athleticism of classical dance is reinterpreted as naked power and villainy when the male changes color. These black men hung out in the Parisian subconscious somewhere between desire and disdain with a hefty dose of awe thrown in.

Enter Debussy. Despite the fact that only a tiny fraction of Debussy's output is devoted to cakewalks, it turns out that a very large portion of what's been written about cakewalks is devoted to Debussy. Golliwogg, that black ragdoll who came to literary fame in 1895, firmly ensconced Debussy in the annals of cakewalk history, and yet Debussy's own attitudes about the dance remain mysterious. To accuse him of intentional racism for having embraced a dubious genre seems excessive. But to note, at the very least, insensitivity to racial stereotyping (shared, undeniably, by most of his countrymen) is more than deserved. Remember that his close contemporary, Maurice Ravel (1875–1937), was, like Debussy, entranced with American ragtime but eschewed the cakewalk. Instead, he took another stance. His song "Aoua" from *Chansons madécasses* is notable for its embrace of the black man's rage against the white. So, while it is true that the racist attitudes described in this chapter go well beyond anything ever verbalized by Debussy, and that one can happily enjoy his cakewalk music now without approving of its origins, it is also true that Debussy was no more averse to the racism of the times in France than was Stephen Foster in the United States. His deep friendship with Robert Godet, who was famous for translating and supporting the shockingly racist philosopher Houston Stewart Chamberlain, who preached the perils of the "black hordes,"[13] does nothing to place him on higher moral ground.

Of course, the question of where the worst of racism resides in the cakewalk wars of the early 1900s is none too easy to settle. Both sides, those who favored and those who detested the provocative fad, were culpable, and Debussy can well be regarded as a progressive populist for eventually espousing the dance. The cakewalk and the "nègres" who purveyed it were seen by social conservatives as a pernicious threat to "Frenchness" at the turn of the century. France stood for tradition and dignity and of course for whiteness as well. Suddenly there was an invasion from abroad. It came most directly from North America but indirectly from Africa, and blacks from both countries were seen as the ultimate "Other." The dance schools that had seen the French gavotte as eternal were horrified; they feared for both their livelihood and the moral fate of the nation. Debussy, once he succumbed, was scolded by the critic Louis Laloy, who warned that "the cakewalk of Debussy will corrupt children, who, bit by bit, will clumsily imitate the well-known postures of that *nègre* dance."[14]

The following is a rough translation of a dance manual at the turn of the century:

> We must say that for a long time we've considered the question of whether this negro dance, imported from North America, would figure in our Treatise of Dances of the Salon.
>
> Even after having finally decided to include it, we had a hard time trying to treat its eccentric movements as a dance worthy of our salons, and that after having ordered it and emended its exaggerations as we have done here.
>
> But "la mode" makes its demands; it has decided; the cakewalk is causing a furor in the most elegant salons of Paris, contrary to healthy notions of grace and good taste. Therefore we have resigned ourselves to publish a theory of the cakewalk here . . . unless the popularity of this dance, with little to recommend it in our opinion, happens in the near future to vanish as quickly as it came.[15]

Against its better judgment, the school commenced with lessons. Accompanying diagrams indicate, however, that it taught a decidedly sedate and manicured version of this dance normally filled with kicks, prancing, and irrepressible high spirits.

Figure 4.1. "On s'efforce de singer le grand monde parisien!" (One tries hard to ape [mimic] the great Parisian world!) *L'illustré national,* Christmas 1902. Bibliothèque nationale de France.

A less compliant school sniffed: "Gossips assure us that one will revisit this winter the odious cakewalk in the salons. I don't want to believe it. One should leave to the joyous negros the success of this amusing dance."[16]

It's not hard to see the disconnect these august institutions perceived between their hallowed traditions, their "belle époque," and the subversive forces now taking hold. Note the central place of the "joyous negros" in their compendium of complaints. Numerous cartoons make clear the remote—ergo barbaric—origins of the threat they posed. The dance appears to emanate from some distant desert replete with palm trees, lions, elephants, and—always, grace à M. Darwin—dancing monkeys.

Perhaps you can't quite distinguish the monkeys and the dancers in figure 4.1. That's not your lack of visual acuity. They blend. And the visual similarities apparently had repercussions for mental abilities as well. A contemporary "scientific" account of Negro anatomy proclaimed that "the Negro facial angle approaches that of a monkey. . . . This relative weakness of intelligence that is revealed by the . . . facial angle will be confirmed . . . by the example of the brain."[17]

What Parisian would want to admit that they too share facial characteristics with monkeys? The cakewalk cartoon in figure 4.2 portrays a hierarchy of dancing couples: the primitive monkeys harking from the jungles of Africa, the black folks said to sport the facial angle of a monkey, and finally the elegant French. It can be no accident that Darwin's theories of evolution had

LE CAKE-WALK
— Comme quoi la Parisienne tient à nous démontrer que nous descendons du singe.
Dessin de George Edward.

Figure 4.2. "Le Cakewalk: How the Parisian is eager to show us we're descended from monkeys." ***Le Rire*****, February 7, 1903. Bibliothèque nationale de France.**

Figure 4.3. Dance in the Desert: "The monkeys Galipaud, father and son, professors of the Cake-Walk. Lessons by the hour and by the course. Payments in the currency of monkeys are preferred." *Le Rire*, March 14, 1903. Bibliothèque nationale de France.

Figure 4.4. "Il faut savoir prendre aux autres peuples ce qu'ils ont du bien." (You must know how to take the best of what other cultures have to offer.) Bibliothèque-musée de l'Opéra, Biblioteque nationale de France.

recently arrived in Paris—if humans descended from apes, the French wanted a buffer zone between themselves and the monkeys. Black cakewalk dancers were the perfect go-between. They emerged from "the most inferior . . . the most un-civilizable . . . degenerate or incompletely developed races . . . seeming at times to be closer to the brute than to civilized man[, but they had] a particular talent for unaccustomed rhythms [whose] bizarre, almost savage, character lends them a special charm."[18]

Blacks were seen as the perfect amalgam of primitive and beguiling; they were encouraged to dance but several paces behind, if you please. Debussy liked anthropomorphic animals, and music about monkeys and blacks wasn't far removed from music about elephants and the circus. Note the cartoon in figure 4.3 that happily links all the animals under the tutelage of the professorial monkeys.

The "Dance in the Desert," figure 4.3, could hardly be more explicit about the beasts in charge. Cute fiends, they are, and very shrewd. The professorial monkey in figure 4.4, who claims to know precisely what will do his students good, is equally clear about his own role and is probably getting rich in the currency of monkeys.

As recently as 2013, France was rocked by a scandal when a candidate for local office in France compared the French minister of justice who was black to a monkey. She said on national television that she would like to see her "in a tree swinging from the branches rather than in government."[19] Monkeys, deeply physical and coarse, represent lawlessness, delicious and unacceptable. Examine the offspring of the man in figure 4.5 who allowed himself an illicit fling, no doubt after a cakewalk lesson with the monkeys Galipaud.

And then see the cartoon in figure 4.6, which reverses the genders and removes retribution from the scene of seduction.

So it goes, in picture after picture. The cakewalk engenders both vice and delight. We have no record of Debussy participating in actual cakewalk shenanigans, but obviously he found the erratic twists and turns of the novel

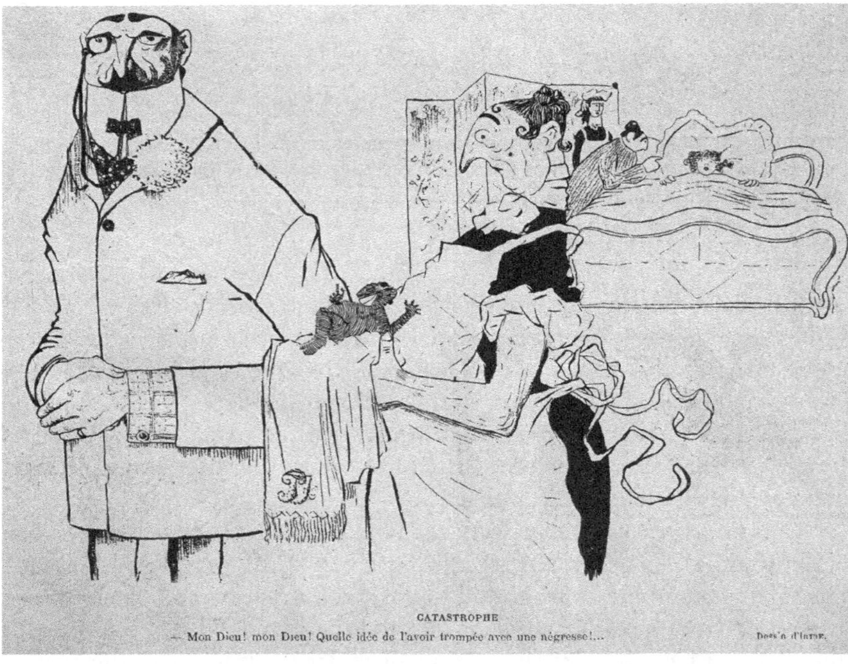
CATASTROPHE
— Mon Dieu! mon Dieu! Quelle idée de l'avoir trompée avec une négresse!...

Figure 4.5. Catastrophe: "My God, my God! What an idea to have cheated with a negress!" *Le Rire*, February 7, 1903. Bibliothèque nationale de France.

Figure 4.6. In the long narrative of a home cakewalk lesson that accompanies this drawing, the female student ends up supine, whereupon she declares that "après tout, ça n'est pas si laid que ça, un nègre" (after all, it's not as ugly as all that, a negro). *Le Courrier français,* July 14, 1901. Bibliothèque nationale de France.

dance a delight. Many French composers resisted the mania; Debussy's enthusiastic surrender was a choice, not a given. His buy-in was partial, however. Whereas the minuet and other dances of the "ancien régime" communicated order, the cakewalk tolerated, nay boasted, chaos, and it was that chaos that engendered the horrifying moral degeneration pictured in these figures. Kick high enough and you lose your moral compass. In the grim language of nineteenth-century moral authorities, "art rises to the moral realm through its salutary or harmful qualities, destroying or preserving life";[20] "the pains . . . of discordant notes and inharmonious colors . . . are each traceable to an actual present disintegration or waste of nervous tissue."[21]

This is all rather extreme and doesn't quite fit the jolly rhythms of Debussy's cakewalks, where nervous tissue appears quite safe. Monkeys and writhing bodies negated his well-bred French values and assumptions, and so his cakewalks are relatively innocent affairs, though notably brazen in comparison with the reticent music that was his normal calling card. The first, and most celebrated, cakewalk in fact occurred in the company of a mere doll, Golliwogg, the black "gnome" Florence and Bertha Upton had created in their children's book *The Adventures of Two Dutch Dolls and a Golliwogg* (1895) pictured in figure 4.7.[22]

The two lily-white dolls, Peg and Mary Jane, are playing when Golliwogg first appears, and he terrifies them. He is "a horrid sight! / The blackest gnome / . . . They scatter in their fright." He turns out, however, to sport a "kindly smile," and all manner of adventures ensue, with Golliwogg alternately a friend and an enemy but no longer an alien. In the end, in fact, the dolls save Golliwogg from a fall through the ice, and all ends on an amicable note. The story is an interesting harbinger of future toys that come to life, particularly those in *La boîte à joujoux*, Debussy's marionette ballet of 1913,

Figure 4.7. Cover of *The Adventures of Two Dutch Dolls and a Golliwogg,* 1895, Bertha Upton and Florence Upton.

and Ravel's opera *L'enfant et les sortileges*, of 1925, where toys rise up to punish an errant child.

Debussy's *Golliwogg*, the final movement of his *Children's Corner Suite*, features the standard duple time signature of the cakewalk, two beats per measure, and it's replete with the requisite ragtime syncopations, or accents off the beat. Its repetitious, jaunty tune makes it ideal for a "children's corner," but the middle section confronts the issues of French identity head on. Here Debussy parodies Richard Wagner, incorporating the famous chord from Wagner's gargantuan and for-adults-only opera *Tristan und Isolde* into his children's creation with apparent glee. "So there," he says in effect, "so much for the overblown music you Germans have produced over the last century. Address yourself to toddlers!" If the cakewalk is about moral degeneration, then Wagner is the perfect exemplar. In Debussy's mind, "he has awakened the secret thirst for the criminal in some of the most famous minds of our age."[23] And for Debussy, the primitive degeneracy of the cakewalk is pure innocence in comparison with that German "egotistical need for glory."[24]

Le petit nègre takes over in 1909 where *Golliwogg's Cakewalk* left off. The term "nègre" in the title is itself ambiguous, lying somewhere between our words "nigger" and "negro" in its overtones. The piece is simpler and shorter than *Golliwogg*, but it is equally filled with alarming syncopations, and its intermediate level implies that "joyous negros" and children (as if the two categories had no overlap) may be partners in the same unsophisticated, simplistic world. *Minstrels* fleshes out that world a bit; it flatters blacks with its charming tunes and rhythms, but its tongue-in-cheek manner still implies paternalism and amused superiority. The minstrels saunter along nonchalantly, with a bit of a limp, and the occasional screeching lurch in harmony and rhythm easily befits their apparent lack of cultivation. Debussy even calls on tambourines to tap out a repeated note motive with an out-of-tune half step thrown in for good measure, and the "espressif" pseudo-lyrical solemnity that follows wickedly mocks any profound thoughts these unpolished blacks may think they're having.

Debussy could easily have notated tambourines in his other "cakewalk" prelude, *"General Lavine"—excentric—*, as well. General Lavine was a bona fide clown, and Debussy's pairing of clown and cakewalk makes clear the all-inclusiveness of that "art of the everyday" so pervasive in early twentieth-century Paris. Simple-minded and jovial though this music appears, clowns were, in actuality, a pretty complicated bunch, and maybe some of the good-humored shrieks General Lavine and those minstrels emit are related to the long history of connections between the cakewalk and poisonous disease or degeneration. The musical syncopations, with their unexpected placement, were early defined as unhealthy, and they are the sine qua nons of the cakewalk. The word "syncope" was, in fact, "first used as a medical term to describe the irregular heartbeat associated with 'sickness of the heart.'"[25] And, if the heart didn't falter when confronted with all those misplaced accents, then the brain would undoubtedly capitulate from the strain of processing such misguided rhythm. Whether the dance caused illness or resulted from it, there's no doubt about the association made in the nineteenth-century medical community. The cakewalk appeared on the scene during the absolute heyday of spurious hysteria diagnoses, and epilepsy, hysteria, and dance formed a close cohort. The cakewalk, in fact, joined a dance known as "the epileptic dance" in music halls. Imagine seeing a seizure as the follow-up to a particularly wanton kick![26]

"Tarentisme," or the involuntary and obsessive dancing of the tarantella, was another of the hysteria diagnoses most in vogue in the late 1800s, and Debussy's *Tarantella styrienne* (republished simply as "Danse" in 1903) was written right in 1890. Tarantellas are among the most curious of musical compositions, and this one is no exception. Ostensibly written to magically cure the poisonous bite of a tarantula, they require extreme exertion on the part of both player and dancer, yet they fail on every factual count. For, as it happens, a tarantula's bites, though unpleasant, are rarely life threatening, and if they were, nothing would spread the poison more quickly and ensure a more rapid demise than a wild dance! Debussy would have killed off the victim in short order with his relentless fast tempo, galloping 6/8 meter (six fast eighth notes per bar, divided into two groups of three), and incessant hemiolas, where those two groups of three eighth notes are conflated at every opportunity with three groups of two eighth notes. No doubt the hapless scorpion, eager to deposit its venom and move along, was baffled and thrown off balance by the shiftiness of those eighth notes. This is delightfully fiendish music, and though there's a brief respite in the lyrical middle section, that relief is short-lived. The *Tarentella* is one of those exceptional Debussy pieces that gallops to a fortissimo, bravura ending, making no apologies for its blazing and unnuanced convictions. The bug is to be slain at all costs!

Syncopations, hemiolas, and jagged accents clearly subverted the natural rhythms not only of spiders but also of society. A look at the pictured scene in figure 4.8 might clarify why. The nude male angel, hands clasped in prayer, who presides over the crowd along with a horned and benevolent devil, could hardly better convey the delicious wages of sin being enjoyed by this motley crowd. The sumptuous, chandelier-bedecked ballroom makes quite clear exactly what is being overthrown, and the rampant disorder, with gendarmes, flying horsemen, Africans, Americans, and French mingling, and varying degrees of undress, is obviously a joy to all concerned. A famous silent movie that appeared in the same year made similar points. Directed by Georges Méliès and entitled *The Infernal Cakewalk*, the film was, like *Le Rire*'s foldout, endowed with smoke, magic, and the devil. It clarified yet further the cakewalk's affiliations with sorcery and the exotic and made equally clear both the origins and the fate of those who danced it. Debussy loved the occult; he joined various societies and flirted with its theories throughout his life. Though his preference was for its more erudite aspects, smoke and magic also had their appeal. A pity he wasn't painted in here; the band in the far right-hand corner was probably playing precisely the John Philip Sousa ragtime that had inspired *Golliwogg*.

"Propriety be damned" might well have been the tag on both film and foldout. Dance, of all the arts, is of course the one that translates most readily into a party, and going just a baby step further, it's the one that's most overtly sexual, though it needs music to help it on its way. This hasn't changed over the century: In 2013, *The New Yorker* reported that "in a story that may be apocryphal . . . a French President, upon being introduced to tango, said, 'In France, we do it horizontally.'"[27] Tango appeared in France very soon

Figure 4.8. Cakewalk supplement to *Le Rire* (foldout), March 1, 1903, Abel Faivre (1867–1945). Print courtesy of the Bibliothèque nationale de France.

after the cakewalk, and as we know from earlier cartoons, cakewalk lessons themselves often started out upright but ended in bed. There appeared to be a downward trend across the board. Dance was allied with nervous illness. Music was taking on rhythms of the jungle. Decadent literature touted physical beauty in opposition to moral good.[28] Painting was obsessed with the primitive. Even artists themselves were often either proudly promiscuous or openly homosexual, delighting in the eroticism of illicit liaisons or adultery. The connections among excitement, perceived pathology, and art were growing in fin-de-siècle Paris.

It bears mention that the last of the cakewalks, *"General Lavine"—excentric—*, dates from 1913, the same year as the infamous debut of Stravinsky's ballet *Sacre du printemps*. Debussy, who heard the Stravinsky work ahead of time, says, "It haunts me like a beautiful nightmare" and speaks of "the terrifying impression it made."[29] The supremacy of rhythm in this music, the lack of melody, the barbarity of the harmonies, and the jangle of the orchestration, along with the pagan subject matter and the explicitly sexual dance, are all elements that brought high art to its knees. Though there are no explicit cakewalks to be seen here, there are early influences of jazz and other parallel trends to be remarked upon. Theater and audience may have been elegant, but the spectacle was anything but, and the coincidence of primitivism in "high" and "low" art is striking. The cakewalk and *Sacre* testify equally to a generation's rebellion. Debussy took an evasive stance in the midst of all this "bed-lam"; he liked to think the immorality was transient, and he placed it artfully between a ballerina's legs: "Immorality passes through the ballerina's legs and ends in a pirouette," he said.[30] Thus, in his imagination, ballet and the new order were reconciled with an elegant denouement that banished past indiscretions. The world, however, was headed in less genteel directions.

• 5 •

A Taste for the Orient

As can be seen from figure 5.1, something of the same prurient interest that drew the French toward primitivism and blacks informed the French attitude toward the Far East and northern Africa: mystery and irresistible attraction ran rampant. If the natives weren't swinging from trees, then they were at the homes of concubines. Sexuality was a very large part of the bundle.

The phenomenon had a name, and it wasn't limited to the French, though they were leaders of the pack. This was "Orientalism," and the Palestinian-born scholar, Edward Said, who helped to define the term and wrote the most famous study of its genesis, has this to say:

> The Orient was almost a European invention, and had been since antiquity a place of romance, exotic beings, haunting memories and landscapes, remarkable experiences. . . . The Orient is not only adjacent to Europe; it is also the place of Europe's greatest and richest and oldest colonies, the source of its civilizations and languages, its cultural contestant, and one of its deepest and most recurring images of the Other.[1]

As one might guess, the relationship of nineteenth-century Europe to the Orient provides a grizzly tale of domination, exploration, envy, and disdain. And since, as usual, Debussy's works are a mirror of what's going on around him, he joins Belle Époque artists and writers in drawing heavily on France's burgeoning relationship with the Eastern world. Works such as *Pagodes*, *Danseuses de Delphes*, and *Canope* refer directly to the larger Orient, and in a bigger sense, the far-off mystery Debussy sought to convey in so much of his music was partially inspired by Orientalism and its bedfellow, colonialism.

The Orient was defined early on to include not only the Far East but also the Middle East, India, Southeast Asia, Turkey, northern Africa, Spain,

Figure 5.1. "Le décolletage à travers les âges. En Orient. (The low-cut neckline across the ages. In the Orient.) *Le Courrier français,* February 3, 1901. Bibliothèque nationale de France.

and even Greece. This was a broad classification indeed and one that covered a vast array of cultures and religions. This enormous territory, much of it previously unknown but now increasingly accessible, literally opened up brave new worlds to the French. First through colonization, then through trade and the Paris World Expositions of 1889 and 1900, the French, and a broad swath of French artists and writers in particular, became utterly infatuated with a fantasy version of what lay outside their borders. Debussy, always eager to escape the quotidian, was heavily smitten. His works fall into three rough categories: those referring to the Arab/Muslim world, which included northern Africa and Moorish Spain; those referring to Southeast and Eastern Asia, which revolved for Debussy around Cambodia, Thailand, Vietnam, and Japan; and, lastly, those referring to India. Africa inspired the most interest among the painters and writers of France and also offers the most interesting case study politically, but Southeast Asia is of particular interest for Debussy, since it was there that he was most heavily influenced by the actual music of the region.

We'll devote a separate chapter to Asia and start here with Africa. Colonialist politics reached its apex there, and the ferment of that exploration was critical to all of Debussy's Orientalist efforts. Without those conquests, brutal as they were, the sense of adventure, the possibility of exploring a world larger than Europe, and, most important, the critical perception of freedom from conventional rules would have been largely lost. Debussy and other French artists were eager to experience life outside France, for they didn't like what they found inside; like many other Europeans, they felt confined by their "law-abiding reality."[2] As the great painter Eugène Delacroix (1798–1863) said of the inhabitants of North Africa when he visited in 1832, "They are closer to nature in a thousand ways: their dress, the form of their shoes. And so beauty has a share in everything that they make. As for us, in our corsets, our tight shoes, our ridiculous pinching clothes, we are pitiful."[3]

And if Parisians felt corseted in 1832, that was well before the Baron Haussmann had taken his toll on the freedoms of the Old City. Beginning in 1852, Napoleon III (Louis-Napoleon Bonaparte) hired Haussmann to make Paris into a modern city—a modern city, that is, that would be immune to the threats of a revolution such as the one that had taken place in 1848. In that year, young revolutionaries had sequestered themselves behind barricades in the narrow, winding streets, making it nearly impossible for the counterrevolutionary forces to bombard them with artillery. Louis-Napoleon, who declared himself emperor in 1851, took these lessons to heart, and it was thus that he set Baron Haussmann to work. The task was mammoth, and the results motley: New and better sanitation and beautiful parks served the city well; impressive public monuments and broad new avenues at the expense of old neighborhoods were more problematic. Critics rued "these new boulevards without turnings, without chance perspectives, implacable in their straight lines,"[4] and further joked that soon even the Seine would be straightened, "because its irregular curve is really rather shocking."[5] The limitless potential of a city with unturned corners was lost; in its place was predictability. Department stores took the place of individual businesses; set prices replaced bargaining. Everywhere, mass urban culture flourished, and Baudelaire announced, "the old Paris is gone." He counted himself among "those who have lost something they may not find / Ever, ever again! who steep themselves in tears / And suck a bitter milk."[6]

In other words, the mystery had been removed from daily life. Especially for a man like Debussy, who decried the excessive use of theory and claimed that "pleasure is the law,"[7] this was a loss beyond measure. Happily, just as Paris was losing its allure to its native artists, the colonialist vistas in northern Africa opened up, compensating for every lost byway in Paris. André Gide (1869–1951) wonders in Algeria at "a path so strange I had never seen the like in any other country . . . twisting and turning. . . . I walked along in a state of ecstasy, a sort of silent joy, an exaltation of the senses and the flesh."[8]

Colonialism was hardly new to the European powers (as Americans may recall from their own regrettable experience as the colonized, rather than the colonizer), but by the end of the eighteenth century, the French had lost most of their earlier holdings in the Americas, and it was left to Napoleon to begin acquiring what came to be known as the Second French Colonial Empire. Interest centered in the as-yet-unclaimed area of northern Africa. Egypt, Algeria, Tunisia, and Morocco were all in play. Any present-day visitor to the medina, or inner streets, of a North African city will understand how captivating the colors, twisted byways, and striking commodities of these exotic cultures must have seemed to the straight-laced European visitor. Indeed, the French took special national pride in the successful relationships they forged. A French account from 1902 boasts that "in Egypt, France is always loved and admired; the Egyptians never stop saying that if we had wanted to, they would have accepted our protection with joy, while they tolerate the British yoke only with impatience."[9]

It's interesting to place *Pour l'égyptienne* (For the Egyptian Woman), the fifth movement of Debussy's four-hand piece *Six épigraphes antiques* (also available in a solo version by the composer), in this context. Though *Six épigraphes antiques* was arranged in 1914, it's taken directly from music written in 1901, the incidental music to *Chansons de Bilitis*. The original *Bilitis* poems, by Debussy's friend Pierre Louÿs (1870–1925), are texts ostensibly written by a BC Greek poetess, and they evoke an ancient, mythical world, encompassing both Greece and Egypt. We'll hear a lot about them later in the chapter as they occasioned many of Debussy's Orientalist musings. This music is all about distance; it is immobilized over a static bass that anchors Debussy in the dream of a long-ago Egypt, a romantic kingdom of fluttering ornaments, unfamiliar scales, and perennial quiet. Egypt may have been in the minds of present-day Parisians because of current politics, but Debussy's Egypt was not the one they knew. In Debussy's Egypt everyone is at peace.

In fact, life for contemporary Egyptians and natives of other colonized African nations such as Algeria, Morocco, and Tunisia, was far from peaceful. An account of French digs in Tunisia, which the French had recently conquered in order to protect their power in Algeria, makes clear the divergent interest of natives and conquerors and has little of the dream to recommend it:

> The Tunisian Department of Antiquities, under the direction of Monsieur Gauckler, has undertaken to extricate the temple from the Arab houses that hide it from view. The natives have, in effect, put their tumbledown cottages side by side against the columns, and the interior of the sanctuary has served them as a stable; thanks to the benevolent concurrence of the French and Tunisian governments, since 1899, one has been able to end this state of affairs, and reveal the anterior portion of the temple and return it, as far as possible, to its earlier appearance.[10]

Clearly, those whose houses abutted the ancient temple valued their homes above archeological advancement. But to the French visitor, those shacks were of little interest compared to an ancient temple. This clash in priorities was not an anomaly; given the newfound interest in ancient art and architecture, similar digs were taking place in Greece, Egypt, and other sites in the Middle East and Asia. This was, in fact, precisely the same destruction of indigenous property that made possible the discovery of the ancient Greek art upon which Debussy based his lovely prelude *Danseuses de Delphes*. Consider the photo in figure 5.2, with its village landscape torn asunder.

This very first of the twenty-four *Preludes* acquaints us not only with a sculpture of ancient Greek dancers that Debussy saw replicated in the Louvre but also with the archeological digs in Delphi from which this photo is taken. Those digs enthralled Paris in the 1890s, and it was no doubt both that publicity and the reflected glory of ancient Greece that inspired Debussy to place this Prelude first in his large series of miniature works. It is filled with grace; the pictured dancers move in a stately procession, subsumed by the ritualistic dignity of their repeating rhythms. The music is simultaneously supple, as befits the dancers, and also static, as a sculpture must remain. Its open harmonies and repeated low octaves speak of distance and tranquility. The digs themselves, however, were less peaceful. They functioned in much the way as the World Exposition of 1889 had—they allowed the French to simultane-

Figure 5.2. ***Delphi: State of Excavation*, November 1892, anonymous, print on paper aristotype, Bibliothèque de l'INHA (Institute national d'histoire de l'art), Collections Jacques Doucet. © INHA Dist. RMN-Grand Palais / Art Resource, NY.**

ously embrace another culture while reaping chauvinistic glory. Though the Greek king had invited the French to Delphi, his enthusiasm was apparently not shared by the people whose village lay atop the excavations. The whole enterprise reeked of colonization, with the villagers subdued only at gunpoint. Though Greece wasn't as remote from France as were its African colonies, it shared antiquity, exoticism, and sunshine, as well as poverty, with more distant locations. The stillness and serenity of Debussy's sculpture, pictured in figure 5.3, beckoned ambiguously, its "strangeness, . . . beauty, [and] nobility" recalling Gide's description of a North African mosque, similarly located in a far-off and impoverished land.[11]

The image of a village torn asunder juxtaposed with the timeless Egyptian lady of *Six épigraphes antiques* and the noble figures from *Danseuses de Delphes* puts a spotlight on the moral ambiguities of Orientalism. Its imaginative art often entailed destruction, and the single villages lost were, of course, small prey compared to the conquests of entire nations that were its larger legacy. The French takeover of Algeria, which resulted in magnificent works of art, music, and literature, is a particularly egregious example. The French were ruthless in their tactics, killing many thousands of civilians and

Figure 5.3. *Dancers of Delphi,* probably fourth century BC, Delphi Archaeological Museum. Photograph by Yair Haklai, October 14, 2008.

uprooting countless others, removing legal rights from the native populations, destroying Muslim educational systems, and inadvertently, but nevertheless catastrophically, introducing lethal diseases such as cholera and typhus to which the natives had no immunity. The story is painfully reminiscent of Americans' treatment of Native Americans. By the First World War, the settlers controlled education, trade, and government and had all but annihilated indigenous Muslim culture and prosperity. Newspaper reports were remarkably oblivious to any opposition, and it was not until long after Debussy was dead that loud voices challenged government policy. In 1939, George Orwell asked with prescience, "How long can we keep kidding these people? How long before they turn their guns in the other direction?"[12] And of course he was right—the 1950s saw an eight-year bloody conflict between Algerians and the French, until the French finally withdrew in 1962.

Debussy and his countrymen didn't see it coming; they reaped the profits but not the ultimate costs. While he was interested in assimilating cultural artifacts and delighted by exotic peoples and their art, Debussy didn't question his nation's "mission civilisatrice," with its concurrent destruction of the culture, scenes, and institutions that gave rise to precisely those artifacts. *Babar, le petit éléphant*, of international children's book fame, is the perfect fictional example of this colonialist mentality. Though written in 1931, thirteen years after Debussy's death, French attitudes hadn't changed much in those intervening years. The engrossing story made it into the annals of music because Francis Poulenc (1899–1963), French composer par excellence in the generation following Debussy, set it to music for piano and narrator just a few years after the Jean de Brunhoff book was written. As the story goes, both with and without musical accompaniment, Babar came back to the jungle to become king after having "lived among men and learnt much." The French were, of course, the men, and the Algerians were, just as unsurprisingly, the elephants; they were regarded, in their natural barbaric state, as seriously in need of learning. Babar was the exceptional crossover Algerian, the "evolué" or "evolved one," who wore the fine clothes, drove the luxury car, and adopted the ceremonies of the West. He was the purveyor of the civilizing mission, and Poulenc marks his coronation as king with music of extraordinary pomp and circumstance. Debussy didn't live long enough to celebrate the rise of Babar, but his own children's music inspired the children's music of Poulenc, and Debussy's famed black Golliwogg doll, adopted benevolently by white children, played a role similar to Poulenc's elephant: Both were curious objects for the white child to study and adore, and each, in his own story, was eventually enveloped by that white culture, with his own heritage effaced.

The civilizing mission that Babar protected is of course what made it possible for artists to head for Africa, and they flocked to the safe French

Figure 5.4. *Odalisque*, 1870, oil on canvas, Pierre-Auguste Renoir (1841–1919), National Gallery of Art (NGA), Chester Dale Collection, Washington, DC. NGA Images.

ports of Algeria and Morocco. Debussy almost went along; in 1893, he was invited to accompany his friend, the poet Pierre Louÿs, on a trip with André Gide, to Biskra, Algeria. That must have been quite a trip, for Algeria was then replete with French luminaries of every description. In fact that same year, a whole Société des Peintres Orientalistes (Society of Orientalist Painters) had formed. They were following in the steps of Delacroix, Gerome, and Renoir, who had already visited and delivered scenes of wild animals, harems, baths, slaves, and snake charmers back to their native France, enticing the next generation and even inspiring exotic fashions like harem pantaloons.[13]

Composers went too, well aware of Africa's attractions. The French composer, Camille Saint-Saëns, who had traveled to Algeria already in 1876, returned to northern Africa on numerous occasions and composed a *Suite Algérienne* for orchestra, an *Africa Fantasy* for piano and orchestra, and a movement entitled "Vision Congolaise" for violin and piano. There was, in fact, an outpouring of music, particularly opera and symphonic music, exploiting the exoticism of Arab lands, but relatively little directly from Africa for piano, perhaps because the instrument itself was so foreign to the culture. Saint-Saëns's "Egyptian" piano concerto (Piano Concerto no. 5) and Debussy's *Pour l'égyptienne* are today's best-known explicit reminders.

It's tempting to imagine what we might have heard had Debussy experienced Africa firsthand, but he did receive personal correspondence from Biskra in Algeria, and the journals he read extolled and expounded upon the colonialist enterprise daily. His most vivid impressions of the region were probably formed at the Paris World Expositions of 1889 and 1900, with their replicas of entire African villages, complete with artifacts, indigenous food, and "natives" singing, dancing, and purportedly going about daily life. When Debussy sent his friend Louÿs off to join Gide in 1894, he cheerfully assured him that "Biskra will teach us new games."[14] And ever eager to snub Richard Wagner and Bayreuth, home to Wagner's opera productions, he snidely lauded Louÿs for his last-minute change in travel plans, announcing, "I'd never doubted for a moment that the 'inversion' of Bayreuth was Biskra, but Heaven knows the second's the chord I prefer."[15] For this proud Frenchman, Wagner's famous Tristan chord played second fiddle, in any of its inversions, to the imagined charms of primitive Algeria.

That charm was only part of the picture, however. The Arab legacy was complex and did not correspond entirely to the French primitivist fantasy that reduced these foreign cultures to images of desire—beautiful interiors, luxurious fabrics, mysterious religious rites, wild animals, and most important, stunning women unconfined by the rites of marriage. The painter Henri Regnault characterizes the Moors as "both terrifying and voluptuous."[16] Henri Matisse confesses that "the Arabs who were nice to me at first disgusted me in the end—I found them too downtrodden."[17] There was a massive cultural clash between the colonizer and the colonized, and the tantalizing sensuality Debussy imagined and Matisse appropriated was part and parcel of a culture that was frightening and about to disappear to boot. As Théophile Gautier, the famous poet and critic, noted:

> Having seen [Bab-Azoun Street] recently, I can say that it has not gained from our civilizing presence. . . . So varied, so picturesque, so interesting in former times, [it] will soon be nothing more than a prolongation of the Rue de Rivoli. . . . That abominably fine road, which cannot stretch past the Louvre, has jumped the Mediterranean and toppled the elegant Moorish buildings so as to continue its frightful arcades.[18]

The French presence in Africa was destroying the very paradise these artists sought, and yet were it not for the French presence, the artists would never have set foot in the paradise. A catch-22 if ever there was one. And those things that were most alluring, such as harems and illicit sex, were at the same time most distasteful. The "law-abiding reality" of France was butting up against a formidable adversary.

Fascinated by both the region and their own reactions to it, French writers reported copiously on their attraction and their repugnance. Like Debussy, they all sought to live "anywhere out of the world,"[19] rather than in it, and northern Africa came close to fitting the description.

Gide, whose autobiographical book *If It Die* describes precisely the trip Debussy chose not to take, reports, "There was a gathering of Aïssaouas [an Algerian tribe] in a little mosque, which surpassed in frenzy, in strangeness, in beauty, in nobility, in horror, anything I have ever seen since."[20] His novel *The Immoralist* presents a promised land "free of rules or moral scrutiny,"[21] and Michel, the first-person narrator, lives like someone foraging for depravity, with a "stubborn attachment to evil."[22] He has found a land unsullied, like the Garden of Eden: "Tranquil, as if outside time, . . . quivering with . . . the soft cooing of the doves, the sounds of a child playing the flute . . . sitting, virtually naked."[23] But he simultaneously savors images of moral trespass: "When night fell . . . I slunk out like a thief. . . . The most even of paths seemed dangerous."[24]

Gide and his tale were far from an abstraction to Debussy. He knew him personally, but more important, Gide was close to his friend, Louÿs. Louÿs and Gide stayed together in Biskra, and when Louÿs reached Algeria, he excitedly wrote Debussy about "a young personage of sixteen, whose morals are extremely depraved" to whom Gide had introduced him.[25] The young woman, Meryem ben Ali, so entranced him that he was inspired to write a number of those *Bilitis* poems that later gave rise to Debussy's *Six épigraphes antiques*. These sexually explicit, and frequently lesbian, texts purporting to be by a Greek poetess of the sixth century BC make clear that Louÿs was transported by the possibilities of sexual promiscuity in far-off Africa. His hoax of false authorship added another layer of titillation to an already forbidden encounter.

Louÿs not only dedicated the poems to Gide but also made special mention of M.b.A., a.k.a. Meryem ben Ali, whose virtues—or rather, extreme lack thereof—he'd excitedly reported to Debussy. He then returned to Algeria in 1897 and this time came home to Paris with more *Bilitis* poems and a bona fide Algerian mistress, Zohra ben Brahim. Figure 5.5 provides a striking photo of Debussy with ben Brahim at Louÿs's home, the composer looking relaxed and pleased with his company.

No doubt she helped inspire his own numerous efforts on behalf of Bilitis. He was clearly as infatuated with the poems as Louÿs had been with the woman who inspired them: Debussy set three for female voice and piano in 1897; arranged twelve of the poems for two flutes, two harps, celeste, and narrator in 1900; and revised six of these yet again for the piano duet (or solo), *Six épigraphes antiques*, in 1914. It is not only the one mentioned earlier, *Pour l'égyptienne*, that is erotic in its title and attitude; all six of these miniatures feature flute-like arabesques that invoke Pan in his role as God/suitor with pipes in hand; they remind us also of the naked boy Gide encountered playing the flute who "was only twelve and . . . very handsome."[26] The music is lonely and indeterminate, never quite fully grasping a harmony or cadence

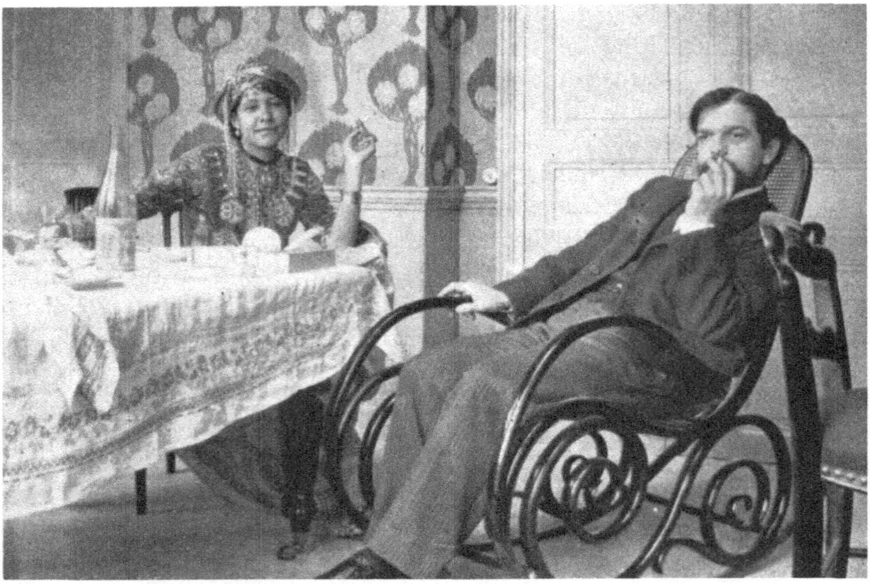

Figure 5.5. ***Debussy with Zohra-ben-Brahim,*** **1897, Pierre Louÿs.**

or even indulging in a full-blown melody. Grace notes enhance the curving lines, making them more like embellishments than resolute structures. These are delicate caresses, and Debussy spoke cunningly of "putting the finishing touches on *Bilitis* . . . if I may thus express myself,"[27] enjoying the fantasy that his music might allow for actual touching. Gide wished to touch the boy; Louÿs, the woman; and Debussy, his manuscript. That was suggestive enough, for even the titles, whether invoking a propitious night ("Pour que la nuit soit propice") or an exotic dancer ("Pour la danseuse aux crotales"), imply sex lurking in the shadows.

Francis Poulenc, who owned that famous photo of Debussy with Zohra ben Brahim, tells us that this ben Brahim was the "sister of the little Arab thief in [Gide's] *L'Immoraliste*."[28] That boy, Moktir, lived a life of the body without rules, and Debussy, who in the same year had yearned for that "india-rubber for removing adultery," had similar proclivities.[29] "It's pointless expecting this same man to follow strictly all the observances of daily life, the laws and all the other barriers erected by a cowardly, hypocritical world," he proudly announced of himself.[30] Laws were his nemesis, and he was at home in a culture without them. The aversion spread across both social mores and musical forms. Nary a symphony or piano sonata is to be found in his catalog. His one completed play, *Frères en art* (1898–1899), proposes anarchism as the solution to artists' ills. "Those around me resolutely refuse to understand that I've never been able to live in a world of real things and real people. . . . I have this imperative need to escape from myself and go off on adventures which seem inexplicable," he explained.[31]

Debussy's fascination with Moorish Spain grants him those adventures, and it's yet another indication of the appeal of Arab and North African culture. The Moors of Spain came directly from Africa, and even the famous Spanish habañera rhythm hails from Africa. The French happily mounted an enormous exhibition entitled *Andalusia in the Time of the Moors* in the 1900 World Exposition in Paris, and any number of Orientalist painters shared Debussy's pleasure in exploring their non-European neighbors to the south. The Alhambra came to be the symbol of that Moorish culture, especially fascinating because it was transplanted into Europe. This enormous structure in Granada that had housed Moorish royalty since the twelfth century was a fairy-tale palace big enough to hold every fantasy, and Debussy returns to it in three Spanish piano works: *Lindaraja* (for two pianos), *La puerta del vino*, and *La soirée dans Grenade*. All three illustrate powerfully the sensuality and abandon the French imagined in their neighbors to the south; they are aural images as powerful as the painted images of Matisse, who also found the Alhambra an irresistible inspiration.

Lindaraja, written already in 1901, refers to a hall and gardens of the Alhambra, perhaps brought to Debussy's attention through his reading of Sir Walter Scott. It's not played often, but that's probably due to the awkward logistics of acquiring two pianos, rather than to a lack of appeal in the music. This is a nice showpiece; it's filled with spikey Spanish rhythms, ostinatos or repeated patterns that make the body itch to dance, and insinuating colors, all augmented by the power of two keyboards.

La puerta, written a full ten years after *Lindaraja*, was reportedly inspired by a postcard Debussy received picturing the "Door of Wine" at the palace, shown in figure 5.6. Even in the opening, one hears black notes clashing with white, as if the confining rules of civilization had been removed and the Fauvist obsession with wild, savage color had set loose the dancers. They flirt, glide, and slink, accompanied always by the same tireless dotted rhythm in the left hand. That bass figure disregards every dissonance it creates; its two entrenched pitches have a steely resolve and insist absolutely on their own rectitude. Bizet's gypsy *Carmen* lurks in the shadows: beautiful, amoral, and insinuating. Debussy even prefaces *La puerta* with the instruction to play "with the brusque opposition of extreme violence and passionate sweetness." He wanted Carmen at the piano.

Though *La soirée dans Grenade*, written in 1903, edges up more delicately, its sinuous lines also ally us with the dancers' very physical and sexual

Figure 5.6. *Puerta del Vino at the Alhambra*, photograph by Michael Clarke, February 26, 2010.

pleasure. Carmen's habañera rhythms parented all these later Spanish seductresses. Here again, even the very first melody note is deeply at odds with the prevailing harmony. This is a world of conflicts and contrasts. Rhythms cross and contradict one another, accents appear where they shouldn't, a third staff invites in third-party voices, and everywhere that Spanish dotted rhythm prevails, an inextinguishable life force, infinitely beguiling. Matisse had said, "Il fallait sortir de l'imitation" (It's necessary to go beyond imitation),[32] and Debussy succeeded in doing precisely that; we hear the guitars and castanets in these pieces, but more importantly, we are given a unified sensation of sounds, scents, and movement for a very particular location.

Spanish life, however, teeming with high-voltage energy, was not Debussy's native habitat. More frequently, we see him accepting Baudelaire's "L'invitation au voyage," where "tout n'est qu'ordre et beauté, / Luxe, calme et volupté" (all is but order and beauty / Luxury, calm, and voluptuous pleasure). That link between "calme" and "volupté" is a delightfully unexpected pairing, one precisely attuned to Debussy's susceptibilities and music. Can you imagine Mozart's Don Giovanni, for example, demanding "calme" as the sidekick to his "volupté"? Tranquility was an important and surprising aspect of Debussy's Orientalist mindset, though it's hardly appropriate to the Spanish works. It was also, of course, at odds with the primary colors that dominated most of what was written and pictured about Africa. Works such as Saint-Saëns's *Africa Fantasy* are outright flamboyant, and many of the paintings and novels are unabashedly violent. Debussy's favorite author, Gustave Flaubert,[33] wrote an Orientalist masterpiece, *Salammbô*, which Debussy briefly tried to set, and it zeroes in on barbaric bloodshed and exotic beasts: "The elephants . . . stifled the men with their trunks, or else snatching them up from the ground delivered them over their heads to the soldiers in the towers; with their tusks they disemboweled them, and hurled them into the air, and long entrails hung from their ivory fangs like bundles of rope from a mast."[34] Debussy was sometimes taken with a violence in literature that he abjures in his music—Poe is a case in point—but my guess is that he preferred Baudelaire's take on the Orient: no unbridled force or orgies but rather perfumed lassitude and endless leisure, a life "outside time" for his romantic encounters.

The omnipresent arabesques of his flute, closely associated with the Arab boys in this chapter,[35] will prove to be a crossover artifact into the next. They conjured muted sensuality with no hint of brutality, and they served Debussy well in "The Flute of Pan," and the *Six épigraphes antiques* for piano duet or solo. He commented, in fact, that "my favorite music is those few notes an Egyptian shepherd plays on his flute."[36]

They will reappear in the curvaceous lines of the piano music associated with Asia. The piano proved to be the ideal purveyor of gentle sexual innuendo; it could conjure both loneliness and companionship, veiled approaches and delicate joinings. Debussy's piano specialized in the colors of wafting harmonies, those "sounds and perfumes turning in the night air" that could cross the world.

• 6 •

Asia on a Pedestal

Debussy's sounds and perfumes found new and radical inspiration in East Asia, where the swirling erotic mystery of his music could incorporate exotic scales, harmonies, and colors unfolding at infinite leisure. Debussy was both aware and pleased that this indolent music had erotic implications; his dictum "It is necessary to abandon yourself completely, and let the music do as it will with you" could as easily have been applied to an amorous tryst as a concert hall.[1] And while Africa and Spain were lands of bright hues, the vast majority of Debussy's music is more aligned with the pastels of Asia, where the culture was Buddhist and the women less overtly suggestive. Here he could immerse himself in "l'extase langoureuse" (the languorous ecstasy) and "la fatigue amoureuse" (the fatigue of love) that both he and his friend, the poet Paul Verlaine, had extolled in the song cycle *Ariettes oubliées*.[2] Here he found a native land for the ennui, the slow tempos and soft dynamics, that brought both laments and murmurs of pleasure in their own good time.

So we'll leave behind the "alluring horrors" and "sultry promise" of Arabic nations for other ports of call.[3] For not only northern Africa, with its Arab culture, but also Southeast Asia, with its Eastern religions, fell prey to French colonialism, and other countries, such as Greece, despite having their independence, were still subject to the whims of the greater colonial powers. French Indochina, comprised of previous conquests of Vietnam and Cambodia, was formed in 1887, with Laos added a few years later. And to top it off, France had additional holdings in Shanghai and southern China. With this colonization, the completion of the Suez Canal in 1869, new trade treaties, and the century's massive industrialization, trade grew exponentially between the East and West. And alongside trade, naturally enough, came increased curiosity about Asian cultures. Japanese prints, for instance, so striking to

Debussy that he named his great piano set, *Estampes* (meaning "prints"), in their honor, began to arrive in Europe in the early 1800s. They arrived first as wrapping paper, but eventually people actually looked, and the art had an immense impact on Impressionist and post-Impressionist painters in France. Dozens of these artists, including Toulouse-Lautrec, Degas, and Bonnard, all acquaintances of Debussy, embraced the resulting vogue of "japonisme" and emulated the prints' flat surfaces, detailed brushwork, and cut-off designs. Orient-inspired figures, wallpaper, and fabrics are rife in any exhibit of these artists' works.

Exposure to this wider world expanded with the Paris World Expositions of 1889 and 1900. Had there ever been any doubt for Parisians that their city was the center of the universe, particularly during the prosperous Belle Époque, the question was fully settled in 1889, for the Champ de Mars now boasted pavilions from around the world, as exemplified by figure 6.1. It seems no accident that Champ de Mars, where the exposition was held, translates as Field of War, for the exposition had been planned to celebrate the centenary of the French Revolution and was filled with nationalist implications. Though the exposition was hardly the site of a literal war, it certainly depended on the subjugation of foreign peoples. The French were dazzled by what they saw from Java, Vietnam, and Egypt, yet they were at pains to construct the Eiffel Tower as a monument "before which oriental peoples would stand in awe,"[4] and to perform their national anthem, "La Marseillaise," at every possible occasion. Admiration was again mixed with domination.[5]

One unthreatening way of admiring a culture from afar while simultaneously asserting one's power is to acquire indigenous objects, effectively divorcing the things from the people that made them. And in the second half of the nineteenth century there was a veritable storm of acquisition, heavily associated with a movement known as aestheticism. Debussy remarked in his letters, "Desire is everything. One has a mad but perfectly sincere craving for a work of art." The work of art may be a "Velasquez, a vase of Satsouma or a new kind of tie. What joy the moment one possesses it. This is really love."[6] The movement featured a strong desire for the exotic, and foreign objects, particularly from the East, figured heavily in the marketplace. From a young age, Debussy made "a clean sweep of tiny Japanese objects which entranced him,"[7] and throughout his life he immortalized chosen objects in his music. Among the objects that lived with him in close quarters were his Chinese porcelain frog Arkel, the Japanese lacquer panel of a goldfish that inspired *Poissons d'or*, and the Greek burial jars that inspired *Canope*.

He was far from the first to exhibit such tastes. Witness Charles Baudelaire, who "was the great apostle of dandyism . . . [and who] frequently talks about the purchase of a Japanese print . . . long before such bizarre objects

Figure 6.1. Pagoda of Angkor (Cambodia), Exposition Universelle, 1889, National Gallery of Art, Washington, DC. NGA Images.

bought randomly were à la mode."[8] And then there was Joris-Karl Huysmans, who was the quintessential spokesman of the aestheticist/decadent movement in France. He privileged art and beauty over nature, action, and even morality in his book *A rebours*, or *Against Nature* (1884), and the book was greeted eagerly hot off the press by Debussy and his artist companions.[9] The hero, Jean des Esseintes, reportedly the inspiration for Oscar Wilde's *Picture of Dorian Gray*, escaped from all relationships and obligations into a cornucopia of possessions, most of which came from distant lands. He enjoyed experiments of the most bizarre nature, outfitting a live tortoise with embedded jewels to match his oriental carpet, and mixing liqueurs to conjure the tones of musical instruments. His living quarters reflected his opulent tastes: "[H]e had fitted out a boudoir with delicate carved furniture in pale Japanese camphor-wood under a sort of canopy of pink Indian satin."[10] And here it was, in the "shelter of this haven of his" that he evaded "that gale of human folly that had battered and buffeted him of old!"[11] The interiors of homes, decorated with such obsessive attention, came to represent interiors of minds.[12] Amusingly, Debussy even speaks of himself becoming "a Japanese vase on the mantelpiece,"[13] and had he succeeded in the conversion, he might have found that he hadn't escaped the interior of his own mind after all. Baudelaire avowed that "taking up an Oriental chest, / . . . One comes, perhaps, upon a flask of memories / In whose escaping scent a soul returns to life."[14] Debussy's music is replete with such flasks.

Take a look at *Canope*, a striking example of a beautiful object musically embodied. An homage to two Egyptian burial vases that Debussy owned, pictured in figure 6.2, this prelude takes us many, many miles and years from Debussy's Paris. The lonely C-sharps you hear near the beginning seem like markers of a distant time and place, floating in and out of the C-naturals preceding them, as if two worlds, both veiled, could exist simultaneously. The foreign pitches appear so unobtrusively that they create no disruption, and yet they don't belong to the preceding music at all. The music seems to take enormous comfort in this calm acceptance of contradiction, and as such it espouses one aspect of the Oriental experience in striking contrast to those Western "punctilious, pedestrian minds" that insist on rational choice.[15]

Danseuses de Delphes offers the same sort of serenity and comfort. The statue, unearthed in Delphi, and pictured in the previous chapter (figure 5.3), was not an object Debussy could himself acquire, but writing music provided proxy ownership: The sculpture could become a repository of emotions, and Debussy's gaze could join centuries of others lavished on these ancient women.

And *Poissons d'or*, another musical rendition of one of Debussy's own prize possessions, also provides solace, though of a more active sort. Here a Japanese lacquered wood panel carefully renders two extraordinarily elegant goldfish with every scale intact. These fish are very much in motion, and Debussy must have imagined an active inner life for them—the shimmer with which the piece commences is only the beginning; later one hears them frolicking, by turns impudent and sensual, and by Debussy's direction, "capri-

Figure 6.2. ***Bouchons de vases canopes,*** **Musée Claude Debussy, Saint-Germain-en-Laye.**

cious and supple." The goldfish are a foil for the other two very quiet pieces in this set of *Images, Book 2* (1907), and the creatures' constant movement, darting, splashing, and leaping, is another, far brasher, version of the dream objects can provide. These stylized fish, cavorting without care, provide memories of the living; they are preserved in action rather than immobilized in death. You can admire them in figure 6.3.

That carefree attitude was the antithesis of Debussy's usual mindset, and it's unusual to find it in his music. He lived in terror of losing hope and, with it, the ability to work. He occasionally speaks of suicide and suffered pitiably from "illness, rehearsals, jangling nerves . . . the full, horrible gamut of Parisian life,"[16] admitting that "from time to time humanity disgusts me."[17] He needed those beautiful objects, his external life buoys, for his art was about fragility and that was not always an easy place to reside. If we look at *Images, Book 2*, we can't help but be astounded by the remarkable stillness and delicacy of *Cloches à travers les feuilles* (Bells across the Leaves) and, even more notably, *Et la lune descend sur le temple qui fut* (And the Moon Descends over the Temple That Was). *Cloches à travers les feuilles*, the first of the set, "paints a tone picture of hardly stirring boughs lulled in a sweet silence, a tranquil green shade touched but not disturbed by far-off vibrations sustained, quiver-

Figure 6.3. Japanese goldfish lacquer panel that inspired *Poissons d'or* (Goldfish) by Debussy. Claude Debussy Centre, Saint-Germain-en-Laye, the Art Archive at Art Resource, NY. Photo by Ginni Dagli Orti.

ing, by the pedals," according to the famous French pianist Alfred Cortot.[18] And Louis Laloy, Debussy's early biographer, believed the evocative title for the piece came from a description he sent Debussy of church bells he'd heard: "[B]etween vespers and the mass for the dead . . . the bells toll from village to village, across the golden woods in the quiet of the evening."[19] Both descriptions, particularly the first, strike me as overly contented and lacking the emotional complexity that quiet can signify, but, regardless of the source, the title is an unusual combination of visual and aural imagery. This is one of those many pieces by Debussy that seem to be so much about textures. One is reminded of the importance of exotic fabrics to Matisse, particularly when the almost inaudible rapid notes introducing the second section herald the arrival of "iridescent mist" (comme une buée irisée). The sheer physicality of the touch in Debussy's writing is akin to the pleasure of running one's hand over delicate fabric, harking back again to the silks, yarns, and satins pouring in from Asia. Beautiful as this music is, I wonder if it can ever be quite as wonderful to simply hear it as it is to also feel it under the hand. Debussy was a sensualist in every regard, and the yearning in the music becomes a physical reality in playing it.

Like so many of Debussy's (and Ravel's) pieces, this piece uses bells to summon memories, in this case not so much personal as archetypal. The bells evoke longing, and they arrive first as even gong strokes, celebrating that omnipresent whole-tone scale on three staves, in multiple voices, rhythms, and directions. Debussy often likes to write on three staves instead of the customary two, as if pretending that the pianist had sprouted a third hand, or at the very least, a third ear, the better to hear multiple speakers. In this case, he's celebrating all the different speeds, registers, and directions a whole-tone scale can simultaneously inhabit. The bells' rhythms quickly morph into grace notes, tiny sparks played before the principal notes, and we hear small cells darting through space, linked not by melodic line but simply by harmony and free association.

The second part of the set is a piece deeply about the past and distance. Its title, *Et la lune descend sur le temple qui fut*, is an alexandrine, the twelve-syllable line used in early French modern poetry. Its evocation of a "temple that was" puts the entire experience in the realm of imagination; the moon is descending in the present tense, but the temple "was" only in the past, and at that, "fut" is a literary past tense no longer employed in everyday speech. The dynamic level of the piece never rises above piano and only rarely above pianissimo; everything must take place in deep recesses of the mind. And those recesses reverberate with echoes of the middle ages in the opening harmonies and of the Far East in the whole-tone harmonies and pentatonic passagework we encounter in so much of Debussy's music.[20] Most striking, perhaps, is the

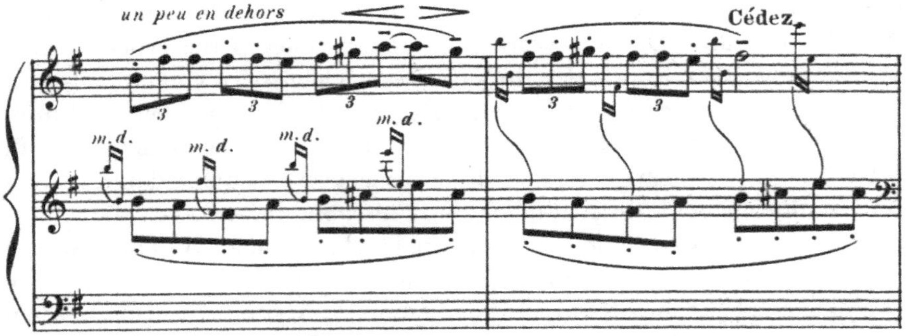

Figure 6.4. ***Et la lune descend,*** **mm. 14–15, in** ***Images, Book 2,*** **by Claude Debussy (Paris: Durand, 1908). Digital image from Hathi Trust Digital Library.**

hint of an Indian influence in that chant-like passage shown in figure 6.4 where all harmony disappears, and we're left with the otherworldly texture of single lines patiently exploring their own reverberations.[21]

Gongs vibrate, reiterating each pitch struck, at first in utter loneliness and then in tandem with a haunting and hollow melody in the soprano. The piece drifts in and out of major and minor triads as if completely unbeholden to any laws concerning harmony. This is a piece that, like *Canope*, seems to exist outside the march of time; the moon's radiance over its temple is not of this earth.

This temple, and its haunting gongs, in turn reminds us of *Pagodes*, the first piece from *Estampes*. *Estampes*, written in 1903, four years before *Images, Book 2*, presumably served as a laboratory for some of the ideas developed in these later images. It holds a special place in any discussion of Orientalism, for it was Debussy's first serious homage, not only to Japanese prints, but also, more importantly, to the gamelan, the orchestra of gongs he had found so astonishing when he first heard it at the Javanese pavilion of the 1889 World Exposition. Debussy's response to it was life changing: "If we listen without European prejudice to the magical beauty of Javanese 'percussion,' we are obliged to admit that our own is a barbarous noise fit only for a travelling circus."[22] One can imagine this twenty-seven-year-old Frenchman, who had barely traveled outside Europe, suddenly encountering sounds, costumes, dances, and beliefs that were entirely remote from his sphere of experience. For a composer seeking to free himself from Wagnerism and the musical hegemony of the Austro-Germans, the sense of liberation must have been staggering, and *Estampes* plays it out. *Pagodes* is almost obsessively concerned with the pentatonic, or five-note, scale, seen most easily on the black notes of the piano and also, like *Les cloches*, with layering. It represents a clear effort to transfer the sounds of an orchestra of gongs onto the Western instrument best suited to imitate it. Like the gamelan, the piano functions as a percussion instrument, and the pedal serves to create the desired reverberations.[23] Robert Schmitz reports that, not surprisingly, "Debussy regarded the piano as the Balinese musicians regard their gamelan orchestras," and warned, in anticipation of indelicate virtuosos, that the keys "must be struck in a peculiar way, otherwise the sympathetic vibrations of the other notes will not be heard quivering distantly in the air."[24] No scale used on Western instruments fully matches the Eastern scales of the gamelan, the slendro, and pelog, yet the naïve Western listener can easily be persuaded of similarities. The pentatonic scale probably comes closest, but the whole-tone scale is another option. Built of all identical intervals, its very essence rebuts the assumptions about tension and resolution crucial to Western harmonic language. By making all intervals uniform, the whole-tone scale asserts that all pitches are equally significant; it has no half-step resolutions that pull irresistibly toward a primary or tonic pitch. Milan Kundera describes the conventional tonal organization metaphorically: He says the system of major and minor keys is like "a king's court in miniature. It is ruled by a king (the first step) and his two right-hand men (steps five and four)."[25] Debussy was clearly opposed to such musical monarchies and their privileged advisors; a great deal of his music is devoted to their debunking.

And that indeed is what qualifies him as such a revolutionary. Hierarchical and goal-oriented language is essential to Western music, and that language is deeply wedded to Western belief systems. Music that does not drive toward one pitch is much more likely to float; time is at its disposal, for it needn't push toward cadence and resolution. Likewise, Eastern religions strive for quiet, meditative states not measured by worldly achievements or ambition. Interestingly (and mistakenly in my opinion), Susan McClary and others have posited that "feminist" music, if it existed in greater quantity, would likewise be circular, rather than linear, and that the "climax principle" is a male construct, unleashed in particularly violent fashion in the works of Beethoven.[26] Debussy, in his own time, was often accused of writing effeminate music: his was an "amorphous and hardly virile art . . . women appreciate it."[27] Perhaps it was these same ostensible qualities that linked it to the Far East! Sergei Prokofiev, presumably in a fit of macho pique, called the music "jelly"-like and "spineless."[28]

Prokofiev's experience of Debussy must have been severely limited. One wonders, for instance, if he'd ever heard the second piece in the set of *Estampes*, *La soirée dans Grenade* (The Evening in Granada) or the other Spanish-tinged music mentioned in the previous chapter. Filled with buoyant rhythms and decidedly un-jelly-like, these pieces leave the Buddhists and

Hindus to their own ascetic devices. The contrast between the evocation of a pagoda, a place of worship, and the Spanish dance culture is striking—Debussy, like his compatriots, wanted it all, and in naming his piece *Estampes* he presumably wanted to indicate the same breadth of subject matter that prints encompass.

Indeed, he moved on from Spain to gardens right at home in the third and last piece of *Estampes*: *Jardins sous la pluie* (Gardens in the Rain). Perhaps Debussy had seen one of the many Japanese prints portraying rain showers, or perhaps he just wanted a vehicle for the two children's songs he embedded in this piece, the same two he quoted in the equally celebratory *Rondes de printemps* from the orchestral *Images*. One of them—"Do, do l'enfant do" (Sleep, the Child Sleeps)—is a lullaby,[29] though played at an extremely wakeful tempo in Debussy's rendition. And the other—"Nous n'irons plus aux bois" (We Won't Go to the Woods Anymore)—is, text-wise at least, more appropriate to the subject matter at hand, rain having apparently put a damper on forest excursions.[30] This piece is lighthearted, virtuosic, and enchanting. It has little to do with Orientalism except as it completes a set called *Prints* and reminds us that a composer who can effortlessly transition from mysterious temples to seductive dances and to French children's songs has a broad worldview at his disposal!

Except for the merest hint of a raga in *Et la lune descend sur le temple qui fut*, one far-flung location is still missing from Debussy's catalog and that is India. We finally arrive there in *La terrasse des audiences du clair de lune*. The mysterious title of that prelude turns out to be a direct quote from a 1912 report by René Puaux in the Paris newspaper *Le Temps*, describing the crowning of King George V of England as Emperor of India. In it, Puaux carefully describes "the Hall of Victory, the Hall of Pleasure, the Gardens of the Sultans, the *Terrace of audiences in the light of the moon*" (italics added).[31] Earlier yet, in 1903, Pierre Loti, the author of numerous Orientalist popular novels, had entitled a chapter in his book *L'Inde sans les Anglais* (India without the English) "Terraces for Holding Council by the Light of the Moon." That chapter begins, "The full moon, still pale, suspended in the sky at dusk, hasn't begun to spread its light."[32] So Debussy had no shortage of poetic images connecting India and the moon. And this hall for receiving audiences that Puaux and Loti mention appears to be a familiar part of Indian architecture; E. M. Forster even refers to it in *A Passage to India*: "It was an audience hall built in the eighteenth century for some high official. . . . Little rooms, now Europeanized, clung to it on either side, but the central hall was unpapered and unglassed, and the air of the garden poured in freely."[33]

The French, who had been defeated by the English in their attempts to control India more than a hundred years earlier, continued to be fascinated by the country itself and by the majesty of the English presence there. The Europeanized rooms Forster describes, alongside the openness of the original central hall, encapsulated the European/Indian duality implicit in that colonial relationship. Puaux, who wrote the initial report quoted above, was so taken with what he saw that he wrote an entire book, entitled *Le beau voyage*, to describe the scene:

> The Arabs, big horse-dealers turbaned in silk and gold, swaggering in carriages superbly hitched, their servants coming from Portuguese fortresses, the snake charmers hurrying in front of the hotels in order to show a stunned cobra and toothless mongoose—all these bronze beings whose bare feet made little sound . . . are perfectly picturesque. One wanted to stop certain ones, like the two women just met carrying on their heads large bamboo baskets on which hooded peacocks were perched.
>
> Do they know they are the subjects of His Majesty George V? Do they have a precise notion of the extraordinary honor that the King of England has done them of leaving his royal kingdom to visit them? . . .
>
> And when the "tiwana" [an Indian regiment] has, with a supreme effort and in a voice hoarse with emotion, vociferously proclaimed "God save the king," the silver trumpets resound, the gigantic orchestra attacks the national anthem, and the entire amphitheater rising, makes one dream of a spring breeze making millions of petals wave in the most extraordinary garden of the world.
>
> This made the historic moment, of which the symbolism strikes the imagination and will remain profoundly close to the English heart.[34]

The colonialist enterprise had found a sympathetic chronicler indeed, one quite struck with the strangeness of local customs and one quite certain that a nation filled with barefoot inhabitants needed an English king to set things right. But Debussy, in reading about the event, clearly fixated not on the political implications but on the mystery, elegance, and distance of the crowning ceremony. This is one of the longest and most complex of the preludes; it speaks to a substantial occasion with its slow, swaying dance rhythms, its stately gongs, and its exquisite embellishments. It seems to be about the materials of the terrace—its wood and its decorations—as well as the breezes that weave through it. The huge span of registers conveys the vastness of the space Debussy envisioned. And coincidentally it can also signify the vast distance between Parisian daily life and the turbaned Indians. Strangely enough, as if to bridge that gap, the prelude begins with a distorted version of "Au clair de la lune," the old French evocation of Pierrot,[35] as if not only the moon over the terrace but also the masked nature of a foreign people brought to mind this song of Debussy's very French childhood.

India returned to haunt Debussy when he started writing *Toomai of the Elephants*,[36] the prelude based on Rudyard Kipling's tale in *The Jungle Book*. It was originally intended to be the penultimate prelude of the second book, but Debussy later discarded it in favor of *Alternating Thirds*, a prelude resolutely lacking in national origin. India reappears too in the "old Hindu chant" that Debussy inserted into *La boîte à joujoux*, probably basing it on material he was no longer using in *Toomai*.

So much for an extremely condensed version of Orientalism, both Arab and Asian. While its one-sided vision reduced foreign subjects to stultifying formulas, it simultaneously freed the artists at home from the formulas they themselves found so confining. André Gide had spoken admiringly of Algeria in words that applied to Asian colonies as well: "A land unencumbered with works of art. I despise those who can't see beauty until it is transcribed and interpreted. What is so wonderful about the Arab people is that they live their art; they sing it and dissipate it on a day-to-day basis. They don't preserve it, embalm it in works of art."[37]

Paradoxically, in response, Gide and others did their best to embalm those cultures for eternity in their own art. They seem to have noted, as had Forster while observing an Indian ceremony, that these cultures "achieved what Christianity has shirked: the inclusion of merriment,"[38] and they chased that merriment, as well as the serenity that was its companion-piece, with a very Western-style determination. Baudelaire said it well when he advised his beautiful "Girl from Malabar" to avoid "the brutal corset's crushing grip" and stay far from the "filthy mists" of France.[39] Her merriment was part and parcel of her homeland, and in abandoning it she would sell her soul. Debussy had no choice but to reside among the "filthy mists," but he chose to transform them.

• 7 •

Child's Play and Make Believe

In Debussy's mind, Charles Baudelaire's "happy child" of Malabar was alive and well in France and, in fact, a very real version of her lived with him. Throughout his adult life, Debussy was drawn to the music, toys, and stories of childhood, and his own daughter, Chouchou (cabbage-cabbage or, less literally, darling) (1905–1919), afforded his most treasured relationship. His *Children's Corner* for piano is his most obvious homage to her, but it doesn't stand by itself. She was perhaps the only human being about whom he was unambivalent, and he eventually went so far as to say "if my little Chouchou weren't here I'd blow my brains out."[1] His letters refer to her with terms of endearment and the sort of easy warmth that is rarely evident in this acerbic man. Witness this letter, written from Vienna in December 1910, perhaps the most tender of the lot:

Vienna
2 December 1910

The memoirs of "outre Croche"

1. Once there was a papa who lived in exile . . . 2. and every day he missed his little Chouchou. 3. The inhabitants of the city saw him walking past and murmured "Why does that gentleman look so sad in our gay and beautiful city?" . . . 5. So Chouchou's papa went into a shop run by an old, very ugly man and his even uglier daughter, he politely removed his hat and using deaf-mute gestures asked for the most beautiful postcards they had, so that he could write to his darling little daughter . . . The ugly old man was very moved by this and as for his daughter, she died on the spot! 6. The said papa went

back to his hotel, wrote this story which would make a goldfish weep, and put all his love into the signature below, which is his greatest claim to fame.

LepapadeChouchou.[2]

Or a later one, also from "a papa who lived in exile":

St. Petersburg Grand Hotel d'Europe
11 December 1913

Ma chère petite Chouchou

Your poor papa is very late replying to your nice little letter. But you mustn't be cross with him . . . He's very sad not to have seen your pretty face for so long or heard you singing or shouting with laughter, in short all the noise which sometimes makes you an unbearable little girl, but more often a charming one.

How is that genius M. Czerny getting on? Do you know:

the "air de ballet" for fleas?

And old "Xantho"? [the Debussy dog] Is he still being good? Is he still digging up the garden? You have my permission to give him a thorough scolding!

At the Koussevitsky's house in Moscow there are two lovely bulldogs with eyes like the frog in the salon (we're great friends, I think you'd like them) and a bird which sings almost as well as Miss Teyte.[3]

It's all very nice but don't imagine I can forget you even for a second. Far from it, the only thing I think about is when I'm going to see you again. Until then, love and lots of kisses from your old papa.

C.D.

Be very nice to your poor mama; do all you can to see she doesn't get too worried![4]

Debussy's interest in childhood is, in the parlance of social scientists, overdetermined, and, though he adored his daughter and the music of *Children's Corner* is dedicated to her, it's doubtful that she alone accounts for his inclinations. His own childhood too must have played a role, though surely not as a positive model. His early years were thoroughly miserable; he felt unattractive with his strange bony forehead protuberances, and his parents were curiously uninvolved and incompetent. His father was unstable, constantly changing and losing jobs, and his mother "did not like children,"[5] despite giving birth to five of them. She foisted their care off on their paternal aunt, and Debussy didn't even attend school as a child. It was small wonder that he might yearn for a fantasyland of cuddly elephants and singing dolls, for it's dubious that any such luxuries followed him as he moved from one unfortunate childhood residence to the next.

Had he been born twenty years later, he would at least have had the assurance of a public school education, for it was in the 1880s that a series of laws, called the Jules Ferry laws, was enacted in France, guaranteeing free, compulsory, and secular education to all French children between the ages of six and twelve. The laws were in large part a response to fears of church-dominated education, but they also cemented the idea that children of every class belonged out of the workforce and off of the streets. Though children had worked hard on farms, that work tended to be within the family. Industrialization pushed them into the public labor market: Child labor in factories was plausible and profitable; the arrival of machinery to handle the heaviest work made physical strength less requisite; and small hands and submissive natures were increasingly desirable. But by the same token, that increasing mechanization eventually made extra workers less necessary. As urbanization led to fewer farming families; increasingly mechanized industrialization to the need for fewer factory workers; and a larger middle class to less need for supplementary income, children were free to attend school, and the image of children as simply miniature toiling adults slowly gave way to a construct of children as creatures with very separate needs and psyches.

The innate innocence or sin of those children was, of course, still open to question, but as secularism and leisure time grew during the Belle Époque, the assumption that children were innocent until shown otherwise became increasingly prevalent. This was not a new idea, but it was hardly an accepted truth in the nineteenth century. It's worth looking at its history, for while we now take it for granted, it required centuries of formulation before taking hold. Jean-Jacques Rousseau, the great French philosopher, already declared in the first sentence of *Emile, or On Education* (1762) that "everything is good as it leaves the hands of the author of things; everything degenerates in the hands of man."[6] And in 1846, the French historian Jules Michelet intoned, "The child is the interpreter of the People. Nay, he *is* the People with their inborn truth before they become deformed, the People without vulgarity, without uncouthness, without envy, inspiring neither distrust nor repulsion."[7] And Michelet not only identified the function children served but also inveighed against their current oppressed status: "They can be happy 'later,' people say; and, to assure the happiness of those uncertain years to come, children are overwhelmed with boredom and suffering, thereby being deprived of the one short moment of which they can be sure."[8]

But even long after Michelet's advice was handed down and absorbed, the plight of the French child had not changed markedly, for the educational system was not given to brightening that "one short moment." While John Dewey proselytized in the United States beginning in the late nineteenth century, France, along with many other European nations, remained more rigid in its approach to schooling. Still, by the early twentieth century Italy had welcomed Montessori Schools (1907), and Germany had given rise to Waldorf Schools (1919), while France had no comparably renowned progressive movement. To this day, its nationalized curriculum entails more memorization and regimentation than a typical American curriculum, and ideas about creativity and independent thinking take second place to the sheer acquisition of knowledge. What holds for French schools in general was, and to a large degree still is, yet more true of the Conservatoire, which Debussy attended for eleven years beginning at the tender age of ten. Here he was surrounded by rules, juries, and ancient traditions, all anathema to this composer who declared, "Some people wish above all to conform to the rules; for myself, I wish only to render what I can hear."[9]

Debussy must have badly needed an alternative universe, unlaced and unbarred. He saw in childhood not only the innocence of pretty toys but also the primitivism of unfettered desires—an appeal markedly similar to that of Orientalism. Note his description of Igor Stravinsky: "There are no precautions or pretentions. It's childish and savage."[10] Debussy clearly associated childhood with an uncivilized state. One must remember too that this was the dawn of psychoanalysis. In fact, Charles Baudelaire (1821–1867), some forty years older than Debussy, had been one of the first artists to undergo psychoanalysis, decades before Freud came on the scene in Vienna in the late 1800s. Psychoanalysis taught that it was the child's desires, "savage" and otherwise, that determined the man. Baudelaire put it well: "It's in the notes relative to childhood that we find the germ of the strange dreams of the adult man, and to say it better, of his genius . . . the small pain, the small joy of the child immoderately enlarged by an exquisite sensitivity, later become, in the adult man, even without his knowing it, the principle of a work of art."[11]

Debussy wrote many "notes relative to childhood," and Baudelaire's suppositions are especially apropos his particular art. Such theories are commonplace today, but they were novel in Debussy's France. The French neurologist Jean-Martin Charcot (1825–1893), important in diagnosing those "nervous disorders" so closely associated with the cakewalk, was in fact an important teacher of Freud's, thus tying him inextricably to much future work on childhood as well. Charcot's student, Pierre Janet (1859–1947), became one of the most influential French psychologists and developed theories similar to Freud's about the association of adult neuroses with childhood trauma or repressed fantasy and the importance of retrieving lost childhood memories from the subconscious. And though France was relatively slow to embrace the work of Freud, by the end of the first decade of the twentieth century, his writings were circulating in Paris; his texts on the subconscious, adult sexual repression as a result of childhood fantasies, and the hypothetical existence of the id, ego, and the superego surely all fed a growing fascination with the mind of a child.

Debussy was far from alone among composers in wanting to explore childhood; in fact, there was a veritable explosion of music for and about children among French composers in particular. Consider Bizet's *Jeux d'enfants*, Fauré's *Dolly Suite*, Debussy's *Petite Suite*, and Ravel's *Ma Mére l'Oye*, all for four-hand piano (is there something about intimate four-hand playing that evokes childhood innocence?), as well as Debussy's *Children's Corner* and *La boîte à joujoux* and Ravel's *Pavanne pour un infant défunte* for solo piano. And one can't resist also mentioning, though it's not for piano at all, Ravel's extraordinary opera *L'enfant et les sortileges*, written to Colette's story of a wild and cruel child whose toys come to life in order to teach him a lesson. Debussy's last song, "Noël des enfants qui n'ont plus de maison," also deserves note, for he wrote not only the music but also the text, and it bears witness to his despair at the calamitous toll of the First World War on French children: They no longer have houses, their schools have been burned, their mothers are dead, and their fathers are soldiers, he says in a repeated and simple lament. Their innocence is destroyed, or as Rousseau had put it 150 years earlier, "everything degenerates in the hands of man."

The song proved a sad final essay on children, but Debussy's earlier works are far more optimistic. Chief among them is *Children's Corner*. It seems the living incarnation of Debussy's avowed promise: "I wish to sing of my interior visions with the naïve candour of a child."[12] Written shortly after the birth of Chouchou, it was dedicated to her and is wholeheartedly devoted to scenes and personages who delighted her or her young peers, complete with English titles to honor her English governess. It was published in 1908, when she was three years old, and it allies Debussy with plush elephants and rag dolls, while German and Austrian composers were opting for generals and gods. To amply underscore the difference, one might note that this is the same year that Alban Berg's ultra-serious, dissonant, and angst-ridden Piano Sonata was published. Had Berg chosen a cover, it might have featured the contortions of expressionist art; by contrast, Debussy's score, figure 7.1, designed remarkably by the composer himself, features adorable toys. The music itself substantiates, for the most part, Debussy's later claim that Chouchou "is unacquainted with

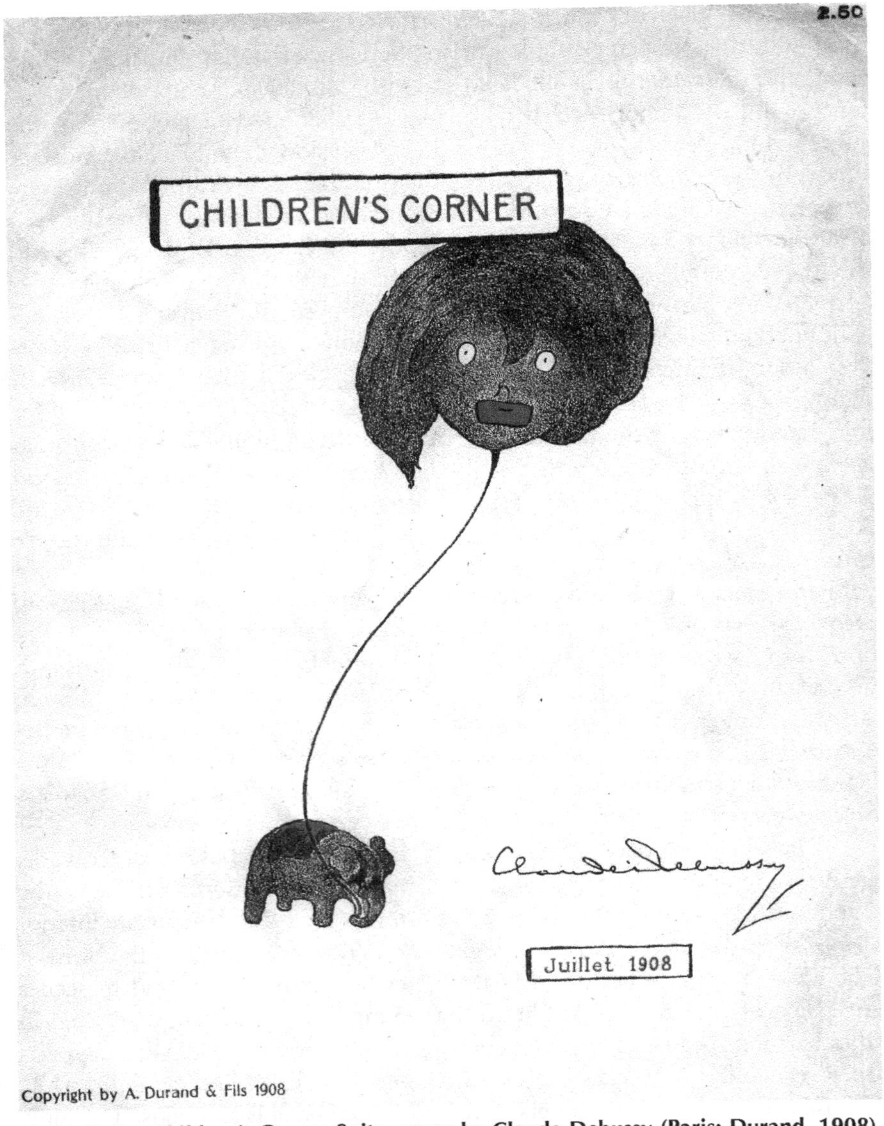

Figure 7.1. *Children's Corner Suite*, cover by Claude Debussy (Paris: Durand, 1908). Courtesy of Sibley Music Library, Eastman School of Music.

the flowers of melancholy."[13] Despite her Parisian lineage, she had apparently escaped "the brutal corset's crushing grip" that so threatened Baudelaire's girl from Malabar. Her father's devotion must have helped, and that same affection provided the basis for music remarkable for its childhood themes and grown-up appeal. Perhaps Chouchou, the toddler, welcomed musical novelty; certainly we find Debussy's very adult ideas about scales and harmony taking up comfortable residence in her playroom. The piece provides a fascinating study in how complexity can be swathed in the simplest of garbs.

The first movement of *Children's Corner*, "Doctor Gradus ad Parnassum," is a kindly takeoff on Muzio Clementi's large-scale set of exercises *Gradus ad parnassum* (Steps to Parnassus); it reminds one of the first *Etude*, which is also a spoof on pianistic dreariness. Apparently Debussy was well disposed toward Clementi however, for this is a lovely piece, whose running sixteenth notes, far from invoking the tedium of boring études, are actually flowing and melodic, marked by Debussy to be played "sans sécheresse," or "without dryness." If the conjecture is correct that this was an étude for Chouchou's imminent piano lessons, then Debussy's later description of her piano teacher as "a lady in black who looks like a drawing by Odilon Redon (1840–1916) or a nihilist caught up in a bomb blast" was not yet envisioned.[14] The title, with its ironic reference to Doctor Clementi, doesn't really capture the warmth of the composition; perhaps as Debussy wrote the actual music he was thinking more about his daughter than about either Clementi or the nihilist piano teacher in the wings. He clearly delights in the gentle parody and mock simplicity of his assignment, however; the entire piece, except for the return of the tune in eighth notes some thirty bars in, consists of relentlessly equal sixteenth notes, and the bombastic C Major cadence at the end would have done Clementi, and even Beethoven, King of the Epic Cadence, proud. Even in top parody form, however, Debussy was unable to resist his own trademarks. In this piece, which pays ostensible homage to rules, he breaks every rule in the book. He adds dissonance to consonant triads, he proceeds from one chord to the next without regard for well-worn rules of progression, and he moves subversively between keys that have no right to appear in close proximity to one another. All this in the simplest of pieces, intended for children. It can only have felt deliciously naughty to inject subtle rebellion into the stiff world of that eminent doctor.

Jimbo's Lullaby, the second movement, is really meant to be *Jumbo's Lullaby*, sung either by or for Chouchou's stuffed elephant, Jumbo. Debussy's goofy English only adds to the charm of the work and this very human elephant. Ironically, though, Debussy's carefully drawn cover to *Children's Corner* pictures Jimbo as anything but Jumbo. He is, in fact, completely dwarfed by the gargantuan head of Golliwogg, who, true to form, has also monopolized posterity's attention to the suite. But Jimbo deserves our notice as well. The lullaby invokes the clumsiness of the elephant, regardless of his name or poundage, with slightly unpredictable offbeat accents and a lumbering gait in the bass half of the instrument. The pianist is even instructed to be "un peu gauche" (a little clumsy). Jimbo must have been a bit of a klutz; his piece abounds in major seconds as well as tritones, that dissonant interval that can't quite make it up or down to a consonant perfect fourth or fifth and used to be deemed an instrument of the devil. The music quotes liberally from the French children's song "Do, do l'enfant do," whose allusion in English to a dodo could hardly be more descriptive of the character in question. In fact, of course, that's not what it means at all. This is a sweet lullaby, which appears also in *Gardens in the Rain*, *Images oubilées*, and the orchestral *Rondes de printemps* from *Images*; it was mentioned in the previous chapter. Its first verse reads, simply (and wishfully), "Sleep, my child, sleep / The child is going to sleep well / Sleep, my child, sleep, the child is going to sleep soon."

Perhaps this elephant was the grandpa of Poulenc's Babar, who appeared in 1940. Does any nation other than France boast such an august family of cultivated elephants? Even Picasso apparently delighted in taming them; regard his dour elephant trainer in figure 7.2 who holds one in the palm of his hand—this from 1905, the year before *Children's Corner* was begun. I think that could be Jimbo, who's not really so jumbo.

Perhaps Stravinsky employed the same trainer; he must have needed one badly for the circus polka he wrote for fifty dancing elephants in 1942, shortly after leaving Paris. This massive and highly intelligent animal took on a large role in the circus and children's book landscape of Paris as well, and Debussy returns to him again in *Toomai des éléphants* and *La boîte à joujoux*. He may have been inspired by his daughter: He reports to his friend André Caplet (1878–1925) that "Chouchou has just finished her first symphonic poem for voice, two paper-knives, and piano ad libitum. The latest title is The Elephant on the Bough. It is extremely dramatic."[15]

The third piece of *Children's Corner*, *Serenade of the Doll*, features spunky dolls indeed, dolls who inhabit a spikey, syncopated rhythmic world. Far from being a lover's romantic serenade, this vignette bursts with brisk good humor; the dolls cheerfully pluck guitars as the dialogue unfolds. They speak to each other in grace notes and melodies drawn from the pentatonic, or five-note all-black key, scale that Debussy loved, and there's a kind of jocularity here, resulting from the "light and gracious" offbeats on all white keys that accompany the black-key tune. The friendly tug-of-war between the hands, featuring the same black key/white key dichotomy that Debussy later used in such pieces as *Brouillards*, *La puerta del vino*, and *Feux d'artifice* results in inevitable dissonance, but there's no rancor implied. Shortly, though, the mood does darken slightly, and the world becomes a more complicated place. I'm reminded of Debussy's re-

Figure 7.2. ***Le Dompteur d'éléphants,*** **1905, Pablo Picasso. © 2016 Estate of Pablo Picasso / Artists Rights Society (ARS), New York.**

mark several years later that "the soul of the doll is more mysterious than even Maeterlinck [author of the play on which Debussy's opera *Pelléas et Mélisande* is based] imagines."[16] These dolls are far from tragic figures, and yet they're not quite as straightforward as the opening would imply. There is a pull toward minor, with its resultant touch of melancholy; there are frequent fluctuations of key, abrupt changes of material, and even a moment of impasse where the right hand, presumably the voice of the doll, is silenced altogether.

We're comforted by the ensuing return of the opening, but the hints of complexity can't be ignored. Debussy revels in doubt: questions hang, and the future is uncertain even if ABA forms and cadential moments provide reassurance. Certain intervals are particularly useful at sowing that ever-present doubt, and like many of his twentieth-century counterparts, Debussy delighted especially in the tritone, which Jimbo already brandished. Because it, like the whole-tone scale from which it's drawn, often negates a key, it's uncomfortable for Western ears accustomed to clear harmonic destinations. Debussy must have sported an especially diabolical smile when, in the following piece, the innocent snow danced to an accompaniment featuring that dreaded "diabolus in musica." This chaste piece, *The Snow Is Dancing*, is an interesting counterpart to Debussy's later snow piece *Des pas sur la neige* (Footsteps in the Snow) from *Book 1* of the *Preludes*, so much more profoundly burdened. The later piece is solemn and glacial; its frozen landscape barely moves, and it emanates from an icy adult world permeated by sorrow. Here the snow is far less oppressive. It sparkles and plays in a world of delicate doubles, first alternating twin sixteenth notes between the hands and then featuring a whole-tone melody subtly doubled in the bass. This is a tender piece, filled with the lightness of childhood, but like the doll, the snow is mysterious. It seems to have a subterranean spirit that belies its innocence; the opening, ostensibly in the key of D minor, is full of modal allusions, patterns that remove it from the familiar world of major/minor. Surprisingly, there's no arrival on the "home" note until the seventh measure, and when it does arrive it's marked "piu [more] pianissimo [extremely soft]," which is about as unboastful as you can get about achieving a requisite goal. The custom of pugnaciously insisting on the tonic from measure one onward has been thoroughly dethroned by this unassuming snowfall. Its sprightly sixteenth notes, presumably wandering flakes of snow, continue unabated throughout the piece, but their merriment comes into question, and they're upstaged by the doubled whole-tone melody marked "doux et triste" (sweet and sad). Its sinking line and accompaniment, drenched in tritones and lacking a secure tonic pitch, do make one wonder how happily this snow can be dancing. The ensuing complexities, involving fistfuls of notes that belie a clear sense of key and rhythms that clash across the hands, are not entirely reassuring; but when the opening music returns, it seems to have regained its equanimity. The piece fades away in a haze of D minor, though still then the accompaniment oscillates between B-natural and B♭. Even in this simplest of domestic settings Debussy can't bear certitude. This was the first piece of the suite that Debussy wrote, and it was originally intended for a piano method book. Lucky young pianists indeed to be treated to this in lieu of Burgmüller or Czerny, whose teaching pieces were hardly known for their flights of fancy.

The Little Shepherd is reminiscent of another prelude from *Book 1*, *The Maiden with the Flaxen Hair*. It too begins with a single undulating treble line that turns in on itself repetitiously: both pieces present lovely examples of that curvaceous arabesque so coveted by Baudelaire and Debussy. And this earlier piece presents exotic harmonies that filter down repeatedly to the fundamentalism of a major triad, just as did *The Maiden*, as if a single lonely, frozen chord sums up the Little Shepherd's life far better than more mobile options. It even shares a principal rhythm with the later, more complex, piece. This shepherd is sadder than his doll and elephant compatriots, and his melancholy affords the entire suite a complexity of emotion and harmony it might otherwise have lacked. His singing repeatedly hovers around the omnipresent tritone, first in the opening tune, stated without accompaniment, and then in the main melody that follows shortly. The lines have a modal tinge, with spare and ambiguous harmonizations that evoke the distant past from which the modes themselves came. When Debussy eventually wishes to allude to more modern tonality, he does so via three pianissimo sustained cadences that punctuate the piece in the gentlest manner possible; order is established with no shrill threats or admonitions.

Debussy had never left tonality entirely behind in *Children's Corner*, but he had certainly evaded its most stringent demands. All these exotic scales and troubled intervals avoid the half-step resolutions that we're trained to crave, and in *Golliwogg* we get yet another take. The cakewalk aspect of this final essay in *Children's Corner* is discussed in chapter 4, but the middle section is more intriguing for us here. The music refers to Wagner's *Tristan und Isolde*, and there are several vain attempts to complete a quote of the opera's celebrated *Prelude*. Instead we get references to the famously ambiguous "Tristan chord," each time intercepted by grace notes that seem to be stuck in a groove, snickering from their superior vantage point. The jaunty interruptions undo every effort to appear grave, and the speedy return of the cakewalk puts the tragedy of the doomed lovers, Tristan and Isolde, in its rightful place. Meanwhile, though, we've gotten yet another take on tonal ambiguity, for it was Wagner who sent the twentieth century hurtling on its path away from what's often called "functional" harmony. He too avoided resolutions, stringing the listener along and spewing "dysfunction" all along the way. Debussy was deeply ambivalent toward Wagner, whom he once characterized as "an old, cynical magician,"[17] but he couldn't help but be influenced. Here he's playing out his determination not to "listen to foreign voices which don't perhaps sing as well in tune as our own,"[18] by listening intently indeed but then sending poisonous darts toward the imposters.

It can't be a coincidence that *Children's Corner* closes with *Golliwogg*; its outer sections are rowdy and confident, and they slay the equivocation of both Wagner and Debussy himself. The music fairly prances off the stage, sustaining the illusion that "all's well that ends well"—at least for a moment. There are no more bona fide children's works until the marionette ballet, *La boîte à joujoux* (The Toy Box), appears on the scene five years later, and its story is larger and more complex.

La boîte, like *Children's Corner*, was a visual as well as a musical venture, but this time the illustrations far exceeded mere cover art (see figure 7.3). Debussy, who collaborated throughout his life with dancers, poets, and painters, composed this music in collaboration with the French children's book

Figure 7.3. ***La boîte à joujoux*, 1913, illustration by André Hellé, music by Claude Debussy. International Music Score Library Project (IMSLP).**[19]

author and illustrator André Hellé (1871–1945), and the score itself could be a museum piece.

The work was written for piano and marionettes, but Debussy later agreed that it could well be acted and danced by children. He intended, but never finished, an orchestration, and though an orchestration was later completed by Caplet, the piano version is extraordinarily effective; it keeps the spectacle on the intimate scale that befits dolls and children. Not performed until 1918, the ballet provides an interesting commentary on World War I, which took place rather precisely between the completion of the score and its first performance. Debussy, typically, didn't find the writing easy; he took his responsibilities to these dolls to heart. The starring doll here is indeed clearly a delicate creature, and she finds herself heavily involved in issues of war, buffeted by the cruelties of Polichinelle, her betrothed, and saddened by the wounds of the soldier with whom she falls in love. She and the other toys come out of hiding at night, and their awakening provides occasion for Polichinelle to abuse both the doll and the soldier. But when the battle is over, the doll is alone with her beloved soldier, and in the aftermath of war they build a world of perfect domestic bliss—so blissful in fact that she is reported to have grown contentedly fat, so fat she can no longer dance! Her musical world and that of the other toys is deeply and touchingly imaginative, and Debussy makes its richness clear by indulging his love of quotation and allusion throughout the tableaus. Just as children dress up and pretend to be other people, so this piece dresses itself in quotations from a vast array of sources, creating its own musical costume ball.

The piece opens with an allusion to *Jimbo's Lullaby*, and then we encounter an elephant dancing to "an old Hindu chant that serves, even to this day, to tame the elephants." Soon thereafter, Harlequin dances to a quote from Debussy's own "*Les fées sont d'exquises danseuses*" (which was itself quoting a Brahms waltz); then an English soldier marches to the ragtime of *Le petit nègre*; and after that Polichinelle provides a fanfare reminding us of *Golliwogg* and *Minstrels*. This is already a veritable medley of tunes we ought to know, but the masquerade isn't even at halftime. Next, the doll herself waltzes to music reminiscent of her earlier incarnation in *Serenade of the Doll*, and the soldiers, youngsters that they are, ready themselves for battle, first to the "Soldier's Chorus" of Gounod's *Faust* and then to the music of Stravinsky's "Dance of the Adolescents" from *The Rite of Spring*, firing their cannons to Debussy's own *Feux d'artifice* (Fireworks). The Third Tableau opens to the scene of a deserted sheep pen, a desolation recalling wartime, evoked with a French folksong *Il pleut bergère* (It Is Raining, Shepherdess), whose lyrics detail the courtship of a shepherdess by a young lad who rescues her from the rain. The shepherd from *The Toy Box* expressively sings music based on *The Little Shepherd* from *Children's Corner*, reminding us of his own family tree, and the music hints at the deeply nostalgic prelude *Bruyères* (Heather), as an added melancholy allusion. As the Third Tableau ends, however, we hear Mendelssohn's "Wedding March" and understand in retrospect the relevance of that earlier shepherdess's betrothal. When Polichinelle makes his return on the scene, twenty years later, now decked out as a sheriff, he's accompanied by the French song "Polichinelle,"[20] which in English is "Pop Goes the Weasel," a most telling commentary on his character. He's clearly been vanquished by the sheer number of the doll and soldier's children, who end by proclaiming joyously the French popular tune "Fan-fan la tulipe," marching ever onward, "En avant," as the tune's refrain enthusiastically counsels them to do.[21]

What an extravaganza, though the music itself is pure and simple! It has an "unaggressive aspect," as Debussy aptly stated.[22] The title of the ballet, *The Toy Box*, is a perfect metaphor for the myriad influences, musical and otherwise, that pervade the score; the characters from the Commedia dell'arte, including Pierrot and Harlequin, who appear here replete with their masks, mute gestures, and melancholy humor, convey in their paradoxes the powerful contradiction between the innocence of childhood and that least innocent of all human pastimes: the making of war. It's the irreconcilability of that combination that ultimately forms the subject matter of this remarkable score, and it seems in its attitude to encompass both the openhearted naïveté of *Children's Corner* and the dread of "Noël des enfants qui n'ont plus de maison."

The remaining children's pieces are mainly contained within the two books of *Preludes*. *Ce qu'a vu le Vent d'Ouest*, "*Les fées sont d'exquises danseuses*," and *Ondine*, as well as the never-completed *Toomai of the Elephants*, all draw upon legends or fairy tales for their source material. They are all based on make-believe, or in French, "faire semblance," a wonderful linguistic construction parallel in the two languages that conveys the essence of pretending; that is, making belief real. These pieces, unlike those in *Children's Corner*, are not dedicated to a child, nor are they childlike in their musical content. To the contrary, all three are among the most difficult of the *Preludes*, both musically and technically. But they call on literature ostensibly aimed at children and requiring a child's credulity and innocence. They require separate chapters to do them justice.

• 8 •

Fairies and Fairy Tales

Fairy tales were very much on the minds of Debussy and his countrymen. The early collections by Hans Christian Andersen and the Brothers Grimm appeared in the first half of the nineteenth century, and these were in fact the first fairy tales to cater to the unsullied imaginations of children rather than the jaded mindset of adults. Posters like the one in figure 8.1 were endemic. The tales are now understood to play an important role in children's comprehension of their perilous world, and psychoanalysts, most famously Bruno Bettelheim, have written extensively about the function of fairy tales in the mind of a child. "The child intuitively comprehends that although these stories are *unreal*, they are not *untrue*."[1]

For a child, the boundaries between reality and illusion are far more porous than for an adult. Even children old enough to "know better" can conjure themselves into a witch at Halloween, embrace Santa Claus at Christmas, and welcome the Tooth Fairy (or "la petite souris," a beneficent mouse who visits only French children) when she alights at their home. Debussy and his contemporary symbolist poets were likewise still able to imagine being as mighty as the wind, as powerful as the elephant, as exquisite as a fairy, and as seductive as a water sprite. They greeted Cupid in Jean-Antoine Watteau's *fête galante* paintings with enthusiasm and attended masked balls alongside the "fantômes" of Pulcinella and Scaramouche. They defied their own limitations by taking on other identities, and since those identities featured eternal life, then, by extension, they defied mortality.

The winds, the fairies, the water spirits, and the elephants, all members of Debussy's musical menagerie, scorned human beings and wielded supernatural power. In each of the stories Debussy chose to portray, a youth is admitted to the company of these unearthly creatures for the first time since

Figure 8.1. *Le pays des fées,* 1889, Jules Chéret (1836–1932). Bibliothèque numérique de Lyon.

creation, he (for he is always male) is transported to an enchanted space, and then he must sacrifice certain aspects of his humanity if he wishes to remain in their good graces. By reading the tales, children grapple in the safety of their bedroom with the challenges, the victories, and the defeats that ensue. They can envision themselves as either the human or the nonhuman, thus flitting effortlessly across otherwise ironclad boundaries; they can imagine themselves as all powerful or entirely helpless, thus covering the entire range of the human condition; they can displace parental fantasies onto elephants and water spirits, thus making anger and jealousy easier to abide; and they can safely barter their sexuality for eternal bliss or their family life for an enchanted garden in a painless experiment with the demands of morality. In brief, they take on the forces of life over which they have no control and triumph over them.

Debussy's prelude *Ce qu'a vu le Vent d'Ouest* (What the West Wind Has Seen) was probably inspired by the Hans Christian Andersen fairy tale "The Garden of Paradise," published in a French translation in 1907,[2] though the music may also have owed a debt to Percy Bysshe Shelley's great poem "Ode to the West Wind."[3] As usual, Debussy is not setting a tale in simple narrative fashion but rather finding a central image or fantasy that sets his musical mind in motion. In the case of *Ce qu'a vu le Vent d'Ouest*, the power and destruction unleashed by ferocious winds also unleashed a primitive energy in Debussy that we rarely see in his music. In the Andersen story, a young prince, bored with ordinary princely pursuits and enchanted by tales of the Garden of Paradise, happens on the Cavern of the Winds. There he joins the mother of the Four Winds as she greets her sons, whose gusts have been spreading destruction across the globe. Debussy's prelude begins immediately with menacing arpeggios. There's no melody in sight; that would be too beguiling. This is about raw power, and the wind rushes by, spitting out fragmentary interjections as it passes. The West Wind of the title has come "from the forest wildernesses . . . where human beings seem to be superfluous." He has "[blown] up a storm so big that it whirled the primeval trees about like shavings. . . . He was indeed a wild boy." The North Wind, meanwhile, has been contentedly causing shipwrecks in the Arctic Seas so that "the crews whistled and screamed"; he greets the prince with the unsettling inquiry, "What sort of feeble creature are you?" The South Wind has returned home from Africa where he blew up sand storms so fierce that the inhabitants "now . . . are buried, and there is a pyramid of sand over them all," and the East Wind has been wreaking destruction amid porcelain towers in China. A friendly crew, and their character inhabits this music. This is an inchoate, primeval world, and nothing fragile could survive the sweep of its ceaseless passagework, tremolos, and rumbling bass. A treble clef doesn't even appear in the piece until page 2, and there the dissonant seconds it engenders, though higher in register than the previous music, are hardly reassuring. We're told they're "plaintif" (plaintive) and "lointain" (far away), but they too are filled with premonitions of evil. They must know the fate awaiting the poor prince. He has been offered a ride to the Garden of Paradise with the East Wind and accepts with pleasure, but the beautiful Fairy of the Garden will prove his downfall. In order to remain in paradise, he must promise not to kiss her; however, his good intentions prove no match for his desire. He sins, much like Adam and Eve, and the loss of paradise is reenacted. Death appears, as the story says, "with a scythe in his hand and great black wings," and the attempt to win eternal enchantment is doomed.

What an expedition has taken place—in both story and music. This Prince, previously rich only in title, has traveled the world, he has met up with powers of indescribable strength and cruelty, he has encountered the irresistible force of his own sexuality, he has seen "the island of Bliss, where death never enters," and ultimately he has had to face the inevitability of his own death. This is no small journey for a child to take, and no wonder that this piece more than any other among the *Preludes* (and really in Debussy's entire piano output) is filled with crashing chords and crackling seconds and ninths, those most dissonant of intervals. The stakes here are enormous, and so are the musical means that convey them. With Lisztian bravura and demonic fervor, Debussy hammers away on broken octaves, alternating seconds, rising sequences, and ferocious harmonies. The piece never once relents; it is arguably the most difficult of the preludes to play and certainly the most atypical. The "great black wings" of death are stridently flapping throughout, and they carry Debussy far indeed from the "whims of reverie" that govern so much of his output.[4]

"*Les fées sont d'exquises danseuses*" (The Fairies Are Exquisite Dancers) whose title is taken directly from the caption to an Arthur Rackham (1867–1939) illustration of J. M. Barrie's *Peter Pan in Kensington Gardens*,[5] written in 1906, also places a young man in a garden of enchantment, but the music could not be more different. Here the enchanted creatures are charming; and the outcome, far less bitter. Rackham's illustrations themselves were a large part of the story's appeal to Debussy, for the great English illustrator was well known to the composer and shared his partiality to children's tales. But in addition, this particular story surely spoke directly to Debussy—it offers a shining vision of a fairyland come alive, and it shares Debussy's dim view of the everyday world left behind. The choices faced by a human trying to gain entry to this fairyland, however, are difficult ones. Peter Pan is able to make the requisite leap across species only by accepting that he shall forever be a "Betwixt-and-Between." When he elects to join the fairies in Kensington Garden, he locks out his own mother. On returning home, he in turn is locked out: "The window [is] closed and there [are] iron bars on it. . . . The iron bars are up for life." He has gained freedom at the cost of human interactions, and even Maimie, the human child who briefly joins him in the Garden, informs Peter that "all [his] ways of playing are quite, quite wrong, and not in the least like how boys play." Loss and death are very present in this tale; at the end of the book Peter is completely without human companionship among the fairies and is digging graves for young babies who have perished in Kensington Gardens.

The music, likewise, is complex, oscillating between euphoria and melancholy. When Debussy's daughter, Chouchou, received the book as a present on her seventh birthday, she and her father must have grieved together at all those very real tragedies befalling Peter. But the losses that would normally devastate a child are compensated, for in J. M. Barrie's universe it is "known for certain . . . that there are fairies wherever there are children," and a magical world is available to overcome grief. We hear the fairies everywhere in this music. They flit about in high registers and rapid notes, and they fly effortlessly in figuration that lies so naturally between the hands that the pianist too feels airborne. These fairies have created a world where thoughts engender reality, unencumbered by actual physical matter. Peter plays "the birth of birds" on his pipe, and the birds "turn round in their nests to see whether they had laid an egg." A listener might be forgiven for doing the same as trill after trill invokes an aerial world. A thimble placed in Peter's palm becomes an actual kiss because he believes it to be so. Indeed, "One of the great differences between the fairies and us is that they never do anything useful. . . . They are frightfully ignorant, and everything they do is make-believe." They have made-believe so effectively that belief has *made* a bona fide world. Debussy likewise shows us a musical world made largely out of little wisps of musical matter, tiny sprigs, be they thimbles, kisses, or bird eggs. They are ephemeral, lasting a fraction of a second, and they are part of a fairy world that happily consists of fleeting bits rather than sustained, more burdensome, statements.

Debussy's music, however, partakes of both fragments *and* full, grammatical sentences, moving back and forth in a mosaic of the two worlds. There are beautiful, long human melodies as well as disconnected snatches of fairy conversation, and often the two are superimposed on one another. This is a binary world, but its natural and supernatural inhabitants meet on the dance floor. We learn, first and foremost, that "the fairies are exquisite dancers," (see figure 8.2) who "never say, 'We feel happy' [but instead say] 'We feel *dancey*'" (see figure 8.3). Their abilities once belonged to humans too, for all human babies begin life by "talking fairy." Debussy playfully incorporates fragments of a Brahms waltz in homage to the exquisite dancers of both species for whom movement and gesture replace words.[6] This is the

Figure 8.2. "The fairies are exquisite dancers." Arthur Rackham (1867–1939), illustration for *Peter Pan in Kensington Gardens* by J. M. Barrie, 1913.

Figure 8.3. "Fairies never say, 'We feel happy'; what they say is, 'We feel dancey.'" Arthur Rackham, illustration for *Peter Pan in Kensington Gardens* by J. M. Barrie, 1913.

Figure 8.4. "Peter Pan is the fairies' orchestra." Arthur Rackham, illustration for *Peter Pan in Kensington Gardens* by J. M. Barrie, 1913.

same quotation he'd included in *La boîte à joujoux*, reminding us that even a German composer such as Brahms knows how to dance. In fact, Brahms isn't the only German quoted here: At the end of the piece we're treated to a whispered reference to Carl Maria von Weber and his opera *Oberon*, a tribute to the King of the Fairies.[7]

The fairies here are captured in all their fragile splendor by Arthur Rackham, the prolific English illustrator whose art accompanied so many of the stories that interested Debussy, including *Undine*, *A Midsummer Night's Dream*, and Edgar Allan Poe's "Fall of the House of Usher." The title illustration, figure 8.2, reminds us how delicate indeed this kingdom is, with a fairy oh-so-perfectly suspended on tiptoe in midair and a gossamer spider web pictured as safety net, despite the fact that such an enchanted creature would never fall. Notice the double bassist who bows while securing one end of the tightrope and the grasshopper clarinetist who serenades the fairy at the other end.

How nice to think that the bassist provides the low sustained notes in the middle of the prelude while the clarinetist flirts with the Brahms waltz above him. "As you know without my telling you, Peter Pan is the fairies' orchestra," Barrie announced and Rackham illustrated in figure 8.4.

For both author and illustrator, orchestras and fairies partake of equal magic; Debussy made their fantasy come true.

Though ousted from its place among the *Preludes* and never completed, *Toomai of the Elephants* surely deserves mention in this discussion. One of eight stories in Rudyard Kipling's *Jungle Book*,[8] it tells the tale of a young boy so trusted by elephants that he is the first human ever included in their rare and ecstatic moonlight dance. This story features elephants that are decidedly clumsier than fairies or sprites, and yet, like those other supernatural creatures, "the ways of elephants are beyond the wit of any man . . . to fathom." When the boy, Little Toomai, reveals that he has followed the herds of elephants hoisted atop his own elephant's gigantic head and seen what "no man has ever seen," the hunters "look[ed] at him as though he were a spirit." He has "heard the elephants talk in their own tongue" and become "of the elephants," and in so doing he has managed to cross over from one universe to the other without the losses that Peter Pan sustained in his own crossover attempts. He has merged with the "broad backs, and wagging ears, and tossing trunks, . . . and the incessant flick and *hissh* of the great tails." He has joined a ritual that has gone on for generations and has thereby put himself outside the limits of a single human lifetime. As with Peter Pan, whose fairies are "dancey," and the winds, who fly at supersonic speeds, Toomai achieves his immortality through superhuman transit, albeit, in this case, the more lugubrious stamping of elephant feet. Debussy left only fragments of this music, so we have no foolproof way of sharing his thoughts, but Robert Orledge has completed a version of the prelude that is tantalizing. Debussy seems to have envisioned a serene landscape, interrupted occasionally by a staccato and jagged bass stampede, and offset by a lonely treble voice, pliable and wise. Might this be the boy who has achieved such perfect harmony with another species?

Now for *The Dance of Puck*, which is neither serene nor subject to stampedes. Shakespeare's *Midsummer Night's Dream*, if not a fairy tale, is surely a tale of fairies.[9] Like *Undine* and *Peter Pan*, it was illustrated by Rackham; this edition came out in 1908, and Debussy had it in his library.[10] Even without those illustrations, though, we know he adored the play. He says in *Monsieur Croche the Dilettante Hater*, his collection of music criticism essays, "The recent foggy weather has made me think of London and of the charming play, *A Midsummer Night's Dream*. . . . A warm night, radiant with stars whose short-lived enchantment lies between a lingering twilight and an impatient dawn. A dream night whose span is but a single dream."[11]

There are plenty of fairies to be had here—a whole kingdom of them—but Puck is the one who takes charge. He is far less cruel than Andersen's Four Winds, who delight in their own destructive powers. Nevertheless, like them, Puck pronounces on humans with no little derision: "Lord, what fools these mortals be!" and brags of his own role as a trickster, "this their jangling I esteem a sport." "And those things do best please me / That befall preposterously." In a particularly creative moment, he allows Titania, Queen of the Fairies, to fall in love with an ass. And he wreaks havoc with the love affairs of Lysander, Hermia, Demetrius, and Helena, turning their amorous world topsy-turvy with misapplied love potions.

It's clear that Puck enjoys fooling with human foolery, but despite all these pranks, in the end he puts things right. His final speech makes his good nature clear:

> If we shadows have offended,
> Think but this, and all is mended:
> That you have but slumber'd here
> While these visions did appear.
> And this weak and idle theme,
> No more yielding but a dream,
> Gentles, do not reprehend.
> If you pardon, we will mend.
> And, as I am an honest Puck,
> If we have unearned luck
> Now to 'scape the serpent's tongue
> We will make amends ere long,
> Else the Puck a liar call.
> So, good night unto you all.
> Give me your hands, if we be friends,

And Robin shall restore amends.

Puck's forgiven, and order is restored. This is by far the cheeriest fairy tale of them all, with reconciliations galore. Debussy's prelude is no less exuberant. The music leaps around, cavorting through multiple octaves, often in tremolos, trills, grace notes, and thirty-second notes so soft and rapid they seem to epitomize Theseus's dictum that "the best in this kind are but shadows." Debussy's frequent instructions (for who can expect a pianist to enter fairyland untutored?) include the words "aérien" (of the air) and "fuyant" (vanishing); the sudden mischievous musical outbursts are surely designed to "mislead night wanderers, laughing at their harm." The very key shifts without warning already in the sixth measure, and thunderous explosions can unexpectedly rock an otherwise dainty world. Even innocent material such as a scale is treated as a zany imposter when it first appears in the opening measures, and yet more so in later appearances that go happily haywire, dispensing with both key and preparation. The music is wholeheartedly "capricieux," just as the pianist is supposed to be if he's obedient to Debussy's instructions.

Debussy also demands that the performance be "leger" (light), and when all is said and done, the audience is given to understand that it has just heard the very enactment of something that never happened. "The lunatic, the lover, and the poet" have all joined together to "giv[e] to airy nothing / A local habitation and a name."

Might one not add children to Shakespeare's list of madmen, lovers, and poets who reside in a world of dreams? For what in fact is make-believe if not "giv[ing] to airy nothing / A local habitation and a name"? And who is more adept at make-believe than a child? Debussy's fairy-tale preludes move from cave to garden to stream to forest, and the inhabitants range from imperceptible fairies to oversized elephants. The pieces feature enchanted spaces in the wilds of nature, inhabitants stronger and smarter than humans, irrespective of their physical stature, and almost always a "Betwixt-and-Between"—Peter Pan, Toomai, the Prince, and as we shall now see, Ondine; these are all characters who suffer the curse of human frailty superimposed on magical powers. Children, as well as Debussy, identify with those "betwixt and between" figures, and in doing so, they come face to face with their own wished-for power and all-too-real limitations. The betwixts and betweens of the following chapter, all part human, part beast, make clear that childhood and its concomitant need to pretend live on in every adult mind.

• *9* •

Crossovers on Land and at Sea

Of all the Betwixts-and-Betweens Debussy befriended, Ondine, the mermaid, is the most tragic, and she introduces a whole new category—the hybrid—part human, part beast. She has also had a singular appeal to composers, and Debussy's *Ondine* is among his most ambitious and magical *Preludes.* It's the single piano title shared with his French countryman Maurice Ravel, whose virtuoso "Ondine" is the first of three movements of the fantastical *Gaspard de la nuit.* And the Ondine legend, according to the renowned pianist Alfred Cortot and others, may also have inspired Chopin's Ballade no. 3 in A♭ Major for piano. Presumably all three composers found this beautiful mermaid a natural subject for an instrument that so easily sparkles and splashes, cavorting across a mighty range of registers and covering the entire gamut of dynamics. They weren't alone. In addition to the piano works mentioned earlier, E. T. A. Hoffmann's opera *Undine* (1816), Hans Christian Andersen's "The Little Mermaid" (1836), Antonín Dvořák's opera *Rusalka* (1901), Alexander von Zemlinsky's symphonic poem *The Mermaid* (1905), and Edvard Eriksen's statue "The Little Mermaid" in Copenhagen (1913) were all inspired by Undine, and these constitute the mere beginnings of a list. The fairy tale itself has been called the ultimate fairy story, and artists of every persuasion have taken it to heart.

As with many fairy tales, there are numerous versions; I have relied on the lengthy one by Friedrich de la Motte Fouqué (1777–1843),[1] who calls her "Undine," rather than "Ondine," so I shall adopt his spelling when speaking of his story. He describes a woman so capricious, beautiful, and mysterious that Debussy's music, with its unpredictable twists and turns and its cascading runs, feels inevitable. Her name comes from the French word "onde," or wave, and she describes her origins to her lover as follows:

> You must know, my sweet darling, that . . . the lakes and streams and brooks are inhabited by innumerable water-spirits. . . . The men and women who live there are very beautiful to look at—far more beautiful than most human beings. From time to time a fisherman is lucky enough to be within earshot, when a delicate sea-maiden rises above the waves to sing. . . . [S]o there are many stories about these strange women, who are commonly called Undines. But you, at the moment, my dearest friend, are actually looking at an Undine.

She continues her tale by explaining, "We'd be far better off than you other human beings . . . if it weren't for one thing . . . we have no souls." Note here the curious inversion of the normal fairy tale, where humans approach fairies in the hope of achieving immortality, rather than vice-versa. Unorthodox though her situation may be, Undine is determined to acquire that missing soul, and in order to do so, she must marry a mortal and defy her wicked uncle, the water spirit Kühleborn, who is equally hell-bent on keeping her in the water kingdom. Here's the complex story, much simplified, but as entrancing now as it was a hundred years ago when Debussy encountered it.

Undine has lived since the age of three or four with a fisherman and his wife, who adopted her when she appeared, unannounced, at their doorstep. Many years later, a handsome knight, Huldbrand, also happens by their cottage. He is eager to find shelter from the unfamiliar surroundings and is utterly charmed by Undine's beauty, so he remains a while. They eventually wed and return together to his hometown, though he is rapidly possessed by the "dreadful thoughts that . . . he had married a fairy, or some evil, mocking creature from the spirit world."

At home, a former sweetheart, Bertalda, awaits, infuriated at her beau's betrayal and eager to torment her new rival. Poor Undine, now the owner of a soul and deeply attached to her husband, is at the mercy of both Bertalda and her vindictive uncle. Kühleborn takes on every possible malevolent guise in his efforts to reclaim Undine for his water kingdom, and Huldbrand gradually realizes that the "gruesome apparitions" encountered during a trip on the Danube are Undine's relatives gone berserk. Enraged, he ousts Undine from their vessel, screaming, "By all the witches in hell, go and stay with them, . . . only leave us human beings in peace, you juggling hag!" His plea is more successful than he might have imagined, and Undine disappears into the waters (see figure 9.1). No longer a "Betwixt-and-Between," the poor mermaid, now again fully of the water, is required by the water spirits to kill Huldbrand so no vestige of her will remain alive in the human kingdom. As befits a water

Figure 9.1. "Soon she was lost to sight in the Danube." Arthur Rackham, illustration for *Undine* by Friedrich de la Motte Fouqué, 1909.

nymph, she chooses to engulf him in water, crying and kissing him inconsolably until she has "wept his life away!"

With that potent kiss, she merges him with her ancient enchanted kingdom. Their union appears everlasting, and a small spring appears, a timeless monument to "the poor, rejected Undine, still clasping her sweetheart in her loving arms." This supernatural creature who was originally denied eternal life now receives and grants it, albeit in precisely the form—that is, water—that she had wished to leave behind. The story's preoccupation with mortality is striking, and it grapples with an "ever after" that shuttles power back and forth between the human and the supernatural kingdoms. Filled with ambiguity, Undine is the perfect example of the mysterious Other in a fairy tale: she is simultaneously an "evil, mocking creature" and a "beautiful darling." She engenders dreams of "furtively leering ghosts that tried to disguise themselves as beautiful women, and of beautiful women who all of a sudden turned into dragons." Belonging to both the water and the earth, she erases barriers between humans and nature, but she is tragically denied her choice of kingdoms.

What can the moral of such a sad tale be? Is *Undine* the story of woman powerless in the face of men's caprices? Or is it the story of men subject to inhospitable Fates and in need of a woman's magical intercession? Is it the story of human sexuality, seductive in its strength, and in the end deadly? Or does it celebrate the ultimate power of sexual union into eternity? Is Undine a castrating female or a virginal innocent? Or is she rather not a woman at all but an embryonic creature, a primeval ancestor emerging from an underwater kingdom resplendent in its mysteries but unknowable and therefore terrifying?

I have no answers to those questions, only more questions, and my guess is that's precisely what attracted Debussy, never a fan of certitude. This music doesn't shout; it whispers and murmurs, only rising above the softest dynamics for a few short moments. The key is unclear; the melody, fragmentary; and the rhythm, fluid. Crossing species is a treacherous and nebulous process. As Huldbrand says, "It all comes of not marrying someone of my own sort. . . . What else can you expect, when a human being goes and gets himself tied up with a mermaid!"

Unlike Ravel's insinuating *Ondine*, conceived just a few years earlier, Debussy's water sprite is a young and naughty girl. She was a "darling child, half-spoilt, half-shy," and Debussy's music is filled with her pranks and mood changes. Just as Ondine's adoptive parents "can't be absolutely sure she didn't drop down from the moon," so the listener wonders more than once how the composer ever got from point A to point B in this rapidly mutating music. Even the delightfully symmetrical opening figure is derailed almost immediately, in the fourth bar, by a sudden splash of tritones, that dissonant interval used for the sirens on emergency vehicles, and here for a more magical water "Siren." The tiny slip of a tune, just three notes, E♭–F♯–E♭, which appears early on, seems to take on Ondine's own nervous and transformative

Figure 9.2. ***Ondine,*** **mm. 30–31, in** ***Preludes, Book 2,*** **by Claude Debussy (Paris: Durand, 1913). Digital image from Hathi Trust Digital Library.**

qualities, reappearing over and over, each time in different and more elaborate attire (see E♭–F♭–E♭ in figure 9.2). Its rhyming up/down motion and its tiny circumference are typical of this piece; the tunes go in circles, though their range of pitch and register fluctuates. Debussy's fascination with masks and metamorphosis has found its perfect match in Ondine: In these musical transformations, note values augment and diminish, intervals contract and expand, and textures and contexts change.

Note in figures 9.2 and 9.3 how the tune appears unaccompanied, as terse single notes, and then reappears, this time "sweetly" adorned and carried by a current of faster notes that create a long phrase and a beautiful, shimmering color.

Those musical surroundings are, like Ondine, more gentle than sinister, but they're capricious as well, spraying and splashing without warning, just as Ondine herself appears in the human world without reason or explanation. Debussy's music re-creates the sensation of a magical creature's movements. It's filled with the hypnotically repetitious figuration of tiny waves and with the quixotic runs of an unpredictable child. Ondine is unstable, constantly flitting from one register to another, from one tune to another, and from one accompaniment to the next. At one moment she's speaking in hollow intervals that are doubled in the two hands; at another she's up in a high register all

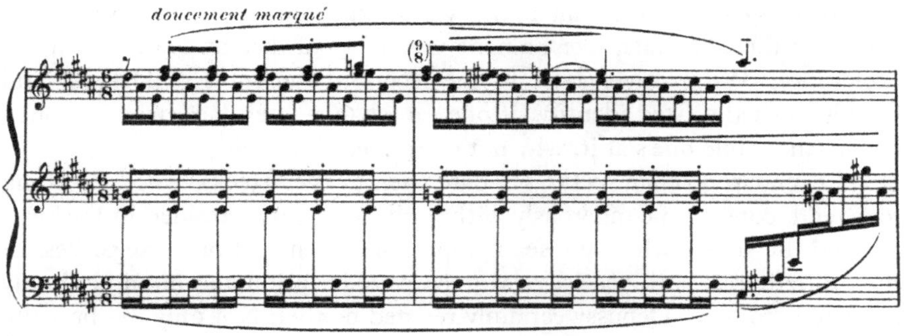

Figure 9.3. ***Ondine,*** **mm. 46–47, in** ***Preludes, Book 2,*** **by Claude Debussy (Paris: Durand, 1913). Digital image from Hathi Trust Digital Library.**

by herself, accompanied only by a distant, murmuring bass; and at yet another she's ensconced in denser harmonies, as in figure 9.3. Near the end, her high voice disappears altogether and the low bass begins to growl ominously as if Kühleborn were lurking. We hear the ghost of Ondine's tune rising, fighting against the bass rhythm, and soon Kühleborn's apparitions are banished. At the end, one hears only the innocent rippling of a spring, as if that's all that remains of the ill-matched lovers. The keys of the two hands playing these glistening broken chords don't agree, but they nevertheless blend perfectly. The musical story ends much more happily than the fairy tale—the hybrid issue appears to have been amicably resolved, and no one seems to have perished.

Ondine isn't the only water nymph to seduce Debussy. We'll look at the legend underlying *La cathédrale engloutie* in the next chapter, but bear in mind even now that it features yet another mermaid, a woman condemned to a watery death and transformed into a water sprite for her wrongdoing. And that young woman, mutated against her will, joins a large mermaid family in the output of nineteenth-century artists and an even larger family of mythical hybrid creatures, of both water and forest, whose magical qualities captivated Debussy and his contemporaries. Like the fairies, these crossover creatures dispense and wield imaginary powers that enchant, and their popularity provides another glimpse of the dream world that lay at Debussy's fingertips. In order to understand them better, we'll have to cross over into other genres as well and investigate paintings, songs, and poems.

It seems that mermaids, with their access to a secret underwater universe and their ambiguous but potent sexuality, have held sway over human imagination across cultures for centuries. But the sex appeal of a woman with the tail of a fish and long hair of seaweed is hardly self-evident. Immersing ourselves in that underwater homeland takes us from Undine to Klimt and Redon, and from naiads to satyrs and ultimately back to fish. The nineteenth-century hunger for exoticism found yet another outlet in these imaginary creatures; their habitats, like France's very real but distant colonies, invited exploration. We're driven back to the recurrent eagerness of Debussy and friends to shed a fixed identity. If one can change one's face, why not one's body? And while one's at it, why not one's species as well?

Legendary women of the sea date back to the Greeks, who, according to legend, consorted dangerously with both naiads, who resided in freshwater, and the sirens, who were sea nymphs and often part bird. Regardless of their differences, both species of women were beautiful and often perilously irresistible to men. Debussy certainly resisted neither: Not only did he write about Undine but he also set Pierre Louÿs's poem "Le tombeau des naïades" as one of his set *Chansons de Bilitis*, and he entitled one of his orchestral *Noc-*

turnes "Sirènes." "Le tombeau des naïades" reproduces a conversation between a man and a woman who purportedly came upon the tomb of the naiads and "broke through the ice / Of the spring where the naiads once had laughed."[2] Peering through the ice, they try to access the mythic time of the satyrs and naiads, and Debussy does likewise in his hypnotic, chant-like setting, filled with the crackling of ice and immobile sixteenth notes that seem to trudge through the centuries. Perhaps this same ice inspired the frozen landscape of the prelude *Des pas sur la neige* (Footsteps in the Snow), which you'll see described in the following "water" chapter. "Sirènes," written for orchestra, features a wordless women's choir that engulfs the listener in the cry of the sirens, those mythical seductresses who ensnared the passing sailors. Odysseus famously evaded them by tying himself to the mast; perhaps he too would have succumbed had he heard Debussy's sirens in full voice. Other French composers were hard at work on the sirens' behalf as well: The sisters Nadia and Lili Boulanger, for instance, both wrote choral works extolling these creatures a few short years after Debussy's.

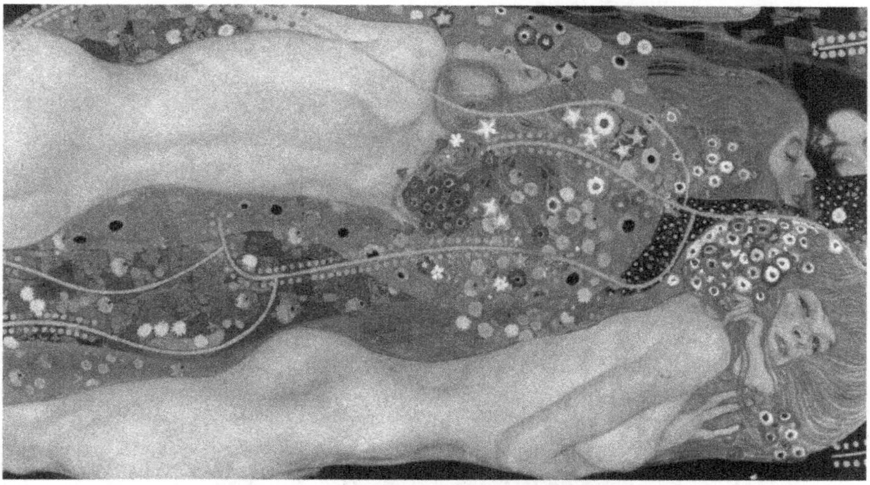

Figure 9.4. *Watersnakes II*, 1907, Gustav Klimt, private collection.

Not all water sprites are so powerful, however, most especially when rendered mute. In Hans Christian Andersen's famous fairy tale "The Little Mermaid," published in 1837 and circulated widely in the nineteenth century, the poor mermaid is so determined to marry her chosen sailor and thus acquire, like him, an immortal soul that she bargains her voice in exchange for receiving a human form. In the end, speechless, mutilated, and ultimately rejected

Figure 9.5. ***Le Courrier français*, October 7, 1900. Bibliothèque nationale de France.**

Figure 9.6. **"Poisson rare,"** ***Le Courrier français,*** **April 8, 1900. Bibliothèque nationale de France.**

by her human suitor, she is condemned to death, rescued only by a substitute ending, conceived after the fact by Andersen, wherein the mermaid's good deeds themselves eventually earn her salvation.

It would appear that crossing boundaries is dangerous on both sides of the border. And yet attraction seems to go in both directions as well: mermaids seek men, men seek mermaids. Gustav Klimt's (1862–1918) sinister and alluring paintings of nymphs, mermaids, and water serpents are a case in point. Debussy and the Austrian painter were exact contemporaries, and one critic even called Debussy "der Klimt der Musik" (the Klimt of music).[3] One can see kinship in their choice of subject matter and their eagerness to create fantasies of dazzling beauty, though Debussy's sexuality is more restrained. His women are likely to be docile blondes; Klimt's, as in figure 9.4, are temptress redheads.

Quite aside from the curvaceous nudity Klimt imagined, more human than fishlike, the undulating body of a fish and its rippling undivided anatomy has inspired many a woman's fashion. Tight skirts and bound feet likewise deprive women of the use of their legs, binding them into one salamander-type figure, able to swivel in one long curve. And as the newspaper clipping in figure 9.5 unmistakably illustrates, even with two legs intact, women and fish can combine in a remarkably felicitous manner to form their own seductive hybrid. Nothing could make it clearer that fish and women are inextricably linked; that masks, desire, and hybrids are all of a package.

Some hybrids conjure no desire, only fear, and Debussy found them fascinating as well. The "Poisson rare," or "Rare Fish," in figure 9.6 is framed with the informative Latin inscription, "This is not all fish," thus leaving its genetic makeup indeterminate.[4] It's clearly up to no good and could be a distant relative of Undine's uncle, Kühleborn, with whom Debussy was well acquainted.

Kühleborn is infinitely mutable, appearing variously as a river, a black object, a white man, and a silvery stream. Coming from the water and returning to it, he is capable of donning all its many forms, and since he can appear anywhere, as anything, humans have no defenses against him. He is a surface on which we can perfectly project "the most evil of those half-tamed demons that inhabit the human breast," as Freud so eloquently put it. He holds power and wants nothing better than to thwart us.[5]

The artist Odilon Redon's depictions of half-human/half-bestial figures in his series *Les origines* (1883) are similarly the incarnation of our own worst fears. Figure 9.7 provides incontrovertible evidence. Redon was himself an accomplished musician, and he and Debussy corresponded and admired one another greatly.[6] Their affection isn't surprising, for the spirit of Redon's symbolist art is closely allied to the music of Debussy. Redon's claim that "all art is the submission of the will to the unconscious"[7] is remarkably similar to Debussy's wish that his music be "supple and chaotic enough to adapt itself to the lyrical movements of the soul, to the undulations of reverie."[8] Luckily, Debussy's subconscious is inhabited by gentler beasts than Redon's, however. Cruelty, lust, and sadism are apparent on the faces of Redon's creatures; these are humans with the souls of fiends and without a superego to monitor their actions or their visage. Their unconscious *is* their will. They are not beasts you will encounter directly when you casually enjoy Debussy at the piano, but they

Figure 9.7. ***Le satyre au cynique sourire*** **(The Satyr with the Cynical Smile), 1883, Odilon Redon. Rosenwald Collection, National Gallery of Art, Washington, DC. NGA Images.**

are a good reminder that Debussy's interests were not limited to the stuffed animals of *Children's Corner*. No one is stuffing these animals anytime soon, and no one is placing them in children's corners. They are repellant—and yet we, along with Debussy, cannot help but gaze at them; they remind us of ourselves.

Satyrs and fauns, half goat, half man, seem to have been particularly fascinating to the French and often represent not unadulterated sin but a wild, orgiastic sexual freedom.[9] They conjure ancient unspoken mysteries, and Pierre Louÿs imagines them as the naiades' contemporaries in "The Tomb of the Naïades." In "The Flute of Pan," also from *Chansons de Bilitis*, and the inspiration for the first of the piano *Six épigraphes antiques*, the satyr takes the form of Pan, the Greek god who is half goat, half man. Pan is shamelessly licentious, seducing an innocent girl as "their mouths unite on his flute." The piano piece begins with the familiar arabesque, allowing the piano to impersonate Pan's pipes, and it's played "in the style of a pastorale," presumably because the word Pan comes from the Greek word "to pasture." All is calm in the poem but not precisely innocent; indeed, the speaker's mother "will never believe / that [the speaker] stayed out such a long time / to search for [her] lost belt." This is a feeble fib, indeed. The piano setting is modal and full of intimations of antiquity. We're hard-pressed to determine a key—Debussy flirts with C Major as well as G minor and undoes every cadential moment as soon as it occurs, preferring to let us float in a land where time has stopped and cadential formulas are unknown. Every up motion is followed by a down, and the music is chant-like and hypnotic, permeated with a single interval, the third. Despite the piece's title, "Pour invoquer Pan, dieu de vent d'été" (To Invoke Pan, God of the Summer Wind), this Pan blows a very gentle breeze indeed, and Pan's more lecherous attributes make no appearance in Debussy's musical depiction.

The famous faun of Debussy's *Prelude to the Afternoon of a Faun*, based on Stéphane Mallarmé's poem "The Afternoon of a Faun," is more obviously licentious: The entire poem is a dreamlike ode to sensual love. The orchestral music again begins with a flute arabesque, one of the most celebrated flute solos in the world. It allows the flute to speak, completely unadorned, in a pulsating voice that seems uncannily human. This faun is of our flesh. When pianists tackle the work in either Debussy's arrangement for two pianos, or Maurice Ravel's four-hand version, or the one-piano transcription by Leonard Borwick, it's their use of the pedal that brings the piece to life. One sound merges into the next, beginnings and endings disappear, and the piano can pretend to have the vibrato of the human voice. Wondrous as an orchestra is, the ability of a single instrument to don so many identities simultaneously is itself extraordinary and fitting. Here the delicate arpeggiations and tremolos,

Figure 9.8. *Le Courrier français,* October 6, 1901. Bibliothèque nationale de France.

the sliding chromaticism of the opening line, and the resonant bass octaves all translate beautifully to the keyboard.

Mallarmé's poem describes love as "the sacred nude burden," and "secret terror of the flesh."[10] His faun is filled with foreboding and melancholy and asks distractedly, "Was it a dream I loved?" That melancholy and the faun's inability to distinguish a dream from reality help explain Debussy's bond with the whole menagerie of nymphs, naiads, and fauns. As Verlaine and Debussy say together in the song "Le faune," the sight of a terra-cotta faun warns of "an unfortunate continuation to these serene moments." Those premonitions darkened all Debussy's days. The fauns' and mermaids' distress was Debussy's own.

Those premonitions must have echoed throughout the streets of Paris; indeed, it appears that these beasts were in line for French citizenship at the turn of the century. Not only the symbolist poets, but also the journals took them up with a vengeance. Debussy probably enjoyed the 1901 *Le Courrier français* take on hybrids. It featured a large two-page depiction of horned satyrs "with the torso of a man and the feet of a goat [who also have] the vices of man and of a goat."[11] Amorous and untrustworthy, the beasts in figure 9.8 cavort in an enchanted forest. There, despite being invested with magical powers and free to pursue their ids' desires, they are consumed by gentle misery. As the *Courrier français* reports, "The amorous satyr / Recounts his martyrdom / In a dolorous voice." Debussy and his poets joined the chorus.

• 10 •

The Floating World

Water is the perfect container for the sundry "Betwixt-and-Betweens," filling the space betwixt and between the floor of the earth and the floor of the sea and housing creatures of every description. France is surrounded by water on three sides, and it's a rare Parisian who hasn't ventured to one coast or another. For whatever geographic or poetic reason, it's clear that water has a potent hold on the French imagination. Debussy, on renting a vacation house at Pourville, remarked on the "fine expanse of sea . . . the sea of infinity!"[1] And what better image for a Belle Époque than a magnificent seascape? Witness the many impressionist paintings of water, especially those featuring the Normandy coast, as well as the extraordinary number of musical compositions by both Maurice Ravel and Debussy that portray water scenes. The most famous of all is, of course, Debussy's *La mer*, for full orchestra, but it hardly stands alone. The Ravel piano oeuvre includes *Jeux d'eau* (Fountains), *Une barque sur l'ocean* (A Boat on the Ocean) from *Miroirs*, and *Ondine* from *Gaspard de la nuit*. And Debussy's contributions for piano include *Jardins sous la pluie* (Gardens in the Rain) from *Estampes*; *Reflets dans l'eau* (Reflections in the Water) from *Images, Book 1*; *Poissons d'or* (Goldfish) from *Images, Book 2*; *La cathédrale engloutie* (Engulfed Cathedral) from *Preludes, Book 1*; *Ondine* from *Preludes, Book 2*; and should one wish to be a bit more liberal about the forms and associations water can have, *L'isle joyeuse* (Joyous Island), *Les collines d'Anacapri* (The Hills of Anacapri) [Anacapri is on the island of Capri] from *Preludes, Book 1*, *Des pas sur la neige* (Footsteps in the Snow), also from *Preludes, Book 1*, *Brouillards* (Fog or Mists) from *Preludes, Book 2*, and *The Snow Is Dancing* from *Children's Corner*. (The title, *Voiles*, given to another prelude from *Book 1*, may mean sails, as well as veils, so though I've dealt with it in chapter 3 on dance, it too deserves inclusion on this list.) And Debussy's famous orchestral nocturne *Nuages* (Clouds) gives notice that incipient rain might count as well.

We know that Debussy spent numerous vacations at the sea, in Normandy and Brittany in France, at Eastbourne in England, off the coast of Italy during his time in Rome, and on the island of Jersey during his premarriage honeymoon with Emma Bardac. His parents had, in fact, thought he'd have a nautical vocation: He reported in a letter, "I was intended for the noble career of a sailor and have only deviated from that path thanks to the quirks of fate. Even so, I've retained a sincere devotion to the sea."[2] And apparently that devotion was passed on to the next generation. In a letter to Jacques Durand, Debussy reports that

> Chouchou has composed a little song in English, a rather ungracious one, saying "the sea is annoyed not to have had a visit from M. and Mme. Debussy or their charming daughter." . . . I expended much eloquence trying to persuade her that this year the sea had gone out so far, people were despairing of ever finding it again; which didn't go down very well. There are times when being a father is a very delicate business![3]

Though Chouchou may have seen the sea primarily as an unattainable tourist destination, her father had more complicated ideas. The phrase "the floating world: shadows, dreams, and substance," used as part of the title for an exhibition of Japanese prints,[4] is highly evocative, and Debussy, with his love of those prints, could have written it himself. Water seems the symbolic receptacle for so many memories, shadows, and dreams. It predates man and the sun; it's primordial and infinitely powerful. Embryos emerge from it. It goes to depths humans cannot plumb, constantly mutating, always in motion. Water reflects light, and it can mirror with accuracy or with distortion. It contains within itself an entire universe of plants and living creatures, an ecosystem that exceeds scientific categorization, and it can, on a whim, send floods and winds to destroy, as well as showers and waterfalls to delight. It represents Nature at both its wildest and most docile.

Debussy's piano works cover the gamut of forms water might take. We've discussed some of these in other chapters, but here they shall be more in the guise of a weather report, and we'll see the ways in which Debussy relates to nature, by turns sanguine, awestruck, or afraid. There's the gentle rain, for instance, of *Jardins sous la pluie*, with its incorporation of children's songs. The song "Nous n'irons pas au bois parce qu'il fait un temps insupportable" (We won't go to the woods because the weather is dreadful) may appear slightly melancholy occasionally due to its harmonization, but the composer is not much worried. After all, gardens need rain, even if children don't. And Debussy's inclusion of the French nursery song "Do, do l'enfant do" (Sleep, the Child Sleeps) in the same movement may even imply that the rain affords the infant a welcome nap. The piece, with its perpetual motion, is decidedly cheerful, and when the two tunes come back synchronized as one continuous tune in the coda, it's positively triumphant. "Nous n'irons pas" has donned a new rhythmic identity in a catapulting triplet figure, and the tune fairly leaps off the page, having obviously shed any untoward regrets about the weather long ago. Certainly this particular downpour poses no serious threats.

The Snow Is Dancing, is also about a relatively amiable "weather event." *Children's Corner*, written under the spell of Chouchou and discussed in chapter 7, is one of Debussy's happiest creations. Nevertheless, despite the pleasure reflected in the title, Debussy's persistent melancholy lurks in the background of the gentle, unceasing snowfall. The piece is in a minor key and never emerges from that shadow, though the snowflakes, in their ceaseless sixteenth-note iteration, are delicate, diaphanous. Snow is actually very rare in Paris, and even adults, let alone a little girl like Chouchou, find it entrancing.

Footsteps in the Snow, no. 6 of *Preludes, Book 1*, is a very different evocation of winter. It could never have taken place in the temperate climates of Paris at all; and there are certainly no young children on the scene. Snow and ice render water immobile; this piece barely moves. The piece boasts one of Debussy's most poetic instructions: "Ce rythme doit avoir la valeur sonore d'un fond de paysage triste et glacé"—literally: This rhythm must have the sonorous value of a landscape sad and frozen. The rhythm is halting and static, and the intervals are small ones; this is arctic tundra and nothing much grows.

The lonely melody is always poised against those unbalanced steps, which shift from one hand to the other; it is separate, more human, trying to be heard. It moves in small increments and arabesques, never asserting itself forcefully against the ostinato and never clarifying that it's in command. This piece brings to mind the tragic couple in Paul Verlaine's poem, set by Debussy, "Colloque Sentimental." They're ghosts. One—let's say it's the melody here—remembers the other as a lover. But that lover, embedded here in the footsteps, has no recollection of any relationship. Are they connected or apart? The melody pleads for recognition in increasingly impassioned terms but then subsides. It makes one further attempt, and in fact the footsteps, so recalcitrant, are briefly vanquished when Debussy writes, "Comme un tender et triste regret," but they return in answer to the melody's increasingly despairing descending line, and the end of the piece, with desolate falling thirds accompanied again by the frozen tread, gives no more hope of a thaw than the poem. "Hope has fled, vanquished, toward the black sky."[5] The two hands of a pianist come in very handy here; they can carry on a conversation with each other, arguing, agreeing, or going their separate ways. This prelude is stark: The more spare the writing, the more exposed that dialogue becomes.

Much of *Brouillards* (Mists), the first of *Preludes, Book 2*, is written on three staves, so the layering and conversation between hands becomes yet more explicit. The voices are enveloped in ocean spray, blurring together in clusters rather than separate particles, and the atmosphere, though certainly not cheerful, is far more about ambiguity than pain. What more nebulous form can water take than all-pervasive mist? This piece, with its constant white-note/black-note dichotomies and insistent use of two keys at once seems calculated to convey the infinite duplicities of water. Yet, though the harmonies contradict each other and undo any sense of key, there's no feeling of active antagonism—Debussy excels at blending opposites and making us forget that they weren't meant to live together. The parallel triads float without anchor or rancor, mixing minor, major, and diminished and surrounded by those quintuplets and sextuplets whose harmonies ought to fight them but don't. They illustrate exquisitely Debussy's wish, quoted earlier, that "the murmuring of the breeze would be mystically mingled with the rustling of the leaves and the scent of the flowers, since music can unite all of them in a harmony so completely natural that it seems to become one with them."[6] The fast notes evaporate only when a ghost of a tune appears like an apparition. Here in figure 10.1 the two hands play in unison octaves, placed at the opposite limits of the keyboard. The resultant color is unearthly, as if the sound came from the ends of the world, rather than a material piano.

The tune comes back fleetingly in double-time toward the end, but it subsides before completing its message and, halting midstream, ends in a separate voice, on a C-natural, despite having begun on C-sharp. The puzzle pieces here don't fit squarely together, but the gaps and discontinuities feel natural and unruffled. This music seems to emanate from some ancient voice; it could be Arkel, the old grandfather from *Pelléas et*

Figure 10.1. ***Brouillards,*** **mm. 18–20, in *Preludes, Book 2,* by Claude Debussy (Paris: Durand, 1913). Digital image from Hathi Trust Digital Library.**

Mélisande, intoning "the human soul is very silent" (l'âme humaine est très silencieuse),[7] or it could be Ernest Renan, a writer Debussy knew well, recording, "Sometimes I stop in order to lend an ear to those trembling vibrations that seem to me to come from infinite depths, like the voices of another world." (Parfois je m'arréte pour préter l'oreille à ces tremblantes vibrations, qui me paraissent venir de profondeurs infinies, comme des voix d'un autre monde.[8]) The tones here have no spikes; they all gravitate toward one another. The water in this mist is all inclusive.

Much of Debussy's music has this sense of resignation, if not outright serenity, and the earlier piano music in particular often emanates repose. The popular *Reflets dans l'eau* (Reflections in the Water) from *Images, Book 1*, though technically demanding, also seems benevolent in spirit. There are no Loch Ness monsters lurking in these waters, and in many ways, this is quintessential impressionist music, much though Debussy dismissed the term as "what imbeciles call 'impressionism.'"[9] Its arpeggios imitate the harp and the ebb and flow of water; the music splashes and surges, always with a transparency that allows light to shine through. And the piece operates in *stream*-of-consciousness mode: The aquatic word choice here is particularly apt and singularly important to Debussy.

The music unfolds as a series of well-hidden transformations, a procedure well suited to shifting reflections. The inauspicious cell that opens the piece assumes a vast array of shapes, some upside down, some truncated, and others extended. Other ideas seem to tumble out of it—a little flourish becomes a mighty waterfall, for instance, at the "Quasi cadenza," where performers are given leave to abandon a strict tempo and let the water's current urge them forward. The principal melodic theme of the piece finally emerges once the waterfall has subsided, and Debussy requests that it be "doux et expressif" (sweet and expressive) (see figure 10.2). Just looking at the score is instructive—you can *see* the waveforms without hearing a note and also get an idea how Debussy encompasses the entire enormous range of the piano while holding one very long bass note within which every other tone vibrates. The tune is in the middle, the most mellow part of the instrument, and it's given its own very distinctive rhythm and shape. Debussy's music is written in layers, and here the image of an ocean floor, with a glistening surface and living matter in between, is particularly apt.

The melody, itself derived from the opening fragment, again mutates in all manner of registers, scales, and rhythms, much as water might surge and diminish. Finally, it climaxes like a tidal wave, in broad triplets, at the single fortissimo in the piece. The moment is chosen, according to the Debussy scholar Roy Howat, based on the Golden Mean. That proportion, "obtained by dividing any fixed length in such a way that the shorter portion bears the

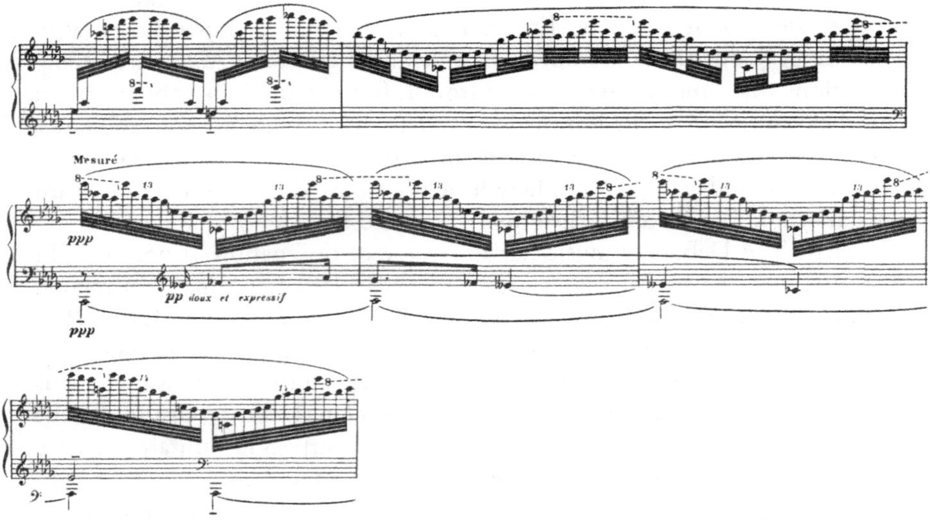

Figure 10.2. ***Reflets dans l'eau*****, mm. 23–28, in *Images, Book 1,* by Claude Debussy (Paris: Durand, 1905). Digital image from Hathi Trust Digital Library.**

same ratio to the longer portion as the longer portion bears to the whole length,"[10] occurs at precisely the climactic and loudest moment of *Reflets dans l'eau*, or bar 59 out of 94.[11] It's a proportion that mysteriously appears in nature, ranging from leaf patterns to human anatomy, and it's frequently found in art too, as in the Hokusai print in figure 10.3, which Debussy chose for the cover of his other great water essay, *La mer.*

After the water settles again, its melody gradually dwindles to a mere trickle, hidden in tiny note values near the end. The piece closes with slow, bare octaves that bring us back to the opening music, moving in a circle befitting of musical waves. Analyzing this piece and attempting to label its themes individually is a bit like trying to separate drops of water in a brook: it's far from clear where one ends and the next one begins. The ending, with its variegated references, leaves us drifting in that slow stream of allusions.

Hokusai's great wave could also have been responsible for submerging the cathedral in *La cathédrale engloutie*, Debussy's popular prelude from *Book 1*. The prelude illustrates the old Breton legend of the cathedral of Is (sometimes spelled "Ys"), in which a cathedral was submerged in the sea as punishment to its sinful inhabitants. The cathedral then rose on occasion to remind future generations of the impiety of their forbears. Many versions of the

Figure 10.3. ***The Great Wave*, 1830–1833, Katsushika Hokusai (1760–1849). Used as the cover for *La mer* (1905), by Claude Debussy.**

legend exist, but the central image of a sea that "rushed in and swallowed Is like a ravenous beast" and that is now "nothing more than a sparkling lake in which [one hears] the peals of church bells" seem common to all. In one version, "The Submersion of Is,"[12] a particularly corrupt daughter of a godly king steals the keys to the protective dike of the city from her father, only to give them to a lover of dubious merits. The sea overflows, engulfing the island; the father escapes, but his villainous daughter "falls into the water with a dreadful howl." In a sequel entitled "Marie-Morgane,"[13] the daughter has become a mermaid, condemned to eternal damnation, and every time she emerges from the water "a terrible storm of the sea-siren [breaks] loose and churn[s] the waters around." A fisherman, caught underwater, finds himself with her in the city of Is, where "bells were swaying and tolling," and he is surrounded by "livid corpses and bleached skeletons." He has the opportunity to complete a mass for the salvation of the inhabitants, but he fails, "and the city of Is still awaits the completion, at long last, of the Mass for its redemption."

Debussy conveys the legend's sequence of events quite literally: One hears the cathedral gradually emerge, to become full blown at a fortissimo with massive chords (see figure 10.4), only to slowly recede again from view, disappearing into pianissimo, as if only a memory of the monumental edifice

Figure 10.4. ***La cathédrale engloutie,*** **mm. 26–30, in *Preludes, Book 1,* by Claude Debussy (Paris: Durand, 1910). Digital image from Hathi Trust Digital Library.**

remained. At one point, the primary theme and its inversion, or upside-down form, appear simultaneously, perhaps representing both the rise and the fall of the church. Indeed, throughout the piece, the melodic lines curve back in on themselves in a hypnotic motion like that of the elusive, seaborne cathedral. Bells toll throughout in every conceivable register, and low sustained bass notes, or pedal tones, abound, setting up vibrations on which the cathedral rests. The piece is the perfect illustration of water as "shadows, dreams, and substance." We encounter the edifice momentarily, replete in all its glory, but it is demolished, and where once there was substance, now there is only shadow and a dream.

It's no coincidence that it's a mermaid who's tied up with all that devastation. Crossed species spell trouble, as we've seen. Not surprisingly, fish that *aren't* crossed with maidens fare better. Think about the lacquer wood panel Debussy owned that is said to have inspired *Poissons d'or*, from *Images, Book 2* (see figure 6.3 for the image). Debussy's goldfish is safe from the savagery of nature and the terrors of mythology; one can imagine the munificent sea where this fish lived as Debussy's "notre bonne mère la mer" (our good mother, the sea, with the words "mère" or "mother" and "mer" or "sea" forming a convenient pun in French).[14]

Here Debussy's music is about motion and light. Like *Reflets dans l'eau* this piece constantly simulates the undulation of water but with few big waves. The fish darts by us, "capricieux et souple," its motions fleeting. The initial dotted rhythm gets isolated as a tiny motto, impossible to grasp before it vanishes, and through much of the piece, rapid thirty-second and sixty-fourth notes whiz by in tiny cells, and often even tiny note heads, that make us understand how ephemeral this creature is, here one moment and gone the next.

This fish sings beautifully as it swims by, sometimes in fragments, sometimes in long phrases. Its opening song, in figure 10.4, is eloquent and confined to a tiny range; unlike most fish, this fish doesn't leap. That tune even-

Figure 10.5. ***Poissons d'or*, mm. 3–6, in *Images, Book 2*, by Claude Debussy (Paris: Durand, 1908). Digital image from Hathi Trust Digital Library.**

tually gives way to a plaintive melody, mostly whole tone, marked "espressif et sans rigueur" (expressive and without rigor), whose exotic scale reminds us that we are witnessing not just any goldfish but a Japanese one. We're taken back to the Far East and also to the first of the pieces in this set, *Cloches à travers les feuilles* (Bells across the Leaves), which is blanketed with layer after layer of whole-tone scales. Playing "without rigor" is yet another way that Debussy takes us away from the march of time, and in the first two pieces of this set, time has slowed to a veritable halt. The goldfish is always in motion, but his life is filled with interruptions and asides. He's quickly bored, given to unexpected flourishes, and one theme blends into the next, as if his darting thoughts refuse definitive punctuation. At one moment he becomes downright villainous, speaking in a low bass voice transplanted from some more brutish creature. Even that long and inexorably rigid episode, however, turns out to be related to the shimmering opening tune, and that pretty melody is not about to tolerate invasion. It returns, "arraché" (ripped apart), in fighting mode, and soon the imposter is no more. The final cadenza without melody or bar lines celebrates the well-deserved victory of its free soul.

The sweetness of the goldfish and the nightmarish quality of the howling mermaid in the "engulfed cathedral" are equally persuasive masks of our floating world. But omnipresent though that water may be, and endlessly enthralling, it's land where people abide. The islands that dot any marine landscape proved equally fertile ground for Debussy's dreams and on firmer, less treacherous terrain. The virtuosic, *L'isle joyeuse* (1904), Debussy's only winning entry for pianists on the competition circuit, provides us, very literally, with an island filled with joy. The physical demands of performing it seem to translate into a joy in physicality itself, an unalloyed pleasure taken in the body. Even Debussy remarks, "how difficult it is to perform . . . since it unites force and grace."[15] Debussy's early biographer, Léon Vallas, reported that the piece was inspired by Jean-Antoine Watteau's painting "L'embarquement pour Cythère" (1717) (figure 10.6), and that's been taken as received wisdom ever since, though it's hardly a unanimous opinion.[16] Surely Debussy's wife to be, Emma Bardac, with whom he was running off to the Isle of Jersey in England (note the title's anglophone "L'isle," as opposed to the French "L'île") was a more concrete motivation, though we do know that much, if not all, of the piece was written before that escape. In any case, it's well worth looking at the Watteau painting and its genre, for this art had an impact on Debussy and his countrymen far beyond a single composition. Francis Poulenc even wrote a piece for two pianos specifically entitled *L'embarquement pour Cythère* in 1953, fifty years later than Debussy; the painting remained in pianistic vogue centuries after it was made.

Like the Commedia dell'arte, the genre provides a challenge to the modern viewer. Its stylization, its mythicized figures, and its air of fantasy superimposed on an ordinary setting unhinge our analytical abilities. The painting doesn't give way to logic. As we examine the painting, we see that everyone going to or from the island of Cythère (there has been debate on the direction of travel) moves in groups of two. Watched over on one side by a statue of Venus and encircled by flying cupids on the other, the couples are clearly creating their own circle of love. Just as the curve of the figures mimics the curves of the landscape and the shores of the island, so it also conveys the sensuality of the figures hidden beneath their ornate costumes. Their finery sets them apart from their natural setting, but their amorous pursuits join them to it in an aristocratic scene that exemplifies the meaning of the *fête galante*. Translated rather vaguely as a courtship party for the rich, this eighteenth-century classification of painting, which originated to describe Watteau's work, inspired numerous other paintings and poems.

In fact, clearly taken with Watteau's idea, Debussy's friend, the poet Paul Verlaine, published a set of more than twenty poems entitled *Fêtes galantes* in 1869; Debussy used the titles of two of them, "En bateau" and "Cortège," for movements in his *Petite Suite* and set a number of them as songs, including two entire sets, which he entitled *Fêtes galantes*. "Clair de lune," probably the

Figure 10.6. *L'embarquement pour Cythère*, 1717, Jean-Antoine Watteau, Musée du Louvre, Paris. Collection de l'Académie.

most famous of those songs, spreads Watteau's landscape out before us as the imagined soul you'll remember from previous chapters: "Your soul is a chosen landscape / Where charming masqueraders and bergamaskers go / Playing the lute and dancing and almost / Sad under their fantastic disguises."[17] The poem captures well the contradictions of this idyllic scene: the artificiality of the costumes in the midst of a natural setting, the immobility of the statue watching over the moving figures, and the reality of the lovers juxtaposed against the imaginary cupids and frozen goddess. Most important, it puts words to the indefinable ambiguity of emotion one senses in the picture. Is this a happy scene or a sad one? For Watteau, Verlaine, and Debussy, emotions were often hybrids, and the creatures pictured here were somewhere between real and unreal, ecstatic and melancholy. Art was the chosen medium for conveying the infinite ambiguity of the unconscious mind.

Debussy's music here chooses ecstasy over agony and embraces wholeheartedly the couples' apparent achievement of paradise. *L'isle joyeuse* is one of his longest works for piano, and, like *Reflets dans l'eau*, it's a masterpiece in *stream* of consciousness, a sort of musical Rorschach test, where one association leads to another. It's fun to trace their exploits. The piece opens rapturously, with a trill spilling over into broken chords, which happen to be augmented triads drawn from the whole-tone scale. The chords circle, rematerializing in a haze, and lead in turn into a Spanish-tinged strummed

Figure 10.7. ***L'isle joyeuse,*** **mm. 8–9, Claude Debussy (Paris: Durand, 1904). Digital image from Hathi Trust Digital Library.**

accompaniment and a rhythmic dotted tune, pictured in figure 10.7. That tune, like the chords, feels insatiable, turning round and round back on itself, and it declares its harmonic freedom by referring simultaneously to A Major, the whole-tone scale, and the Lydian mode. That's a lot of harmonic baggage, but it simply means that rules are in abeyance. Lydian is an ancient church mode with its own whole-tone flavor and decidedly alien tonality, and Debussy uses it as yet another escape hatch from the prosaic predictability of major and minor, here converting "D-natural" into a "D-sharp" and thereby decisively setting this harmonic island off from the mainland of academic harmony.

Those whole tones are everywhere; they give birth to the opening flourishes, and they sneak in again with the circuitous tune that is marked "un peu en dehors" (a little brought out). Debussy needs to provide that instruction because that new tune, as well as the following one, is consigned to the left hand, at first awkwardly crossed over the right hand, slightly hidden and abashed, like an intimate conversation.

Nothing in this piece stays hidden for long, however—this is not one of Debussy's efforts to achieve Far Eastern sublimity. Instead, the opening returns, swirling again in abandon, but leading this time to a slightly

Figure 10.8. ***L'isle joyeuse,*** **mm. 67–68, Claude Debussy (Paris: Durand, 1904). Digital image from Hathi Trust Digital Library.**

melancholy waltz in triple meter (see figure 10.8). It's marked "ondoyant" (undulating). What a wonderful and rare musical instruction: a bona fide ode to Ondine. It encompasses the motion of the water shifting beneath and the flexible movements of a dancer on top. Its spirit is far removed from the simple world of that opening march-like tune, but it carries the same foreign D-sharp into the scale of A Major, puncturing our tonal world with ambiguity and allowing the piece to flow from one subject to another very disparate one, while still making subconscious connections.

The coda makes those connections yet clearer; as we'll see in *Les collines d'Anacapri* as well, this is a veritable banquet of thematic interplay, with contrasting themes coming back and racing toward one another in their eagerness to mate. Whole-tone scales, shifts of meter, and an inexorable, ecstatic crescendo eventually lead back to a portion of that melancholy waltz, which now wears a different costume altogether, and has blithely shed its troublesome D-sharp. In fact, it has so absorbed the spirit of its predecessors that it appears in fortissimo and in happy tandem with a fragmentary version of the awkward theme that previously had to be instructed to be heard at all. Now both are anchored in one place, and the timid theme is shouting, "Très en dehors" (very much brought out) in a kind of orgasmic celebration. The piece culminates in victorious tremolos proclaimed "fortissisimo" or *triple* forte; there could be no clearer sign of fulfillment from this most circumspect of composers. This island has brought the loudest joy that can be mustered from his chosen instrument.

Les collines d'Anacapri, Preludes, Book 1, again takes place on a storybook island, but this one really exists, and the music that describes it is equally elated, though a bit more restrained. Anacapri is a village on the isle of Capri, off Italy. The assumed genesis of the piece is a label from a bottle of Anacapri wine, but Roy Howat, whose theories about the Golden Mean were mentioned earlier in the chapter, hypothesizes that Debussy may also have been inspired by Alex Munthe's contemporary accounts of visits to Capri.[18] In one, Munthe, a physician, recounts leaving Naples, which was besieged by cholera, and arriving by boat at the island as if delivered from hell to paradise.[19] The music, with its quotations of two Italian songs, makes clear its grounding in a far-off place; this piece, like *Poissons d'or*, could also have been a part of the chapter on Orientalism. The piece begins with a series of interruptions, trial balloons, utterly mysterious in their intention. This is an unknown land. The opening gambit is a series of unharmonized pitches with rising open intervals, like plucked strings on a guitar, and Debussy delights in prolonging it. He says, "Laissez vibrer" (let it vibrate) and does so twice. Each time we stop and listen to the aftermath for a long measure afterward, as if unsure what the future will bring. And each time another fragment follows, brief and inconclusive.

We approach this island as an explorer, seeing only vague outlines at first, fairly exploding with excitement, and then drawing nearer and nearer until we finally arrive in the fifteenth measure with a full-fledged tempo and theme, rather late for a piece to find its bearings. Here we're greeted with a tune that's "joyous and light," cavorting up and down in a delightfully carefree manner and never giving any indication that it's derived from earlier material. One idea again spills out of another in this piece with no apparent forethought, as if the universe were simply infinitely fertile. The next thing we know we're in the midst of a "chanson populaire," and Debussy even instructs the pianist to play "with the liberty of a popular song." Debussy is fond of using quotation—remember *Gardens in the Rain*, *Golliwogg*, and *La boîte à joujoux*, among others—and it's a wonderfully effective way to simulate the experience of memory. The listener is taken to a different time and place by the interpolation of familiar material without warning and without context, just as the thought of a past event might cross the mind with no prior notice. Most composers enjoy some use of quotation, but in piano music, the master par excellence, is Robert Schumann, one of the few recent composers whom Debussy greatly admired. Schumann piled quotes upon quotes, and his use of costume balls as the metaphor for his masked musical inventions resonated perfectly for Debussy, who was surrounded by Parisians darting off to just such occasions. Despite different nationalities, eras, and musical styles, the affinities between the two men, both so fascinated with fluid identities and alter egos, are remarkable.

In choosing a popular song as source material, Debussy not only evokes the sensation of memory but also erases the lines between his own creation and the larger world. It's as if he's ceded private ownership, and the communal experience that results is ecstatic. There are no divisions between his original music and the song; instead, the same accompaniment serves both, and in fact, no sooner have we heard one song than another arrives, this one particularly haunting. That second tune, pictured in figure 10.9, is one of the most beautiful in all Debussy's piano music—it's sultry and sun soaked, and though it has hints of melancholy, it emanates from a place we'd clearly like to live, preferably forever.

This one too emerges from pitches introduced earlier, but these derivations are artless and hidden, and even the tune itself is inclined to be clandestine; it's in an inner voice, in a dusky, viola range that's self-effacing. The ease of transformation in this piece is mind-boggling; the opening eighth-note solo query turns out to be equally comfortable as a sixteenth-note accompaniment; it leaps across registers and dynamic levels, happily befriending multiple tunes. Everyone gets along famously here, and even without recognizing the tunes that are being quoted, one knows that one has chanced upon a

Figure 10.9. ***Les collines d'Anacapri,*** **mm. 50–51, in** ***Preludes, Book 1,*** **by Claude Debussy (Paris: Durand, 1910). Digital image from Hathi Trust Digital Library.**

delicious moment of unity and beneficence. Toward the end, Debussy weaves together the opening vibrations, now secure as rapid groups of six, along with his own first theme and the first popular tune; they're happily layered, melded both horizontally and vertically. The certainty of the ending, with its thematic unity and tonal authority, is as absolute and exhilarated an affirmation as Debussy ever conceived. The beauty and mystery of this island has cured body and soul, just as the *Joyous Island,* written six years earlier, gave promise of a past and future Utopia.

It's fun to see this composer, who's generally more at home in murky waters than unclouded shores, opt for such certainty in these last two pieces. We have to remind ourselves, though, that these are islands rather than solid landmasses, and even here fragments, instability, and covered allusion flourish. Debussy doesn't often tread on firm ground.

• 11 •

Fair-Haired Maidens

Witness those mermaids in the infinite sea, the ones who bind water and earth together. They are often wrapped in streams of long hair, and their hair, like the ever-changing water where they live, carries lexicons of meaning, most especially to the French, who were so attuned to symbolic inference. Hair can telegraph personality or enable changes of identity; it is replete with symbolism. It is the only part of the body, aside from fingernails and toenails, which can be modified while remaining both attached and unmutilated. The current mania for piercings and tattoos aside, it's a territory singularly apt for alteration and experimentation, and Debussy's creatures are no exception. They advertise their traits through their plaits. Debussy was even interested in his own hair: When asked in a questionnaire to name his distinctive feature, his answer, surprisingly enough, was simply "my hair."[1]

Debussy introduces us to two women in his piano works, and they both have long hair, the better with which to seduce us. One femme fatale is Ondine, and the other is the "Maiden with the Flaxen Hair." Short though their namesake works may be, these tresses carry a heavy weight in Debussy's oeuvre. And although no other Debussy piano pieces sport actual feminine titles, pieces such as the two *Arabesques* and *Bruyeres* evoke flowing hair without explicitly saying so.

Since that maiden with the flaxen hair moves slowly, and her musical portrait is spare, she attracts younger and more amateur players than any other Debussy prelude, and her attractions lie not only in the fact that she's easy to navigate on the piano but also that her music is so lovely and approachable. This is a lady you can fall in love with at first sight—or sound. She inhabits a sad, but harmonious world, filled with reassuring major triads. Phrase lengths are clear; rhythms, regular; and tunes, singable. This world is circumscribed and soothing. Only the key Debussy has chosen gives pause. Why the difficult key of G♭ Major, a key using all the black notes?

Composers' key choices remain a bit of a mystery; one can easily transpose or change a piece from one key to another, and only a listener with perfect pitch will know the difference. In Bach's day, a theory of affects lent each key a particular emotional symbolism, but those particular meanings gradually faded. Still, particular keys often have very specific, if personal, connotations for composers. In this case, Debussy probably wanted to use all the black notes because they impart a mystery and complexity to both the piece and the tactile sensation of playing it. Sharps would, of course, have accomplished the same thing, but sharps lead up and flats lead down, and this woman seems more likely to lie than stand. We can learn more about her—and why she might be depressed—by looking at some of the other long-haired women Debussy portrayed, in works such as *La damoiselle élue, Pelléas et Mélisande,* and "La chevelure" (The Hair) and also by examining the role hair played in the thoughts of the men Debussy lived and worked among.

It appears that none of these men could resist long hair, particularly if it was blonde. From Maurice Denis's (1870–1943) frontispiece for *La damoiselle élue* (figure 11.1) to Robert Burns's "Lassie wi' the lint-white locks" and Pierre Louÿs's "La chevelure" from *Chansons de Bilitis,* Debussy lived among flowing locks. Even his letters attest to the preoccupation: in 1899, he writes, "When I'm not feverish there's a young lady I love with all my heart (a blond, naturally) with the most beautiful hair in the world."[2] Hair seemed to symbolize many things: innocence (the lass who inspired *The Maiden with the Flaxen Hair,* who sits in the garden with flowers); guilt (Mélisande, the heroine of Debussy's opera who loves her husband's brother); and seduction and sexuality ("La chevelure," where lips and limbs entwine). As Baudelaire's repository for the "memories that sleep within this mane," hair encompassed past and present hopes and fears.[3]

Nothing much has changed. Consider for a moment, before we go further back in time, what hair meant in the later part of the twentieth century. Long hair (for both men and women) signified political radicalism. (Witness the musical *Hair.*) Bleached hair signified movie stardom. An Afro signified black pride. A crew cut signified the marines. A butch cut indicated lesbianism. On and on goes the list. Young girls in particular spend half their adolescence in front of a mirror, confronted with limitless paraphernalia—curlers, clips, conditioners, straighteners, permanents, peroxide, and dyes—and ultimately determined to convey their very essence through the stubborn locks with which nature has presented them. Clearly what is on your head is felt to transmit what is in it.

Figure 11.1. Frontispiece to Debussy's *La damoiselle élue* (1893), Maurice Denis, Morgan Library and Museum, New York. The Pierpont Morgan Library, New York.

One need not look only at recent customs, however, to witness the life-changing power of coiffure. Remember the biblical Samson whose powers resided in his hair and who lost all strength when betrayed and shaved by Delilah. Or consider Medusa, whose hair with snakes twirling in it was, like her psyche, quite literally venomous. These are interesting forerunners to later women, like Salomé, who also destroyed men. Oscar Wilde's play *Salomé* premiered in Paris in 1896, having been banned in London; quite likely Debussy saw it, or at the least, followed the scandals associated with it, but in any case, he knew Richard Strauss's opera based on the play, which arrived in Paris in 1907.[4] The art nouveau drawing in figure 11.2 by Aubrey Beardsley (1872–1898), made for the publication of Oscar Wilde's play, captures all the decadent pathology of the princess whose lust for John the Baptist drives her to behead him. Her own flowing hair is linked by curving arcs to the flowing blood of her victim; both hair and blood fairly ooze.

Medusa and Salomé are women whose hair embodies murderous power over men (and the word *em-body* is particularly apt here, with the bodies of snakes and the blood of victims merging into the body of woman), but of course other magical powers are possible as well. Debussy's beloved artist Gustave Moreau, for example, presents us with a mythical woman, Gelatée, who achingly transforms the blood of her murdered lover into an eternally flowing river that springs from her hair. She, like the others, has the power of a sorcerer; these women are all mythical and magical creatures who walk around with a veritable wand attached. Their hair itself radiates action—it writhes or spikes or grows appendages. Debussy's music is quieter, but he was attracted to both their supernatural powers and to the gentler lines and curves used to convey them.

Those curves of the art nouveau avoid sharp angles and divisions; they meld man to woman, and human to nature; they also allow for spun-out musical phrases. And they opened the way to another sort of woman whose curvaceous hair had milder meanings. In her, hair seems to bring a diminution, rather than an augmentation, of powers. Debussy's favored woman, in fact, was quite the opposite of Medusa and Salomé; she appears pale, wan, and languid. Her hair is tame, straight, and often colorless. In figure 11.3 by Pierre Puvis de Chavannes (1824–1898), one of the early symbolists, there's a homoeroticism implicit in the company of three seminude women, and yet an isolation as well—they never look at one another, and even the sole face that's directed toward us appears vacant. Their proximity to the sea reinforces the maternal symbolism of the ocean, the cloudy sky is as delicate as their fine hair, and their draped attire mimics their hair's curves. It's clear that the women have nothing to do and nowhere to go; languor is their raison d'être.

Figure 11.2. Drawing by Aubrey Beardsley illustrating *Salomé* (1894), by Oscar Wilde, British Library, London (ca. 1906, 1920).

Figure 11.3. ***Jeunes filles au bord de la mer*, 1879, Pierre Puvis de Chavannes, Musée d'Orsay, Paris.**

Should Puvis de Chavannes's indolent women wish to faintly bestir themselves, they presumably comb or caress their own hair. The activity leads nowhere and is utterly solitary. It partakes of masturbation in its sensuality, and it can hardly be coincidental that they are already half nude.

Debussy's Mélisande, from his famous opera *Pelléas et Mélisande*, is, like these pictured women, devoid of ambition. Her long hair blows in the wind, and so does she. Debussy quotes her speaking in "that frail and gentle voice of hers: 'Let your dreams dwell upon my hair.'"[5] In the opera, she stands at the window, combing her hair, and when Pelléas appears, she tells him she is "arranging [her] hair for the night." Hair is the only thing Mélisande arranges in her life. As it flows out the window it gives the sense of liberating her from the terrible confines of her existence: it forms a ladder out of the tower. For Pelléas, it transmits love, like a cord through which current can flow. He cries in ecstasy, "Oh! oh! what is this? . . . 'Tis your hair, 'tis your hair falling down on me! . . . All your beautiful tresses, Mélisande, all your beautiful locks have come down from the tower! . . . They are here in my hands, in my mouth, too, I hold them. . . . They are here in my arms, I have put them all round my neck." The locks take on an identity all their own; indeed Pelléas notes delightedly that "they love me, they love me more than thou."[6]

These tresses in figure 11.4 have suddenly become potent and autonomous, both exciting and dangerous. The text is strikingly close to Pierre Louÿs's "La chevelure" from Debussy's *Chansons de Bilitis*, written only a year later. "He told me: 'Last night I dreamed. / I had your tresses around my neck. / I wore your locks like a dark chain / Around my neck and on my breast. / I caressed them and they were my own; / And we were thus forever united."[7] The connecting power of hair is obvious; it knots two people together and permits a sexual union. Such sexuality is implicit in *The Maiden with the Flaxen Hair* as well, chaste though both the music and the poem that inspired it may appear to be. The music curves around with a kind of lazy languor; there are flutterings of energy, followed again by lassitude; there is a solo voice, which is then wrapped by sympathetic harmonies. This music speaks the symbolists' poetry: Verlaine's "languorous ecstasy" and "lovers' fatigue" is no longer a mere text.[8]

But hair round one's neck can also strangle, and its knots can form an unwelcome bond. So it must have felt to Huldbrand, captured by Ondine under false pretenses, and betrothed to a water sprite in lieu of a beautiful woman. "Beware . . . for she excels all women in the magic of her locks, and when she twines them round a young man's neck, she will not ever set him free again," says Dante Gabriel Rossetti, another of Debussy's poets, apropos Lady Liluth, one of the women he painted.[9] And for Pelléas and Mélisande, the prisoner-captive relationship is gender reversed. "No, no, no I shall not give you your freedom tonight," says Pelléas. "They [Les cheveux] are bound, they are bound to a branch of the willow. . . .You shall never go free . . . you never shall go free . . . you never can leave me anymore." Mélisande's hair has betrayed her authority and attached itself to something other than her.

Figure 11.4. Mary Garden as Mélisande, 1908, Rudolf Eickemeyer Jr. (1862–1932). Wikimedia Commons.

Debussy's Mélisande is instructive here. It is always her fate to be manipulated, and it is no surprise that even a part of her own body turns against her. She will go to her death as a victim, eventually giving birth, but dying in the process, as if that radical action has pained her unto death. The art nouveau women who appeared so like her, with pale hair that dominated their features, were part of a movement very centrally *about* women who seemed equally passive: the artists explored their hair, their surroundings, and their desires. Their art was filled with portraits of the women themselves, surrounded by flowers and leaves that symbolized the fertility of a Mother Earth. When away from their easels, the artists made ornamental objects, glasswork, ceramics, and jewelry that were expressly for women. In fact, women themselves took on the aspect of ornaments. Judging by their demeanors, their existence was not altogether satisfying. They appear to meditate somewhat grimly on their fates, sadly prevented from taking charge of them. Perhaps this was implicit in that well-named "Belle Époque," where beauty got top billing, and substance, little mention at all.

Was it likewise for Debussy's maiden with the flaxen hair, "the lovely one with lips like cherries"?[10] She sits and sings. "The long look of [her] big eyes" invites "love, in the clear sun of summer." The curves and arabesques of the prelude, particularly its opening and oft-repeated theme, mimic the curves of art nouveau.

She's sweetly indecisive, oscillating throughout the prelude between the keys of G♭ Major and E♭ minor, but despite that hesitancy, this is one of the most tonal of the preludes, finding great comfort in the clarity of its cadences. The first closure, in fact, appears straightaway in the third measure, pictured in figure 11.5. The lovely girl's voice is supple, covering a large range and never wavering from the sweetness of the opening legato. Debussy was inspired by Leconte de Lisle's poem "La fille aux cheveux de lin," which he

Figure 11.5. ***La fille aux cheveux de lin*, mm. 1–4, in *Preludes, Book 1*, by Claude Debussy (Paris: Durand, 1910). Digital image from Hathi Trust Digital Library.**

set as a song in the early 1880s, and de Lisle's text was in turn an imitation of Robert Burns's earlier "Lassie wi' the lint-white locks." Leconte de Lisle's poem begins this way: "On the grass, sitting in flowers / Who sings since the fresh morning? / It is the maiden with the flaxen hair / The lovely one with lips like cherries." Robert Burns's chorus has the suitor proposing to a "Lassie wi' the lint-white locks, / Bonnie lassie, artless lassie, / Wilt thou wi' me tent the flocks, / An wilt thou be my Dearie O?" Was he addressing yet another pale girl, hidden by an ample mane, sweetly crooning as she awaits her beloved?

This tempting maiden does not sit alone in Debussy's oeuvre. There is, of course, the song he wrote earlier by the same title. And the early arabesques are similarly curvaceous and equally evocative of tame, though seductive, femininity. They charm without challenging; their range is confined. There was an alternative, however, even in Debussy's era, to both the man-eating ogre whose hair breathed death and the ornamental maiden staring into mirrors or windows, enclosed and enveloped by her voluminous locks. The more daring periodicals of the day abound with illustrations featuring women decked *only* in hair, and, in contrast with more decorous paintings, their faces are proudly showing and they are calling out to the world. The women are empowered, and their hair is a daring symbol of overt sexuality; it's a lure or even a snare. Astarté, the goddess pictured in figure 11.6, is clearly a stand-in for something more immediate than the gods. She reminds us of Zola's Nana and Proust's Odette, those demimondaines unashamed to flaunt their sexuality throughout Paris. This is not a woman to Debussy's taste: His maiden of the flaxen hair is far more chaste, and Mélisande is far more unhappy. Debussy prefers his women lovely, forlorn, and distant, but not all Parisians were, so to speak, on the same wavelength.

Baudelaire, in his poem, "La chevelure,"[11] manages to imagine Nana and the maiden with the flaxen hair entwined, though neither was specifically on his mind. Hair here is simultaneously "languorous" and "scorching." In both "La chevelure" and Baudelaire's prose poem, "Un hémisphère dans une chevelure,"[12] hair is a ship that carries one across the world like a magic carpet; it is an ocean where one is drowned in caresses. It is an entire world, filled with "memory's fine wine." "Your hair holds an entire dream," he happily claims in "Un hémisphère dans une chevelure," and in "La chevelure" its "fleece, billowing even down the neck / . . . perfume charged with nonchalance" offers the perfect vehicle for Debussy's self-stated goals to "seek oblivion" and a "charm [that] is eternal."[13] Baudelaire approaches hair like a synesthesiac—he not only feels it and sees it but also listens to it and hears infinity: "If only you could know . . . everything I hear in your hair!"[14] It falls to Debussy to find the requisite sounds.

Figure 11.6. Drawing by Louis Morin (1855–1938) for the cover of *Astarté* by Victor d'Auriac (1858–1925), *Le Courrier français,* February 22, 1903. Bibliothèque nationale de France.

And Debussy obliges with his usual acumen. The task was confusing, however, for the entire identity of women was rife with contradiction in Debussy's Parisian world, and hair was its obvious symbol. The properties of this wondrous substance that is at once part of our body and at the same time apart from it are remarkable. Hair can be the repository for magical powers, good or evil, functioning like a magic wand, or even a phallus. It can be the gentle twine that connects man and woman, the ladder that allows man to "mount"[15] or the imprisoning rope that forms a hangman's noose. It can be the ornament that makes woman lovely or the trap she spins to ensnare. Its pale lack of substance is corpse-like; at the same time, it is, as Baudelaire said, "the oasis where I dream" of desire.[16] I'm not surprised that Debussy stationed himself there.

As a postscript, it's worth adding that French attitudes toward hair surely have implications beyond mere coiffeur. An interest so strong in ornament implies that substance is secondary. French women didn't receive the vote until 1945 (most European countries granted it in the early twentieth century, the United States in 1920); for many men in power, what went on inside the female head was apparently of less interest than what went on outside it. As recently as 2013, the director of the Paris Conservatory of Music was quoted as saying that he well understood why there were so few women conductors; he was sure their strength couldn't meet that metier's physical demands.[17] Apparently those fragile maidens with the flaxen hair lack the heft for directorial roles. The preference of painters such as Rossetti and composers such as Debussy for docile heads of long blonde hair not only reflected but also impacted their society. The legacy of their delicate women lives on.

• 12 •

Edgar Allan Poe's "Imp of the Perverse"

Charles Baudelaire wasn't the only author who recognized that hair was the "wine of memory." Years earlier, Edgar Allan Poe had spoken of "grey hairs that are records of the past."[1] Here was an author deeply concerned with past memories that haunted the present, and Debussy too often felt surrounded by ghosts of the past. He felt a deep sympathy with this author, and in fact, when asked in 1889 to identify his favorite prose authors, Debussy responded with two names: Gustave Flaubert (1821–1880) and Edgar Poe (1809–1849).[2] The august French novelist was hardly a surprising nomination, but the choice of Poe at first glance elicits astonishment. How could this refined Frenchman enjoy the macabre tales of a poor and alcohol-ridden American? And what would have led him to attempt two operas based on Poe's stories?

Indeed, even American schoolchildren believe that Poe is something to be outgrown: We dutifully memorize "Annabel Lee" in middle school, and by high school, we approach it "nevermore." T. S. Eliot suggested that Poe's intellect "seems to me the intellect of a highly gifted person before puberty."[3] Suspenseful though the tales may be, their language is deemed crude; their plots, juvenile; and their concerns, of no abiding moral importance.

The opinion of contemporary American literary critics and public school teachers, however, was not shared by the nineteenth-century French literati, and Debussy was far from alone in his adulation of the American poet and short-story writer. Astonishingly, Baudelaire was said to pray to Poe daily and, with more concrete results, wrote a large essay on him entitled *Nouvelles sur Edgar Poe* and devoted seventeen years of his life to translating Poe's prose output.[4] (He avoided the poetry because of the difficulty of maintaining the crucial rhythm in translation.) Stéphane Mallarmé learned English in order to translate the poetry; Paul Valéry (1871–1945) and Gabriel Mourey

(1865–1943) undertook the same task, with Mourey, a good friend of Debussy's, eventually translating the entire poetic oeuvre. And Debussy was obsessed with his operatic attempts, persisting through years of discouraging results. His piano music is infused with all the influences he absorbed.

What in the world possessed these dreamy symbolist poets, and Debussy, their musical disciple, to pass their time in passionate study of an American upstart who wrote detective stories? Though, as is suggested by Eliot, part of their fascination may be explained by their clumsy grasp of the English language—and their resultant blindness to Poe's own lack of subtlety—that can hardly explain so widespread an infatuation. Likewise, they may have identified with parts of Poe's biography—his degenerate use of drugs and alcohol, his neglect as a child, and the lack of public recognition for his artistic achievement—but that can hardly account for their intense artistic devotion.

Something at the very core of Poe's thought must have spoken to these men. One claim is that his essay on the "Philosophy of Composition" and other theoretical writings had strong resonance for the poets. Poe peered at his own work with self-conscious calculation; he claims to have "proceeded step by step, to its completion, with the precision and rigid consequence of a mathematical problem."[5] Eliot, in his essay on the French love affair with Poe, "From Poe to Valéry," says that for Poe the poem is far more about its own creative method than about its subject.[6] "A poem should have nothing in view but itself," says Baudelaire in describing Poe's beliefs.[7] For the French symbolists, who elevated the style and sound of language above its narrative content, that self-reflexive attitude struck home. They were less involved in telling a story than in observing and immersing themselves in the *process* of telling a story. The endeavor puts the creator at the center; Poe wished us to watch him at work; the poets wished to draw our attention to the aptness of their art. The approach ultimately questions the primary purpose of art and its function as a mirror of reality. There's a link here to musical composition, where the work is abstract to start with. As a composer who "requires weeks to decide on one harmonious chord over another,"[8] Debussy may have been attracted by Poe's obsessive planning, as well as by his insistence that art was ultimately not about a real, and thereby limited, object but rather about the birth of the art itself, a far wider concern.

The tenuous nature of that thread connecting art with the world of real objects and people—as well as the tenuousness of reality itself—is one of the major concerns of the symbolists, the Dadaists, and the surrealists, all of whom, one generation after the next, had a central presence in the Paris art world. Despite the fact that Poe was incontrovertibly American, there was obviously an intangible "je ne sais quoi" about him that tantalized Francophone artists before, during, and after Debussy's lifetime. For Debussy and his poets—most of them, like him, irreligious, given to biting humor, and often morose—Poe's refusal to clearly divide the rational from the irrational and to delve into the workings of the mind rather than the physical realities of the universe was infinitely intriguing.

Debussy, who you will remember, had declared that "art is the most beautiful deception of all," was all in favor of that conflation of the real with the illusory nature of human perception. "Let us not disillusion anyone by bringing too much reality into the dream," he had cautioned.[9] And like Poe, he aimed to convey the dream through a very particular conception of beauty. Poe specified that refrain and rhyme reigned supreme, and as Eliot points out, he "had, to an exceptional degree, the feeling for the incantatory element in poetry."[10] It's precisely that incantation that brings life to poems such as "The Raven" and "Annabel Lee"; their mesmerizing sound world digs deep into the subconscious. Baudelaire and Mallarmé were equally taken with the hypnotic effects of rhyme and repetition,[11] and I would argue that Debussy was as well. His prelude "*Les sons et les parfums tournent dans l'air du soir*," based on Baudelaire's poetry, is a case in point. The dipping fourths and fifths scattered throughout reverberate in the listener's unconscious, lodging there as in a dream.

Debussy's other Baudelaire homage, the very late "*Les soirs illuminés par l'ardeur du charbon*" (Evenings Illuminated by the Ardor of Coal), makes use of the same sort of ritualistic repetition, much as does the poem "Le balcon," a line of which gives the piece its title. In fact, the music begins with a direct quote from "*Les sons et les parfums tournent dans l'air du soir*" simply transposed down a half step.[12] More even than refrain and rhyme, Debussy and Baudelaire and the later symbolist poets shared with Poe a sense of tone. Poe instructs, "Regarding, then, Beauty as my province, my next question referred to the *tone* of its highest manifestation—and all experience has shown that this tone is one of *sadness*. Beauty of whatever kind, in its supreme development, invariably excites the sensitive soul to tears. Melancholy is thus the most legitimate of all the poetical tones."[13] Those words must have been music to Debussy's ears. No other composer before Debussy had written such a preponderance of slow, soft music. In fact, one of the major challenges in performing his music on the piano is finding a sufficient variety of soft sounds, for the dynamic range often *starts* at "piano" and moves down from there to the barely audible. He consistently eschews violence and celebration for introspection and regret. Baudelaire puts his sentiments into words, writing not one but four poems entitled "Spleen." The word, a stand-in for melancholy, evokes loss and hopelessness, and here Baudelaire could be Poe's doppelgänger. The "low and heavy sky weighs like a lid / Upon the spirit moaning in ennui,"[14] and the poet's memory is "a giant vault / Holding more corpses than a common grave."[15]

The tie-in between melancholy and death is obvious, and those corpses take center stage in another, equally brooding poem, "Le vin de l'assassin" (The Murderers' Wine). Here Baudelaire deals with literal corpses, explaining with a certain Poe-like detachment the irrefutable arguments for spousal murder when overcome by "love with its dark, enchanting pains / Troupe of anxieties from hell, / Its flasks of poison, tears as well, / Its rattlings of bones and chains."[16] Baudelaire's use of the same images one encounters in Poe is striking; the vault, the corpses, the worms, the bells, the cats, the poison, and the chains all sprout with a grotesque vividness. Just as Poe conveys a stultifying ship's hold in *Arthur Pym* or a suffocating vault in *The Cask of Amontillado*, so Baudelaire conveys the prison of a man's mind. The identical choice of images is uncanny, and the images of darkness and death recur in Debussy's piano titles as well: *Dead Leaves*, "*Evenings Illuminated by the Ardor of the Coal*," and *Élégie*.

More explicitly, that same atmosphere conveying desolation and living entombment, though minus the cruelty, pervades the texts that Debussy set in his songs as well. In Paul Verlaine's "Il pleure dans mon coeur" (*Ariettes oubliées*, no. 2), the narrator laments his unceasing languor, crying, "What! No treason? / This mourning has no reason." Against a cause, he could fight and possibly find an exit; a foe could be vanquished, but in a struggle without an antagonist, there is no victory to be had. Debussy said, "I dream of librettos . . . in which the actors don't discuss things but are victims of life and destiny."[17] He was fascinated by victims, and his opera *Pelléas et Mélisande*, with its story by Maurice Maeterlinck (1862–1949), is very much the story of a family victimized by fate. Mélisande appears as if by chance; she has no home, no volition. Maeterlinck draws heavily from Poe in his landscape of "darkness, so thick that it lies in dense and poisoned masses,"[18] and like Poe, he uses ancient castles and the desolation of overgrown landscapes to evoke an ancient and suffering race, a race unable to arrest its own self-destruction. Debussy, in fact, used the castle from Poe's story "The Fall of the House of Usher" as the precise model for the castle in his opera.

Debussy was obviously deeply drawn to this tragic tale of a woman who knows not her own will and a man who kills his brother in order to own her. To accompany its despairing text, he wrote chant-like music that circles around the narrow compass of speech and refuses the conventions of traditional opera and tonality. Clearly, Debussy hoped to delve further into this language and this exploration of the damaged psyche: He was equally drawn to the dark landscapes of Poe's "The Fall of the House of Usher" and "The Devil in the Belfry," attempting both a symphony and an opera based on "Usher" and an opera based on "Devil in the Belfry," though he ultimately completed none of them. The orchestral work, "a symphony on psychologically developed themes,"[19] was begun already in 1889 and eventually dropped; the operatic version of "Devil in the Belfry" occupied him from about 1902 to 1912 and the "Usher" opera all the way from 1908 to 1917. Thus, through most of his professional life and certainly throughout the time that the important piano music was written, Debussy was grappling with the macabre tales of Poe. He identified personally with the gloomy stories as well, announcing:

> And then I've been spending my days lately in *La Maison Usher*, which isn't exactly a house to calm the nerves, quite the opposite. . . . You get into the strange habit of listening to the dialogue of the stones and expecting houses to fall down as though that were a natural, even necessary phenomenon. What's more, if you press me to, I'd admit to a greater sympathy with that house's inhabitants than with . . . many others, who shall remain anonymous.[20]

He describes Roderick Usher, in his opera libretto, as a "figure ravaged by anguish," a description he could equally well have chosen for himself.[21] And in another letter he even appropriates Baudelaire's translation of the opening sentence of Usher, confessing that "sometimes my days are dull, dark and soundless like those of a hero from Edgar Allan Poe"; he was using Baudelaire's "journée fuligineuse, sombre et muette," the French translation of Poe's first sentence, verbatim.[22]

The house of Usher was not just dull, dark, and soundless—it was also filled with characters engaged in possible murder and incest. A brother buries a sister alive and listens to the walls vibrate as she wails and stirs in her underground prison. The strain of destruction and self-destruction runs deep in Poe; just as he watches himself write, his characters watch themselves act. He's fascinated not just by fear but also by our fear of fear and by our instinctive masochism. Poe identifies that masochism as the "Imp of the Perverse," explaining at length that

> through its promptings we act, for the reason that we should *not*. In theory, no reason can be more unreasonable; but, in fact, there is none more strong. With certain minds, under certain conditions, it becomes absolutely irresistible. I am not more certain that I breathe, than that the assurance of the wrong or error of any action is often the assurance of the one unconquerable *force* which impels us, and alone impels us to its prosecution. Nor will this overwhelming tendency to do wrong for the wrong's sake, admit of analysis, or resolution into ulterior elements. It is a radical, a primitive impulse—elementary.[23]

This "imp" is tellingly translated by Baudelaire as a "demon," and a demon he is, cunningly coaxing Poe's characters into self-inflicted disasters. More than fifty years before Freud formulated his theories, Poe was examining the inner workings and pathologies of the human mind: He was fascinated by its helplessness in the face of self-created demons, as was Debussy, who himself in one letter referred familiarly to "that Imp of the Perverse who urges us on to choose the very idea we ought to have left alone,"[24] and in another, ruefully reflects on "orders . . . given to someone who does not obey you, and this someone is yourself."[25]

In "The Black Cat," the narrator proclaims, "Yet I am not more sure that my soul lives, than I am that perverseness is one of the primitive impulses of the human heart. . . . Who has not, a hundred times, found himself committing a vile or a stupid action, for no other reason than because he knows he should *not*?"[26] As Michael Davitt Bell would have it, "The essential Poe fable . . . is a tale of compulsive self-murder";[27] as D. H. Lawrence conceives it, Poe chooses to explore "the disintegration processes of his own psyche."[28] Bleak assessments, both of them. In story after story a character is destroyed through his own choice—most strikingly, the lucky murderers in "The Black Cat" and "The Imp of the Perverse," who have escaped the slightest suspicion of guilt, are driven to confess and suffer mortal punishment, not through moral repugnance at their own acts but simply through an irresistible impulse to bring about their own complete destruction. To a composer fascinated by the hidden workings of the human mind, and subject to constant self-flagellation, the appeal here is obvious.

The lack of moral stance that is a signature of Poe's work no doubt appealed to Debussy as well, who announced that "the man of unbending moral rectitude never inspires me with any confidence whatever."[29] Debussy detested rules and was deeply cynical about mankind's finer instincts. He would have felt quite an affinity for Poe himself and for Mr. Ellison, Poe's wealthy landscape gardener in "The Domain of Arnheim" who is certain there is not "possibility of any improvement, properly so called, being effected by man himself in the general condition of man." Like Ellison, Debussy was "upon the whole . . . thrown back, in very great measure, upon self," having despaired of more cooperative enterprise.[30] Individual artistic endeavor, however, engages both men: Ellison sets about creating the perfect landscape garden and soon finds himself "enwrapt in an exquisite sense of the strange."[31] There is "a gush of entrancing melody . . . an oppressive sense of strange sweet odour . . . a dreamlike intermingling to the eye."[32] Baudelaire's synesthesia, and its heir, Debussy's "*Les sons et les parfums tournent dans l'air du soir*," immediately spring to mind. Poe could not have been more prescient.

In fact, though he doesn't always receive due homage, Poe and his imp are actually hiding throughout much of the piano music. The imp, more friendly than usual, jumps out at us, for instance, in *Etude No. 1, Pour les "cinq doigts"—d'après Monsieur Czerny*, when a bored child, purportedly "sage" or well behaved, slyly inserts wrong notes into every measure of the Czerny he dutifully practices, gaining courage and obduracy as he goes. He begins with a tedious five-note pattern, consonant and predictable, and then, inspired, slams down a note that clashes. Obviously pleased with the results, he speeds up and slams down the note more often. Now the imp is in full ascendance and the piece is off to a rollicking start—rules be damned. This imp reminds me of the comic devil who appears in *The Devil in the Belfry*, one of Debussy's two unfinished Poe operas. This demon disrupts all expectations in the rule-bound land of "Vondervotteimittiss" (Wonder-what-time-it-is), by striking thirteen on a clock that, for centuries, has never experienced life past twelve. He's an amusing, rather than a terrifying, fiend, but the disorder he engenders wreaks havoc in "the ancient order of things";[33] he clearly drew inspiration from an inner Puck proclaiming "this their jangling I esteem a sport."[34]

Debussy must have felt both Puck-like and Poe-like when he composed *Hommage à S. Pickwick Esq. P.P.M.P.C.*, poking gentle fun at Charles Dickens's Pickwick[35] from the beginning to end. The piece begins with a rousing rendition of "God Save the King," Pickwick's very own national anthem, harmonized in a most unconventional and delightfully unpatriotic fashion. It then proceeds to disembowel the anthem, arriving finally, in figure 12.1, at a strident rendition in the upper reaches of the instrument, where the distorted anthem itself is accompanied by a nagging and shrill dotted figure; it's patently unrelated to the anthem and clearly delights in creating disturbance. Debussy again opts for three staves, instead of the normal two, thus creating the maximum degree of visual separation between the competing forces.

Throughout the prelude, we're treated to a close-up view of Dickens's quasi-hero, who roamed England with his coterie of followers, seeking a cause but rarely progressing beyond inebriation. We hear him, pompous and self-satisfied, as he proclaims his virtues at top voice in bombastic, empty-headed triads and, equally smug, as he tweedles his way around England,

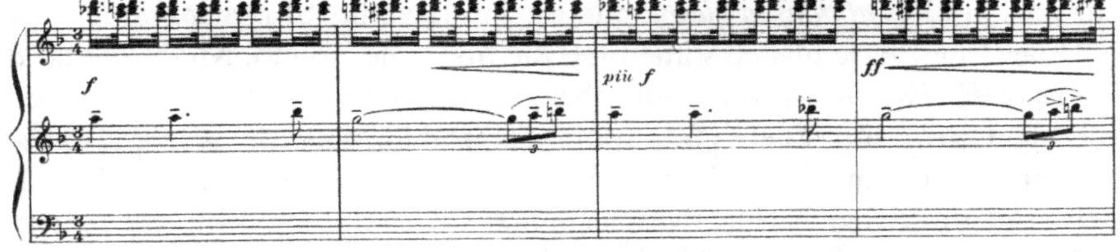

Figure 12.1. ***Hommage à S. Pickwick Esq. P.P.M.P.C.*****, mm. 37–40, in *****Preludes, Book 2*****, by Claude Debussy (Paris: Durand, 1913). Digital image from Hathi Trust Digital Library.**

"lointain et léger" (far away and lightly), spouting the simplest of tunes in a piccolo register. Throughout we are pleasantly reassured that "the gigantic brain of Pickwick was working beneath that forehead" and that there was no doubt as to "the advantages which must accrue to the cause of science" by encouraging the "immortal Pickwick" in his ceaseless efforts "to benefit the human race." Pickwick, apparently almost as popular in France as in England,[36] had equally meritorious sidekicks. Mr. Weller was the proud owner of a face that "had expanded under the influence of good living" and sported "large brass buttons, whereof the two which garnished the waist, were so far apart, that no man had ever beheld them both at the same time." And their acquaintance, Mrs. Leo Hunter, inspired the entire crew with her ode to amphibians: "Can I view thee panting, lying / On thy stomach, without sighing; / Can I unmoved see thee dying / On a log / Expired frog."

Debussy no doubt took the frog's plight particularly to heart, given the frog figurine, Arkel, which he had always at his side; his luckily never expired! Pickwick doesn't sit alone in Debussy's comic oeuvre. Consider the many preludes and études where jangling surprises are charmingly disruptive: say, *The Interrupted Serenade*, *The Dance of Puck*, or even the *Etude, No. 11, Pour les arpèges composés*, which glories in ephemeral beauty until a clown cavorts across the stage, delighting in disruption. It's the graver aspects of that imp, though, that are more puzzling and ultimately even more intriguing. Debussy does not usually convey a sense of the human psyche as deeply pathological, and it's difficult to reconcile such beguiling music with such dark undercurrents. Yet ultimately it was precisely Poe's psychological complexity, his willingness to bare the inner demons of characters such as William Wilson, pursued and destroyed by his own doppelgänger, and Roderick Usher, guilty of his sister's murder and murdered by her ghost, which drew Debussy in.

As Debussy imagined himself living in Usher's desolate "maison" and, over decades, strove to give musical voice to Usher's fanatical ravings, how could the piano music have remained untouched by similar terrors? And so I wonder as I relisten to the cavernous harmonies of *Canope*, the rustlings in *Feuilles mortes*, the shock of *Ce qu'a vu le Vent de l'Ouest*, the ominous undercurrents in *Le vent dans la plaine*, and the implacability of *Des pas sur la neige* whether I may have missed something the first time around. Might the dead leaves of *Feuilles mortes* come from the "the decayed trees, the grey wall, and the silent tarn—a pestilent and mystic vapour dull, sluggish, faintly discernible, and leaden-hued" of Usher?[37] Might the winds of *Ce qu'a vu le Vent de l'Ouest* be those that Arthur Pym encountered "from the southwest . . . with a violence almost inconceivable?"[38] And could the *Footsteps in the Snow* have taken place during "the long Polar winter" Pym later faced?[39] Could perhaps even the light wind of *Le vent dans la plaine*, interrupted so mercilessly by those implacable forte triads at the change of key, be "the wind that came out of the cloud by night, chilling and killing my Annabel Lee?"[40] Perhaps the funeral urns in *Canope* contain the ashes of any number of unlucky Poe victims? Is it even possible that the mysterious endings of many of the tales, with characters such as Arthur Pym and the hero of "Manuscript Found in a Bottle" ultimately unaccounted for, inspired Debussy to end *Preludes* with ellipses and to leave harmonies hanging, as if his music itself had simply vaporized in the same manner as Poe's heroes?

Of all these possibilities, the relationship of *Feuilles mortes* to the spirit of Poe seems to me most undeniable. The prelude is probably named after a collection of Gabriel Mourey's poems, "Feuilles mortes" from *Voix éparses*, and Mourey was both a close friend of Debussy's and a devoted translator of Poe.[41] He speaks of forests "melancholy and cold" and "trees, without leaves, trembling" "in the solitary woods . . . of indecisive paleness," thus placing himself squarely in Poe's uncanny world.[42] Debussy's prelude, marked "lent et mélancolique" (slow and melancholy) may spring from a gentler world than Poe's, but it is equally eerie. It begins with two falling chords, whose descent is then repeated at a wider interval. One does indeed "sense groaning without cease, with all their murmurs, / The hopes, the sighs and the sobs of humans."[43] Already in the second measure, there is a bass undercurrent, like a padded echo, which foreshadows the constant low resonance throughout the piece, as if the prelude, like most of the poems, takes place during "the mysterious night" under cover of darkness and with forebodings of death.[44] From the opening tune, now transformed into a disturbing ostinato, emerges the measure seen in figure 12.2, transported into the bass like a flying leaf dislodged. The piece consists of inconclusive fragments such as this one, which seem to blow aimlessly in the air, perhaps like the bereaved lover of the fourth poem, having felt "dying all hope of return."[45] Buffeted by changing winds, they are never firmly anchored (note the key ambiguity of the musical opening); they float through changes of direction, and they swirl more and more slowly in the air. There are brief energetic triads where the hands interlock and issue a clarion wake-up call to life, but they're soon defeated, eventually falling back near the end, into a slow, deep, tender sort of death. Motives remain incomplete, and the musical ideas gently disintegrate and blend into one another, without goals or closure. Theirs is indeed a voice of "the indecisive evening," with "its sad echoes."[46] The bleakness of the stark octaves introduced in the very beginning seems to win a sad and quiet victory in the lone C-sharps that remain sounding at the end when all other signs of life are gone. Those notes stretch out into a kind of infinity, held after all other notes are released; they imply magical thinking that faint vibrations might last forever. This music is less gruesome than the stories of Poe, but it too is filled with ominous premonitions.

Figure 12.2. ***Feuilles mortes*, m. 19, in *Preludes, Book 2*, by Claude Debussy (Paris: Durand, 1913). Digital image from Hathi Trust Digital Library.**

Debussy said as he worked on *The Fall of the House of Usher*: "I live surrounded by memories and regrets."[47] Those memories and regrets must have been with him when he wrote *Feuilles mortes*.

They were with others as well, artists of all sorts. Odilon Redon one of Debussy's favorites, did a striking series of prints entitled *To Edgar Poe*, which captures those same premonitions and taps into precisely the humor, the terror, and the imagery that felt so irresistible to poets, musicians, and artists alike. See figure 12.3 for just one example.

For all these men, masks, bells, funerals, and gnomes of unidentifiable lineage combine to create a sinister fantasy. Baudelaire calls them "primitive, irresistible," born of the "natural nastiness of man";[48] for Mallarmé, in "Le tombeau d'Edgar Poe," they are "dark flights of blasphemy" and they signify "triumphant death."[49] Perhaps the seductive surface beauty of Debussy's dreamlike music serves to camouflage a more sinister nightmarish quality ensconced within. At the very least, we know that Poe's vision obsessed Debussy, its gloom invading his work and mind. Though no piano pieces bear direct attributions, the piano music surely broods frequently on subjects of irony, death, and fate; we'd probably do well to hear more darkness in its mystery and fewer pastels.

Figure 12.3. ***To Edgar Poe (The Eye, Like a Strange Balloon, Mounts toward Infinity),*** **1882, Odilon Redon, Los Angeles County Museum of Art, Los Angeles.**

• *13* •

The Sounds of Nationalism

Unfortunately, Edgar Allan Poe's imp of the perverse did not remain within the covers of storybooks. The European powers elected to set it free from 1914 to 1918, and it wreaked a self-destructive havoc far exceeding any novelist's imagination. Debussy did not live to see the end of World War I, but he died only eight months short of Armistice Day, and he had the misfortune to witness a large part of the war's massive destruction firsthand. The Belle Époque had come to a crashing end.

A social history of Debussy's life and works cannot steer clear of World War I's catastrophic events; they left no French citizen untouched. But it is above all the history of French nationalism, a cause well prized by Debussy, which interests us here. Particularly with the advent of World War I, Debussy's letters are filled with scathing political commentary about both the enemies of France and the failings of the French themselves to live up to their country's heritage—and not only his letters but his music as well. Early on, he'd written homages to the great French composers Jean-Philippe Rameau and François Couperin, and made clear his essential debt to that French heritage; later on his patriotism becomes more aggressive. The French national anthem, "La Marseillaise," appears in a prelude, the Belgian national anthem appears in a lullaby, and a German Lutheran hymn is pitted against "La Marseillaise" in the two-piano masterpiece *En blanc et noir*. After 1914, he begins to sign himself "musicien français"; and that identity becomes supreme.

A bit of background is in order here, for Debussy was born in 1862, only eight years before the Franco-Prussian War, and it was a war in which France suffered a bitter defeat. This was just the last of a series of conflicts that had torn the country apart in the previous century, beginning, of course, with the French Revolution in 1789 and followed by the smaller revolutions of 1830 and 1848. Throughout the century, the struggle between monarchy and republicanism persisted, the 1789 revolution having opened the door not only to radical ideology but also to instability and dissension. Monarchies, empires, and republics followed each other in rapid succession, with struggles over voting rights, labor unions, censorship, and the role of the Catholic Church apparent in each iteration.

While the wars of 1789, 1830, and 1848 were internal, the war of 1870 confronted an external enemy on home territory. Emperor Louis-Napoleon had foolishly declared war on Prussia in July 1870 and was quickly defeated. German troops captured Paris, and France was eventually forced into an ignominious peace treaty involving massive indemnities and the loss of Alsace-Lorraine. Unwilling to stand by passively, sympathetic soldiers and citizens took over Paris in March 1871, declaring a socialist government with an extremely progressive agenda in the capital city under the so-called Paris Commune. This short-lived but extraordinary experiment placed France temporarily under two governments, until, after two months, the Commune was defeated during "la semaine sanglante" (the bloody week), at a loss of thousands of lives.

Though Debussy, who was only eight years old when the war broke out, would presumably have been little involved, he couldn't help knowing about the Commune early on, for his father, Manuel-Achille Debussy, fought for it, and his mother, as a result, moved the family to Cannes to escape Paris. Though he spoke of it rarely, there can be no question that the French defeat at the hands of the Prussians, as well as the internal conflicts that climaxed in the calamitous defeat of the Paris Commune, set the stage for the vehement nationalism and deep insecurity that beset both Debussy and the country as a whole in the lead-up to World War I.

If the Paris Commune and its aftermath had polarized the French, the Dreyfus Affair was no less significant and divisive, but again we know little of Debussy's inclinations. In 1894, a Jewish army officer, Alfred Dreyfus, was accused of handing over military secrets to the Germans. Despite his protestations of innocence, he was convicted in a secret trial and exiled to Devil's Island, off South America. A couple of years later, evidence came to light that definitively placed the blame for the leak elsewhere, but the whistle-blower, a conservative army officer, Lieutenant-Colonel Georges Picquart, was banished; the guilty man, exonerated; and the evidence, suppressed. Rampant anti-Semitism and a predilection for buttressing authority at any cost easily vanquished facts. In 1898, the famous novelist Émile Zola published an angry letter, "J'accuse," demanding that the case be reopened, as indeed it was in 1899. But again, Dreyfus was convicted and Zola took refuge in England to escape his own resultant trial. It was no small matter, in a country proud of its freedoms, for the nation's leading novelist to be forced into exile! Despite his conviction, Dreyfus received a pardon and was allowed to live as a free man in France, but it was not until 1906 that he was reinstated in the army and all the charges against him, which had, of course, been entirely fabricated, were removed.

Again, the conflict called citizens' loyalty to the state into question. One could be viewed as a traitor on either side of the question, but feelings ran high across the nation, with friendships ending, accusations hurled, and jobs lost. On one side stood the nation's army; on the other stood its system of justice. And overlooking it all stood the large and ugly specter of anti-Semitism. It was a conflict whose repercussions and implications have lasted till the present day, and it dominated French news for more than a decade. Even today, no French citizen is ignorant of the shameful affair, and it continues to raise doubts about religious equality in the French nation.

Despite the fact that Debussy never declared his position on Dreyfus, and generally held politics in little esteem, he cannot possibly have been impervious to the battles ranging around him. His friends were on both sides of the Dreyfus case, with Pierre Louÿs, Debussy's close friend and the author of *Chansons de Bilitis*, strongly opposed to Dreyfus, and René Peter, Debussy's longtime acquaintance and early biographer, defending him. Debussy himself caustically minimized the scandal, weighing in only indirectly through disdain for Edvard Grieg and his Dreyfus-inspired boycott of France. Even though Dreyfus may have meant little to Debussy, the bitterness resulting from both the war and the internal conflict seeped more and more into the musical landscape. Music was becoming increasingly politicized, and when it came to French nationalism, Debussy weighed in. He had a stake here, both musical and practical, for the sheer existence of artistic institutions in France was, and always had been, tied to the largesse of government.

Whereas in the United States art and politics are largely separate entities, with the government providing little funding for the arts and arts education, in France, to the contrary, the arts are seen as a central part of French statehood. The Paris Opera was founded way back in 1669; the Paris Conservatoire, in 1795; and both were fully funded by the state. The tradition grows out of aristocratic traditions: Kings were patrons, their interests gave birth to cultural institutions, and after the revolution those traditions were carried on by the government, despite the shift from monarchy to democracy. To this day, the French government plays a large role in the arts, with a national theater and national opera dominating the arts scene, and every arrondissement, or district, in Paris sporting a highly subsidized Conservatoire for children.

Thus, when in the early twentieth century nationalist French identity became a burning issue for the government, the role of music and the other arts was paramount in building that identity. The French traditions in classical music were seen as crucial evidence of French supremacy—a sharp contrast to the United States, where it would be considered laughable to cite leading American composers such as Mrs. H. H. A. Beach or Edward MacDowell as proof of American prowess on the world political stage. In 1906, Debussy, ever eager to secure France's preeminence, announced in a letter to Louis Laloy, "I'm delighted about your enthusiasm for Rameau. He deserves it for all the qualities in his music which ought to have protected us against Gluck's deceitful grandiloquence [and] Wagner's bombastic metaphysics."[1] And in 1911, in the midst of travels, he dismissed Vienna as "an old city covered in make-up, overstuffed with the music of Brahms and Puccini, the officers with chests like women and the women with chests like officers."[2] From early on, he worried already that "French music is still in the position of a pretty widow who, having no one by her side strong enough to direct her, falls, to her cost, into alien arms."[3]

To complicate matters, however, Debussy's own music was not universally perceived as sufficiently pure to pass all litmus tests, and it posed a new cause for controversy in the never-ending debate on what was worthy of the French patrimony. Beginning already in 1905, criticisms of the composer were posed in grandiloquent terms, with Émile Vuillermoz announcing that "Debussy is the most problematic of all our contemporaries" and comparing controversy over his works to the Dreyfus Affair. "Achille Debussy and Alfred Dreyfus have the two same initials . . . [and] it won't take more than that to create confusion [between them] in the minds of our descendants," he declares with an astonishing lack of historical perspective.[4] The conflict was revisited in earnest in 1910 with the publication of a book entitled *Le cas Debussy* (The Debussy Case), and there was endless pontification in the press on whether Debussy was sufficiently glorious to pass muster in this increasingly chauvinist world. His "curious" style was derided, with one critic commenting, "There are notes and sounds, but there is no music. . . . Take out rhythm, melody, and emotion, and you will just about have it."[5] The famous writer and filmmaker Jean Cocteau, one of the most xenophobic of all, announced that France must "free itself . . . from the vapors of Debussy and Mallarmé";[6] the two had apparently hopelessly erred by incorporating foreign influences into their artistic output. In Cocteau's warped view, Debussy would have been a superior composer had he never encountered the likes of Bach, Mozart, or Wagner. Fortunately, he had, and to his credit, he refused to join the most xenophobic of his colleagues in a National League for the Defense of French Music that recommended outlawing the public performance of all recent German and Austrian music.

Despite that honorable stance and the controversy surrounding his own work, Debussy had no doubt that he was unmistakably French through and through and might himself have preferred to remain untainted by Germanic influences. By the time World War I arrived, he was unapologetically censorious and anti-German, announcing incisively that "30 million Boches [a derogatory term used to describe Germans] can't destroy French thought" and that "beauty" was being "destroy[ed]" by the "meticulous brutality that is unmistakably 'Made in Germany.'"[7] And finally pontificating at more length:

> In these last years, when I smelled "austro-boches" miasma in art, I wished for more authority to shout my worries, warn of the dangers we so credulously approached. Did no one suspect these people of plotting the destruction of our art as they had prepared the destruction of our countries? And this ancient national hate that will end only with the last German! But will there ever be a "last German?" For I am convinced that German soldiers beget German soldiers.[8]

The music, of course, bears witness at a far earlier date to Debussy's determination to support his patrimony and move away from that detested "affection of German profundity" aimed at "a collection of utter idiots who understand nothing unless [they] are first compelled to believe that the moon is made of green cheese."[9] In a conversation with Debussy in 1891, Erik Satie avowed his desire to create "a music of our own—if possible without any Sauerkraut,"[10] and Debussy surely tried to fulfill their mutual wish, doing so already in *Suite Bergamasque* (1890, published 1905) and *Pour le piano* (1896–1901), both modeled on suites by the French clavecinistes, and in the sarabande, "Hommage à Rameau," which forms the centerpiece of *Images, Book 1* (1905). A bit later came various parodies, most pointedly that of Wagner in "Golliwogg's Cake-Walk" from *Children's Corner Suite* (1906–1908), with its hilarious adaptation of Wagner's Tristan chord in the midst of a panegyric for a rag doll.

Later, signs of heartfelt patriotism multiply, and their presence becomes more significant as World War I approaches. Significantly, "La Marseillaise" is incorporated into *Feux d'artifice* with strains of the national anthem floating unexpectedly into the last tones of this last prelude, written in 1913 (see figure 13.1).

In that same year, *La boîte à joujoux* is born, Debussy's children's ballet portraying a doll torn by war, maligned by a wicked fiancé, Polichinelle, on the one hand, and grieving over the injuries to the soldier she loves on the other. Finally, during the war itself, we hear the *Berceuse héroïque*, written in 1914 for inclusion in the Belgian relief project *King Albert's Book*. It is, as Debussy says, an "homage to so much patient suffering."[11] Even the name is instructive; most lullabies are gentle rather than heroic, but Debussy here has mobilized a musical army: The brief dirge-like composition quotes directly from the Belgian national anthem and is filled with march rhythms and bugle calls. The piece was written only the year before "Noël des enfants qui n'ont

Figure 13.1. ***Feux d'artifice*, mm. 91–94, in *Preludes, Book 2*, by Claude Debussy (Paris: Durand, 1913). Digital image from Hathi Trust Digital Library.**

plus de maison," Debussy's last song, for which he himself wrote the desolate text. That piece is another small-scale effort but touchingly personal; in it, he despairs of the plight of children in wartime, bereft of toys, schools, homes, and parents. And yet at the same time he calls fiercely to vanquish the enemy and "avenge the children of France."

Debussy was no pacifist, and he took every opportunity, short of actually fighting, to let his enmity be known. In September 1914, he wrote, "I'm doing a little piano-playing again, notably on a Bechstein; my only excuse is that it's not paid for! It can go under the heading of 'War Contributions.'"[12] Nice to see the piano put to a bona fide political purpose! Despite his determination that "French art needs to take revenge quite as seriously as the French army does,"[13] he was incapacitated by the onset of the war and his progressing illness, and he wrote that he felt like "nothing more than a wretched atom hurled around by this terrible cataclysm."[14] His depression is hardly surprising; a very partial list of the losses suffered by the artistic community alone makes one weep with incredulity. By the end of the war the Spanish composer Enrique Granados had died on a torpedoed ship; the Austrian pianist Paul Wittgenstein had lost his right arm; the poet Guillaume Apollinaire had suffered a head wound of which he would later die; and the English poet Wilfred Owen, so famous for his antiwar poetry, had died in battle.[15] And that is only the very beginning.

More remarkable than the depression itself is the fact that Debussy emerged from it at all. And he did so with a vengeance. In the summer and fall of 1915, he worked feverishly, composing the *12 Etudes*, which stand as one of the mainstays of the solo piano literature, at extraordinary speed. These succinct masterpieces moved Debussy into a style more modern than anything he had previously written. They are, by turns, acerbic, violent, comic, and achingly beautiful, often within a page. They leave behind entirely the descriptive allusions of his earlier works, nor are there references to the war. But they represent a distillation of his style that shoulders the burden of both the historic moment and the need to make a final statement. He noted that he had "rediscovered my ability to think in music, which I'd lost for a year. . . . I've been writing like a madman, or like a man condemned to die the next morning."[16] Other composers too have written their finest works when faced with death—Franz Schubert, in particular, comes to mind—and, at this moment, Debussy was faced not only with his own mortality but also with the incalculable losses of the war.

In the same year, a bit earlier, he edited the compositions of Chopin in order to save them from sole residence in a German edition, now unavailable in France because of the war effort. And in a more significant war gesture, he composed *En blanc et noir* for two pianos (1915), another monumental work to emerge from Debussy's last years. Each movement is preceded by a quotation; part 1 features a quote from Charles Gounod's opera *Romeo and Juliet*: "He who stays in his place and does not dance, quietly admits to a disgrace," probably a reference to his own lack of active military service, which embarrassed him greatly. Part 2 is dedicated to a friend who had died in the war, and it is headed by a wrathful quote from François Villon's "Ballad, against the Enemies of France," which closes with the words, "For unworthy is he of any virtue / who wishes ill for the Kingdom of France." And part 3 quotes Charles d'Orléans: "Winter, you are nothing but a villain," presumably a reference to the atrocious first winter of the war.[17] More importantly, the music itself makes its patriotic point irrespective of text, for the second movement incorporates "Ein feste Burg ist unser Gott," the German Lutheran chorale, interlaced pointedly against a "modest carillon sound[ing] a foreshadowing of the Marseillaise" near the end of the movement.[18] As Debussy says, "You see what happens to the Lutheran hymn for having imprudently wandered into a French caprice."[19] The war casts its shadow over the entire structure, and quotation is used as a weapon that opens onto a whole world of outside reference. Those references could not be more different from the popular songs quoted so optimistically in *Les collines d'Anacapri* or the children's songs quoted so innocently in *Gardens in the Rain*, but they are just as potent a tool for accessing human memory. Debussy made clear his yearning to participate in the war effort in a letter of 1916: "Let us hope they [the French soldiers] will realize that there are many paths to victory! Music, fertile and admirable, is one of them."[20] He was consumed by both patriotism and despair.

"*Les soirs illuminés par l'ardeur du charbon*" (Evenings Illuminated by the Ardor of the Coal), written in February or March 1917, and Debussy's last composition for the piano, can't compete with the *Etudes* or *En blanc et noir* in profundity; it lasts a mere twenty-four measures. As a personal commentary on the miseries of war, however, it cannot be surpassed. Paris was exceptionally and unremittingly cold the winter of 1917, as if some unmerciful god had chosen to heap yet more indignities on that ravaged city.[21] Debussy writes, "The cold, the race for coal, that whole life of domestic and other miseries makes me more distraught every day."[22] And so it was that he chose a particularly appropriate line of Baudelaire's poetry, one he had set thirty years earlier as a song, to register his sadness and muted protest.[23] The beautiful manuscript that resulted was a present to his coal merchant, who'd kept the household warm in spite of every obstacle.[24]

This last essay and the brief *Elégie* for piano that came a year before it are diffident, outside the fray. But where does all the earlier, more blustery oratory, in both music and speech, leave us? Do the nationalist politics bear strongly on the music in the end? The answer isn't straightforward, but in the final analysis, all the rhetoric is far too simplistic for the music. Debussy's greatest music, so filled with subtlety, could make allusions to battle, it could posit ostensible winners and losers, but in aiming for "that graceful profundity, that emotion without epilepsy" that Debussy ascribed to "our old harpsichordists who produced real music in abundance," he left the simplicity of black and white in the dust and eschewed the epilepsy of the battlefield.[25] His devotion to France imbues his music with fervor, his feeling for the French language determines his setting of text, and his admiration for Couperin and Rameau encourages delicacy reminiscent of the French baroque. But this is only part of the picture; if it were all, he would have composed only graceful national anthems and strict French dances. In his early years, Debussy spoke no party line. In his later years he may have spoken one, but his music remained singular. Try as he might, the music he wrote could not be contained by definitions of French tradition or the narrow simplifications of political propaganda. The "Cas Debussy" offers an interesting study in political and musical entendre, but in the end, the music leaves politics trailing in the dust. That Debussy died during the German bombardment of Paris provides a cruel footnote to the universality of his musical language.

Afterword: In Conversation with Baudelaire and Proust

He knew that the very memory of the piano falsified still further the perspective in which he saw the elements of music, that the field open to the musician is not a miserable stave of seven notes, but an immeasurable keyboard (still almost entirely unknown) on which, here and there only, separated by the thick darkness of its unexplored tracts, some few among the millions of keys of tenderness, of passion, of courage, of serenity, which compose it, each one differing from all the rest as one universe differs from another, have been discovered by a few great artists who do us the service, when they awaken in us the emotion corresponding to the theme they have discovered, of showing us what richness, what variety lies hidden, unknown to us, in that vast, unfathomed and forbidding night of our soul which we take to be an impenetrable void.

—Proust, *Swann's Way, Remembrance of Things Past*[1]

How can one possibly write a fitting conclusion to a piano romp that encompasses satyrs and the Belgian national anthem, Edgar Allan Poe and Tarentisme, and then the quote above? I don't believe there is any other composer quite so omnivorous in his tastes or given to such disparate inspirations as Debussy. It all goes back to that quote from Oscar Wilde, Debussy's irrepressible contemporary: "Man is least himself when he talks in his own person. Give him a mask and he will tell you the truth."[2]

And so Debussy sought masks—voraciously. And then he told you the truth. But his truth was not hard-edged, despite the times in which he lived. The fin de siècle was a time of radical change across the Western world, and artists were grappling with the end of tonality in music, the end of realism in art, stream of consciousness in literature, and a world in deadly political turmoil. And yet, Debussy's music eschewed the primitivism of Igor Stravinsky, the contortions of Arnold Schoenberg, and the shrillness of Charles Ives, all of whom were his contemporaries. It studiously avoids all the tonal and formal stability sought so assiduously by earlier composers, but its insistent instability rocks gently rather than jolts. His music resides in a world of irrational dreams, it is immersed in sensuality, it initiates in physical gesture—and yet it rarely shocks; it seduces rather than affronts. It chooses beauty over contortion, harmony over radical dispute. His Parisian sensibility, no doubt

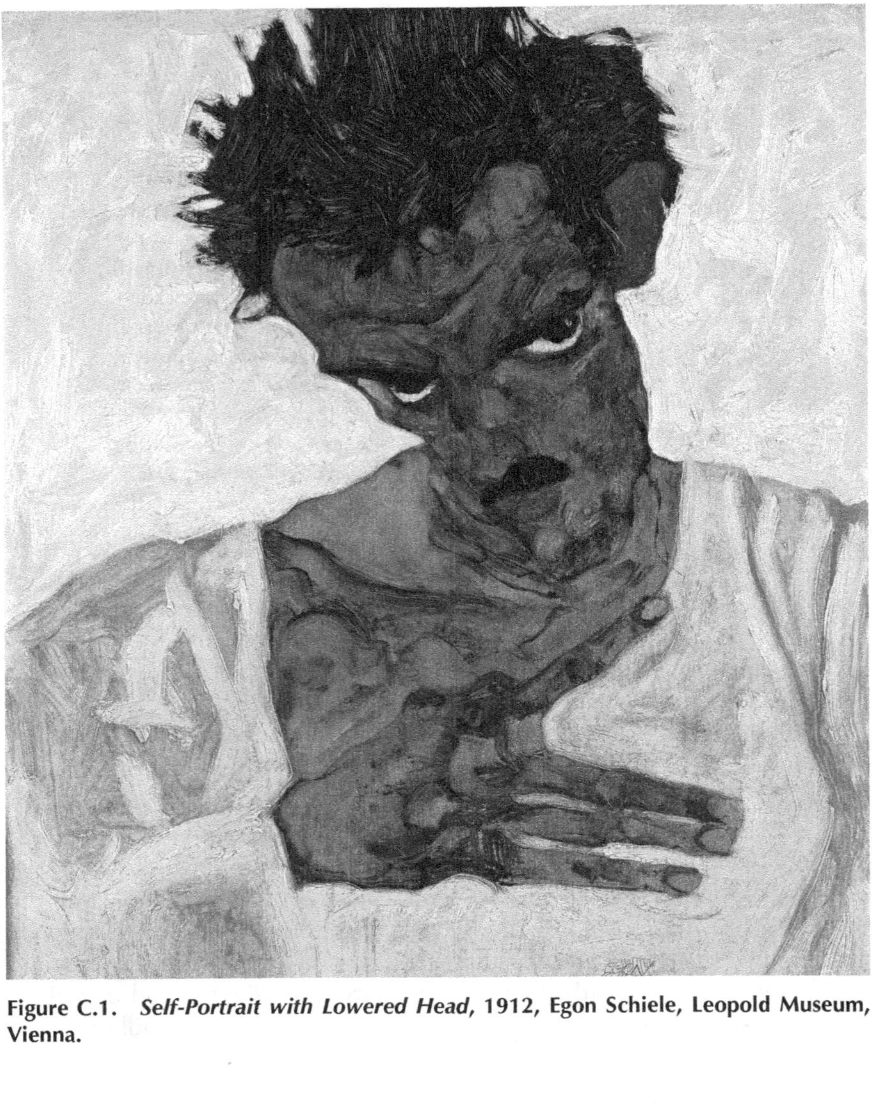

Figure C.1. ***Self-Portrait with Lowered Head,*** **1912, Egon Schiele, Leopold Museum, Vienna.**

impacted by the overall emphasis on aesthetics in the Belle Époque, provides a striking contrast to the expressionist torment taking Schoenberg's Vienna by storm in precisely the same time frame. There, painters such as Egon Schiele (1890–1918) and Oskar Kokoschka (1886–1980) display their pain, as is evident in figure C.1. For them the normal disingenuous face presented to the world is a mask, and brutal honesty requires its removal; their figures appear unnatural and tormented in their UN-masked state.

Likewise, the composer Arnold Schoenberg (1874–1951) whose painting is as revelatory as his music, shows us a truth that is literally glaring and deeply uncomfortable and surely as far removed from "belle" as one can possibly be (see figure C.2).

Parisians saw masks differently; they were less eager to avidly display their neuroses. Masks were highly entertaining; among other things, they made lewd desires acceptable—witness the numerous risqué masked women, such as the one in figure C.3, featured weekly in the *Le Courrier français*. And even when more serious, they could be liberating. The paintings of Picasso in which he himself donned the apparel of Harlequin among the *saltimbanques*, remind us that a mask is just another possible face we wear, none more clearly a true self than any other, and outright despair no more authentic than a clown's makeup. Even when not specifically about masks, much of the visual art Debussy loved dealt in various forms of camouflage and ambiguity: Impressionism reveled in mist, Turner in fog, and Redon in hybrids. Obscurity was sought rather than frowned upon. Realism had fallen upon hard times.

In fact, as we have seen, the concern with masks and disguises in the nineteenth century permeated all the arts. Debussy's interest in alternative identities parallels the obsession with dreams that dominates symbolist poetry and art, and it converges clearly with the birth of psychoanalysis as well. Dreams are, of course, another way for people to carry on a double life, a reinterpretation of their humdrum quotidian persona. No one was more concerned with getting to the root of that alternate persona than Charles Baudelaire, the so-called father of the symbolist poets, and a father figure to the entire late nineteenth-century French imagination. His experiments with hashish and opium, mentioned in chapter 3, were just such an attempt to penetrate beyond everyday selfhood: "The eyes pierce the infinite. The ear hears sounds that are almost imperceptible. . . . Then the hallucinations begin. . . . Through some odd misunderstanding . . . you feel yourself vanishing into thin air, and you attribute to your pipe (in which you fancy yourself crouched like packed tobacco) the strange ability to *smoke you*."[3]

Picasso becomes a Harlequin; Baudelaire packs himself into a pipe. Both change reality via their art—or claim that reality is not a singular entity. Another French writer comes to mind here, one whom Debussy knew casu-

Figure C.2. *Gaze*, 1910, Arnold Schoenberg. Courtesy of the Arnold Schoenberg Center, Vienna. © 2016 Belmont Music Publisher, Los Angeles / Artists Rights Society (ARS), New York / Bildrecht, Vienna.

Figure C.3. "Bals masques," *Le Courrier français*, January 27, 1901. Bibliothèque nationale de France.

ally and who greatly admired Debussy's music: Marcel Proust. They met but never became close. Still, not only did Debussy live at the same time and in the same city as Proust, but also his second book of *Preludes* came out in the same year as Proust's magnum opus, *In Search of Lost Time*, and the two men had fundamental affinities. Both men wished to slow the passage of time, to live within memories and dreams, and to understand how music conveys human experience where words cannot. Debussy may have provided Proust with evidence that music trumps words, but Proust in turn provides us with words with which to better understand Debussy. As Alex Ross, the music critic of *The New Yorker*, says, "Proust captures the imaginary dimension of musical experience—the ability of the mind to conjure inner worlds under the influence of charged sound."[4]

That formulation sounds remarkably similar to Baudelaire's charged experience with drugs and probably to Picasso's charged experience with paints. We've now moved entirely to a world within the mind, and it's one where Debussy felt very much at home. Hallucinations, supernatural beings, and masks have much in common with one another. "After all," says Debussy, "an artist is by definition a man accustomed to dreams and living among apparitions."[5]

Proust is engaged in a constant effort to write of those apparitions, to capture the fleeting nature of experience and the mystery of memory and sensation. The apparitions that interest him are those generated from within, but of course in the end, what apparitions aren't? Proust speaks of "all the various lives we lead concurrently,"[6] and he elaborates, as an example, in recalling his childhood:

> The zone of melancholy which I . . . entered was as distinct from the zone in which I had been bounding with joy a moment before as, in certain skies, a band of pink is separated, as though by a line invisibly ruled, from a band of green or black. . . . I was now so remote from the longings by which I had just been absorbed . . . that their fulfillment would have afforded me no pleasure.[7]

He had become a different person in a flash; he wore a different color, a different inner mask. Like Debussy, Proust was immersed in the mysteries of childhood, not least of all its plasticity.

Because memory and sensation do not lead forward on a single, directional path, Proust's writing, like Debussy's music, requires patience—it does not catapult the reader through suspense-driven plots and white-water adventures; rather, it circles round and round the crevices of the human mind, exploring not events but the perception of those events. It does not function through the buildup and release of tension but rather by a search that incites wonder rather than excitement. The effort is to stop time, to search for the "lost time" of the past, rather than to propel us eagerly forward. As time moves backward into memory, the author conjectures that "reality takes shape in the memory alone."[8] Clearly this reality, which is for Proust "the deepest layer of my mental soil,"[9] wears a different mask than the mundane experience that may have initially generated it. This is Poe's imp and Freud's unconscious and Baudelaire's flower of evil probed deeply. Personalities subdivide and splinter in this subterranean layer of the mind.

In excavating that layer, both Proust and Debussy explore the senses and the most ephemeral aspects of human existence, often the characteristics of daily life for which France is best known.[10] Proust tried to take "impressions of form or scent or colour—[and then] to perceive what lay hidden beneath them."[11] The concern is always with what is hidden from view. It's hard not to recall here the attraction Debussy felt to Eastern religions; mystery was found in the invisible. In gazing at church steeples, Proust worried that he "was not penetrating to the core of my impression, that something more lay behind that mobility, that luminosity, something which they seemed at once to contain and to conceal."[12] And in coming to know people too, he sought out the "luminous section cut out of the unknown" that their personality contained.[13] Those luminous sections are strikingly redolent of Debussy's music, a music so concerned with transparency and light.

Proust knew that that luminosity could not be contained or fully expressed in language. What emerges then as an unbidden thread in the life of Swann, Proust's hero, is something wordless: a tiny theme of music that he hears at a party and then encounters again, unexpectedly and with boundless pleasure. He never learns its provenance, but he knows it belongs "to an order of supernatural beings whom we have never seen, but whom, in spite of that, we recognise and acclaim with rapture when some explorer of the unseen contrives to coax one forth."[14] It is "veiled in shadow, unknown, impenetrable to the human mind."[15] And Proust tries to understand: "Was it a bird, was it the soul, as yet not fully formed, of the little phrase, was it a fairy—that being invisibly lamenting[?]"[16]

He is at pains to describe in words a theme that interests him precisely because it cannot possibly be reduced to words.[17] An insoluble, but fascinating, conundrum.

Ironically, Debussy himself complains bitterly that in his profession "all . . . has to be expressed with doh, ray, me, fah, soh, lah, te, doh!!!"[18] But, in truth, perhaps no other syllables are nearly so capable. As E. T. A. Hoffmann had remarked many years earlier, "Such is the power of music's spell that it . . . can only burst the fetters of any other art."[19] The disappearing fetters include every other sort of syllable.

Those paltry syllables vanquished, Debussy said apropos the *Prelude à l'après-midi d'un faune* that he hoped to give us "the dream left over at the bottom of the faun's flute,"[20] and others have said that appreciating beauty consists of "unselfing."[21] Perhaps that's what Proust's fairy and Debussy's dream help us to do: shed our noisy, busy selves. When all the layers are gone, we're left with the quiet that's at bottom. Proust, Baudelaire, Debussy, and the many artists we've viewed "unselfed" variously through masks, drugs, and mysterious "little phrases." The art that emerged as a result was, as Proust put it, "like an iridescent bubble that floats for a while unbroken . . . supernatural, delicious [and] frail."[22] How striking that Paris, this city of massive steam trains, teeming crowds, and garish music halls, nourished some of the most delicate art the world has ever known. Was it that very cacophony that nurtured such interior silence? Perhaps. It cannot be coincidental that so much activity produced artists of an uncommon stillness. Debussy was deeply a son of Paris, and though his genius was hardly bound by his nation's proclivities, the city where he lived—its art, literature, politics, and nightspots—provided an irreplaceable stimulus to his remarkable imagination. All that bustling activity must have been critical, but ultimately it was just one more mask. Debussy lifted it to find the "dream left over," and we are the lucky beneficiaries of his tireless search.

Notes

A BIOGRAPHICAL NOTE

1. Quoted in Roger Nichols, *The Life of Debussy* (Cambridge: Cambridge University Press, 1998), 34.
2. Ibid., 41.
3. Elliott Antokoletz and Marianne Wheeldon, eds., *Rethinking Debussy* (New York: Oxford University Press, 2011), 150. https://books.google.com/.
4. Claude Debussy, *Debussy on Music*, collected and introduced by François Lesure, trans. and ed. Richard Langham Smith (New York: Knopf, 1977), 16–17 (quoted from *La Revue Blanche*, April 1901).
5. Quoted in Edward Lockspeiser, *Debussy: His Life and Mind*, vol. 1 (New York: Macmillan, 1962), 28.
6. Claude Debussy, "Open-Air Music," in *Monsieur Croche the Dilettante Hater* (as published by Noel Douglas in 1927, trans. B. N. Langdon Davies, Viking Press, 1928), in *Three Classics in the Aesthetic of Music* (New York: Dover, 1962), 33.

INTRODUCTION

1. See Vanessa R. Schwartz, "Public Visits to the Morgue," in *Spectacular Realities: Early Mass Culture in* Fin-de-Siècle *Paris*, 45–88 (Berkeley: University of California Press, 1998), for a detailed discussion of this particular Parisian obsession.
2. Claude Debussy, letter to André Caplet, November 25, 1909, in *Debussy Letters*, selected and edited by François Lesure and Roger Nichols, trans. Roger Nichols (Cambridge, MA: Harvard University Press, 1987), 216.
3. Quoted in Roger Nichols, *The Life of Debussy* (Cambridge: Cambridge University Press, 1998), 58.

4. Walter Benjamin, *The Writer of Modern Life: Essays on Charles Baudelaire*, ed. Michael W. Jennings, trans. Howard Eiland, Edmund Jephcott, Rodney Livingston, and Harry Zohn (Cambridge, MA: Belknap Press of Harvard University Press, 2006), 30.

5. Charles Baudelaire, *The Painter of Modern Life and Other Essays*, trans. and ed. Jonathan Mayne (London: Phaidon, 1995), 9.

6. Benjamin, *The Writer of Modern Life*, 31, quoted from Sigfried Giedion, *Bauen in Frankreich* (Architecture in France) (Leipzig, 1928), 3.

7. Julien Tiersot, "Promenades musicales à l'Exposition," *Le Mènestrel* 55 (1889): 165–66, at 165, quoted from Annegret Fauser, *Musical Encounters at the 1889 Paris World's Fair* (Rochester, NY: University of Rochester Press, 2005), 146–47.

8. Debussy, letter to Jacques Durand, July 8, 1910, in *Debussy Letters*, 220.

9. Michel Leiris, *Documents*, 1930, quoted on wall posting at the Centre Pompidou, Paris, summer 2014.

10. G. Willow Wilson, *The Butterfly Mosque: A Young American Woman's Journey to Love and Islam* (2010), quoted in Pauls Toutonghi, "App for the Ancients," *New York Times Book Review*, August 12, 2012.

11. Claude Debussy, "The Orientation of Music," in *Debussy on Music*, collected and introduced by François Lesure, trans. and ed. Richard Langham Smith (New York: Knopf, 1977), 85; Debussy, letter to André Poniatowski, February 1893, in *Debussy Letters*, 41.

12. *Masques, Mascarades, Mascarons*, Louvre exhibition, organized by Françoise Viatte, Dominique Cordellier, and Violaine Jeammet, Paris, June 19–September 22, 2014.

CHAPTER 1

1. Claude Debussy, *43 Songs for Voice and Piano*, ed. Sergius Kagen, trans. Edith Braun, Waldo Lyman, and Kathleen Maunsbach (New York: International Music Company, 1951), VII. See chapter 3 for further discussion of the poem.

2. Ibid.

3. See *Musik zu einer Faschingspantomime für zwei Violinen, Viola und Baß*, KV 446 (416d), composed in 1783. In addition to this explicit foray into the Commedia, many of Mozart's operatic characters, such as Leporello and Figaro, both of them loyal and mistreated servants, bear close resemblance to Commedia personages.

4. A. G. Lehmann, "Pierrot and Fin de Siècle," in *Romantic Mythologies*, ed. Ian Fletcher (New York: Barnes & Noble, 1967), 117. From Théophile Gautier, *Pierrot posthume*, scene 14.

5. Claude Debussy, *La boîte à joujoux* (Paris: A. Durand & Fils, 1913), International Music Score Library Project, http://imslp.org/. (Unless otherwise noted, French translations throughout are by the author.) "Les boîtes à joujoux sont en effet des sortes de villes dans lesquelles les jouets vivent comme des personnes / Ou bien les villes ne sont peut-être que des boites à joujoux dans lesquelles les personnes vivent comme des jouets." For more about *La boîte*, see chapter 7, "Child's Play and Make Believe."

6. Claude Debussy, letter to Jacques Durand, September 27, 1913, in *Debussy Letters*, selected and edited by François Lesure and Roger Nichols, trans. Roger Nichols (Cambridge, MA: Harvard University Press, 1987), 278.

7. Paul Verlaine, "Pierrot" (1868), in *Paul Verlaine: Seventy-Three Poems*, trans. A. S. Kline, Poetry in Translation, 2010, accessed March 12, 2017, http://www.poetryintranslation.com/.

8. "Au clair de la lune," Mama Lisa's World, accessed March 12, 2017, http://www.mamalisa.com/.

9. Drug-induced states had similar advantages and were perhaps more easily achieved. Many of the great poets experimented with opium, and Baudelaire wrote an entire book, *Les paradis artificiels*, detailing his experiences with drugs. Charles Baudelaire, *Artificial Paradises*, trans. Stacy Diamond (New York: Carol Publishing Group, 1996).

10. "Gemeinheit," no. 16, from Albert Giraud, *Pierrot Lunaire*.

11. George Tis, "Chanson de la lune rouge," Palestro, February 5, 1903, from *Le Courrier français*, no. 9, March 1, 1903.

12. Edgar Allan Poe, "The Fall of the House of Usher," Edgar Allan Poe Society of Baltimore, accessed December 2016, http://www.eapoe.org/.

13. *Le Courrier français* 18, no. 25, June 23, 1901, 7. "Il est pâle comme un mort, de blanc vêtu tel un fantôme: il ferait peur s'il ne faisait rire, cet être muet qui sort les nuits au clair de la lune."

14. Charles Baudelaire, *The Painter of Modern Life*, trans. and ed. Jonathan Mayne (London: Phaidon, 1995), 9.

15. Quoted in Robert F. Storey, *Pierrots on the Stage of Desire* (Princeton, NJ: Princeton University Press, 1985), 128–29, from Théodore de Banville, "Preface" to [Richard Lesclide], *Mémoires et pantomines des frères Hanlon Lees* (Paris: Reverchon et Vollet, [1880]), 12–13.

16. Jules Laforgue, "Pierrots," in *Poems*, trans. and introduced by Peter Dale (London: Anvil Press, 2001), 205. I: "Une face imberbe au cold-cream, / Un air d'hydrocéphale asperge."

17. Jules Laforgue, "Locutions de Pierrot," in *Poems*, 230. XVI: "Je ne suis qu'un viveur lunaire."

18. Jules Laforgue, "Complaint of the Outraged Husband," in *Poems*, 151–55.

19. Debussy, letter to Pierre Louÿs, February 9, 1897, in *Debussy Letters*, 88–89.

20. *Le Courrier français* 18, no. 25, June 23, 1901, 7. "Pierrot est poète et comme ce n'est pas un métier—du moins avouable—il est tout ce que notre imagination veut qu'il devienne. Il joue tous les rôles et comme il a tous les vices il nous incarne, tous, sans peine successivement, admirablement."

CHAPTER 2

1. Charles Baudelaire, "The Old Showman," in *Paris Spleen*, trans. by Keith Waldrop (Middletown, CT: Wesleyan University Press, 2009), 28.

2. "Clown" ("Manquer son coup, c'est se casser et net le cou"), *Le Courrier français* 18, no. 22, June 2, 1901, 6.

3. Théodore de Banville, "Le saut de tremplin" (The Jump from the Springboard), Les grands classiques, accessed December 2016, http://poesie.webnet.fr/.

4. René Peter, *Debussy*, 2nd ed. (Paris: Gallimard, 1944), 90–91, quoted in Paul Roberts, *Images: The Piano Music of Claude Debussy* (Portland, OR: Amadeus, 1996), 225. Roberts has an excellent discussion of the role of the circus in both art and music in fin-de-siècle Paris.

5. Claude Debussy, *Monsieur Croche the Dilettante Hater* (as published by Noel Douglas in 1927, trans. B. N. Langdon Davies, Viking Press, 1928), in *Three Classics in the Aesthetic of Music* (New York: Dover, 1962), 22.

6. Quoted in Rae Beth Gordon, *Dances with Darwin, 1875–1910* (Aldershot, UK: Ashgate, 2009), 160, from Cocteau, "Portraits-Souvenirs," 63.

7. Quoted in Martin Green and John Swan, *The Triumph of Pierrot* (New York: Macmillan, 1986), 169.

8. Quoted in Joris-Karl Huysmans, *Against Nature*, trans. Robert Baldick (London: Penguin, 2003), 97.

9. Robert F. Storey, *Pierrots on the Stage of Desire* (Princeton, NJ: Princeton University Press, 1985), 133, quoted from Théodore de Banville, *Ouevres complètes*, III, 225.

10. *Picasso et le cirque* (Martigny, Switzerland: Fondation Pierre Gianadda, 2006), 315, exhibition catalog, Museu Picasso, November 15, 2006–February 18, 2007; Fondation Pierre Gianadda, March 9–June 10, 2007.

11. Edmond de Goncourt, *The Zemganno Brothers*, 1879, trans. Leonard Clark and Iris Allam (London: Alvin Redman, 1957), 61, 117.

12. Ibid., 118–19.

13. Roberts, *Images*, 225, quoted from Jean Cocteau, *Paris Album, 1900–1914*, trans. Margaret Crossland (London: W. H. Allen, 1956), 55.

14. Charles Baudelaire, *The Painter of Modern Life*, trans. and ed. Jonathan Mayne (London: Phaidon, 1995), 8 (italics in original).

15. Alfred Frankenstein, "A Curious Literary Progress from Man to Mechanism," *San Francisco Chronicle*, March 11, 1945.

16. Roberts, among others, points this out. *Images*, 224. I would certainly have missed it otherwise.

CHAPTER 3

1. Claude Debussy, "Du Gout," *Revue S.I.M.*, February 1913, quoted in Brian Hart, "The Symphony in Debussy's World," in *Debussy and His World*, ed. Jane Fulcher (Princeton, NJ: Princeton University Press, 2001), 181.

2. Debussy appears to have been generally cynical about politics. His letters offer few opinions. In January 1912, he wrote to Jacques Durand, "Here it's raining—your sympathy accepted—but we have a new government, which is bound to bring back

the sun and put an end to the taxi strike." In *Debussy Letters*, selected and edited by François Lesure and Roger Nichols, trans. Roger Nichols (Cambridge, MA: Harvard University Press, 1987), 255. So much for government. See chapter 13 for more details.

3. For a more extensive discussion, see Jann Pasler, *Composing the Citizen: Music as Public Utility in Third Republic France* (Berkeley: University of California Press, 2009), esp. 501–7.

4. Partial quote. Entire poem found in "Parisian Cake Walks," by Davinia Caddy, *19th Century Music* 30, no. 3 (Spring 2007): 316. "Un nouvel arrivant, un nègre / Semblant plutôt gris, / Dans les salons pénètre, allègre / Et saute, cassant tout, plus ouistiti qu'humain."

5. Paul Roberts, *Images: The Piano Music of Claude Debussy* (Portland, OR: Amadeus, 1996), 91.

6. Charles Baudelaire, *Journaux intimes, fusées* (1855–1862), Wikisource, last updated February 7, 2017, accessed December 2016, https://fr.wikisource.org/, 79 ("Le dessin arabesque est le plus spiritualiste des dessins").

7. Claude Debussy, *Debussy on Music*, collected and introduced by François Lesure, trans. and ed. Richard Langham Smith (New York: Knopf, 1977), 27 (from *La Revue Blanche*, May 1, 1901).

8. See Roy Howat, "The Exotic via Russia and Spain," in *The Art of French Piano Music*, 126–44 (New Haven, CT: Yale University Press, 2009), for a lengthier discussion of the Russian influences.

9. From Paul Verlaine's "Clair de Lune," "Votre âme est un paysage choisi / Que vont charmant masques et bergamasques, / jouant du luth et dansant, et quasi / Tristes sous leurs déguisements fantasques" (Your soul is a chosen landscape / Where one finds charming masked ones and dancers from Bergamo / playing the lute and dancing, and almost / Sad under their fantastic disguises). Translation from Debussy, *43 Songs*, ed. Sergius Kagen.

10. Jonathan Bellman, ed., *The Exotic in Western Music* (Boston: Northeastern University Press, 1997), 174.

11. Claude Debussy, letter to Jacques Durand, August 17, 1916, quoted in Robert Orledge, *Debussy and the Theatre* (Cambridge: Harvard University Press, 1982), 128.

12. Roger Nichols, *The Life of Debussy* (Cambridge: Cambridge University Press, 1998), 141. Debussy's comments were made in an interview with an Italian journalist.

13. Orledge, *Debussy and the Theatre*, 156–57.

14. Debussy, letter to Jacques Durand, September 5, 1912, in *Debussy Letters*, 262.

15. Claude Debussy, letter to Robert Godet, June 9, 1913, in *Debussy Letters*, 272.

16. A projected collaboration between Fuller and Debussy on *La boîte à joujoux* (see chapter 1, "Pierrot Conquers Paris," and chapter 7, "Child's Play and Make Believe") never materialized, because, Robert Orledge hypothesizes, Debussy had, by that time, lost patience with Fuller and her unruly troupe of youthful veiled dancers. The only clue to his reluctance is a letter from Debussy's wife to Fuller pleading her husband's illness as a reason to be excused from their further work together. See Orledge, *Debussy and the Theatre*, 157–58, for further discussion.

17. Charles Baudelaire, *The Painter of Modern Life*, trans. and ed. Jonathan Mayne (London: Phaidon, 1995), 30.
18. Ralph Locke, in *Musical Exoticism: Images and Reflections* (New York: Cambridge University Press, 2009), 228, also makes the suggestion that those veils might belong to women in Algiers, thus folding together exotic women and exotic scales.
19. Quoted in Edward Lockspeiser, *Debussy: His Life and Mind*, vol. 2 (New York: Macmillan, 1962), 176.
20. Loie Fuller, *Fifteen Years of a Dancer's Life* (London: Herbert Jenkins, 1913), 66, http://archive.org/.
21. Quoted in Ann Cooper Albright, *Traces of Light: Absence and Presence in the Work of Loie Fuller* (Middletown, CT: Wesleyan University Press, 2007), 185 (interview published in *Éclair*, May 5, 1914).
22. F. de Ménil, *Histoire de la danse à travers les âges* (Paris, 1904), 340–41, quoted in Carolyn Sinsky, "Loie Fuller," Modernism Lab at Yale University, accessed December 2006, http://modernism.research.yale.edu/.
23. E. T. A. Hoffmann, "Kreisler's Musico-Poetic Club," in *Musical Writings: Kreisleriana; The Poet and the Composer; Music Criticism*, ed. David Charlton, trans. Martyn Clarke (Cambridge: Cambridge University Press, 1989), 134.
24. Hoffmann, "Extremely Random Thoughts," in Charlton, *Musical Writings*, 105.
25. Charles Baudelaire, *Artificial Paradises*, trans. Stacy Diamond (New York: Carol Publishing, 1996), 49–50, 58.
26. Debussy, letter to Jacques Durand, September 12, 1912, in *Debussy Letters*, 263.
27. See Joris-Karl Huysmans, *Against Nature*, trans. Robert Baldick (London: Penguin, 2003), 41.

CHAPTER 4

1. See Rae Beth Gordon, "Natural Rhythm: Africans and Black Americans in Paris," in *Dances with Darwin, 1875–1910*, 145–97 (Aldershot, UK: Ashgate, 2009), for a detailed history and discussion of Parisian attitudes toward the shows. I owe an enormous debt to this resource for the information in this chapter.
2. Interestingly enough, a similar format is just now becoming popular for classical concerts. Witness (*Le*) *Poisson Rouge* in New York City, a multimedia art cabaret that aims to take the starch out of classical music by serving wine and jazz alongside thorny new music.
3. See Rae Beth Gordon, "Natural Rhythm: La Parisienne Dances with Darwin, 1875–1910," *Modernism/Modernity* 10, no. 4 (November 2003): 617–56, doi:10.1353/mod.2003.0077. The article draws fascinating connections between Darwinism, primitivism, and the popularity of black performers on the Paris night scene.
4. Gordon, *Dances with Darwin*, 173, quoted from Marshall Stearns and Jean Stearns, *Jazz Dance: The Story of American Vernacular Dance* (New York: Da Capo Press, 1994), 22.

5. Claude Debussy, *Debussy on Music*, collected and introduced by François Lesure, trans. and ed. Richard Langham Smith (New York: Knopf, 1977), 180–81.

6. See Sue Peabody, *"There Are No Slaves in France": The Political Culture of Race and Slavery in the Ancien Régime* (Oxford: Oxford University Press, 1966), Google Books, http://books.google.com/.

7. Quoted in Robert Orledge, *Debussy and the Theatre* (Cambridge: Cambridge University Press, 1982), 135.

8. Claude Debussy, letter to Jacques Durand, September 12, 1912, in *Debussy Letters*, selected and edited by François Lesure and Roger Nichols, trans. Roger Nichols (Cambridge, MA: Harvard University Press, 1987), 263.

9. Arthur Gold and Robert Fizdale, *Misia: The Life of Misia Sert* (New York: Morrow Quill Paperbacks, 1981), 198.

10. Joris-Karl Huysmans, *Against Nature*, trans. Robert Baldick (London: Penguin, 2003), 13.

11. "Nègre," *Le Courrier français* 18, no. 28, July 14, 1901, 7. "Li petit nègre, li bon nègre aimer beaucoup son frère blanc, les larges dents claires et blanches nous font songer qu'il est encore par-ci par-là des anthropophages, le frère blanc a la chair tendre."

12. *Le Courrier français* 19, no. 45, November 9, 1902.

13. Houston Stewart Chamberlain, quoted in Wikipedia, from Geoffrey Field, *The Evangelist of Race: The Germanic Vision of Houston Stewart Chamberlain* (New York: Columbia University Press, 1981), 252.

14. Quoted by Matthew F. Jordan in *Le Jazz* (Urbana: University of Illinois Press, 2010), 37, from Louis Laloy, "To Dance or Not to Dance," *Revue S.I.M.*, June 1914, 57.

15. Lussan-Borel, *Traité de danse, avec musique, contenant toutes les danses de salon, avec une théorie nouvelle de valse et boston du cotillon et du cake-walk*, RO9933, ed. Ernest Flammarion (Paris: BNF Arts du spectacle, n.d.), 236. "Nous avouerons que, longtemps, nous avons balancé la question de savoir si cette danse nègre, importée de l'Amérique du Nord, figurerait ou non dans notre Traité de Danses de Salon. / Même après nous être enfin décidé à l'admettre, nous avons de la peine à considérer ces evolutions excentriques comme une danse digne d'être admise dans nos salons, même après avoir été réglée et émondée de ses exagérations, comme nous l'avons fait ici. / Toutefois, la vogue a ses exigences, la mode a décidé, et le Cake-Walk faisant fureur dans les salons les plus élégants de Paris, contrairement aux saines notions de la grâce et du bon goût, nous nous sommes donc résigné à regler une théorie du Cake-Walk, que nous publions dans ce volume et que paraîtra aussi dans les éditions ultérieures de cet ouvrage, à moins que la vogue de cette danse, peu recommendable à notre sens, ne vienne, d'ici-là, à s'évanouir comme elle est venue."

16. Huguette Fancy, quoted from "La pavane au cake-walk," *BNP Arts du Spectacle*, Ro 9768, 1903. "De mauvaises langues assurent que l'on reverra cette hiver l'odieux cake-walk dans les salons. Je n'en veux rien croire. Il faut laisser aux joyeux nègres le succés de cette danse amusante."

17. Louis Figuier, *Les races humaines*, 556–57 (Paris: Hachette, 1880), quoted in Gordon, *Dances with Darwin*, 104.

18. Jordan, *Le Jazz*, 152, quoting from Julien Tiersot, "Notes d'ethnographie musicale: African Continent," *Le Ménéstrel*, March 22, 1903, 89.

19. From an interview with France 2's "Envoyé Special," quoted in Priscilla Lalisse-Jespersen, "Is France Becoming Racist?" *Washington Post*, November 7, 2013, https://www.washingtonpost.com/blogs/she-the-people/wp/2013/11/07/is-france-becoming-racist?.

20. Hippolyte Taine, *Philosophie de l'art* (Paris: Fayard, 1985, originally published in 1866–1869), 415–16, quoted in Gordon, *Dances with Darwin*, 109.

21. Grant Allen, *Physiological Aesthetics* (London: King and Co., 1877), 194, quoted in Gordon, *Dances with Darwin*, 109.

22. Florence K. Upton and Bertha Upton, *The Adventures of Two Dutch Dolls and a "Golliwogg,"* Project Gutenberg, accessed March 14, 2017, http://www.gutenberg.org/ebooks/16770.

23. Debussy, "Prince L.-F. of Bavaria," in *Debussy on Music*, 97.

24. Ibid.

25. Jordan, *Le Jazz*, 28. Quoted from the Litrée Dictionary (Paris: Hachette, n.d.).

26. Here, as in the next paragraph, and indeed throughout this chapter, I am extraordinarily indebted to the information and insights in Rae Beth Gordon's *Dances with Darwin*.

27. Joan Acocella, "The Love That Kills," *The New Yorker*, September 2, 2013, 66.

28. See both Joris-Karl Huysmans's *Against Nature* and Oscar Wilde's *The Picture of Dorian Gray* (1891).

29. Debussy, letter to Igor Stravinsky, November 5, 1912, in *Debussy Letters*, 265.

30. Debussy, letter to Jacques Durand, September 12, 1912, in *Debussy Letters*, 263 (refers to *Jeux*).

CHAPTER 5

1. Edward W. Said, *Orientalism* (New York: Random House, 1978), 1.

2. Louis Menand, "Silence, Exile, Punning: James Joyce's Chance Encounters," *The New Yorker*, July 2, 2012, 75.

3. David Rosenthal, *The Near East in French Painting* (Rochester, NY: University of Rochester Press, 1982), 44, quoted from *Delacroix Journal*, 1832.

4. T. J. Clark, *The Painting of Modern Life* (New York: Knopf, 1985), 35, quoted from Edmond and Jules de Goncourt, *Journal des Goncourts: Mémoires de la vie littéraire* (1891): 1:345–46.

5. Ibid., quoted from Edmond About, *L'homme à l'oreille cassée* (1862), 196.

6. Charles Baudelaire, "Le cynge" (The Swan), in *The Flowers of Evil*, trans. James McGowan (Oxford: Oxford University Press, 1993), 173.

7. Quoted in Edward Lockspeiser, *Debussy: His Life and Mind*, vol. 1 (New York: Macmillan, 1962), 207, from a conversation between Debussy and his former professor, Ernest Guiraud at the Conservatoire, as reported by Maurice Emmanuel.

8. André Gide, *The Immoralist* (1902), trans. David Watson (Harmondsworth, UK: Penguin, 2000), 35.

9. *Le Monde illustré* 46, no. 2381, November 15, 1902, 464.

10. "Les Fouilles de Dougga Depuis 1899 (Tunisia)," *Le Monde illustré* 46, no. 2383, November 29, 1902, 506.

11. André Gide, *If It Die*, trans. Dorothy Bussy from first edition of *Si le grain ne muert*, 1920 (Harmondsworth, UK: Penguin, 1982), 246.

12. Quoted in Andrew Hussey, *The French Intifada: The Long War between France and Its Arabs* (London: Macmillan, 2014), 291. Google Books, https://books.google.com/.

13. Mary McAuliffe, *Twilight of the Belle Époque* (Lanham, MD: Rowman & Littlefield, 2014), 221.

14. Claude Debussy, letter to Pierre Louÿs, [July 20, 1894], in Lockspeiser, *Debussy*, 1:174. "Biskra doit nous apprendre de combinaisons nouvelles."

15. Claude Debussy, letter to Pierre Louÿs, [July 20, 1894], in *Debussy Letters*, selected and edited by François Lesure and Roger Nichols, trans. Roger Nichols (Cambridge, MA: Harvard University Press, 1987), 70.

16. Roger Benjamin, *Renoir and Algeria* (New Haven, CT: Yale University Press [along with Sterling and Francine Clark Art Institute, Williamstown, MA], 2003), 9, quoted from *Correspondance d'Henri Regnault*, ed. Arthur Duparc (Paris: Charpentier, 1872), and quoted in Lynne Thornton's biographical essay on Regnault in *Orientalism: Delacroix to Klee*, ed. Roger Benjamin, exhibition catalog (Sydney: Art Gallery of New South Wales, 1997), 249.

17. Henri Matisse, letter to Henri Manguin, undated, in *Orientalist Aesthetics: Art, Colonialism, and French North Africa, 1880–1930*, by Roger Benjamin (Berkeley: University of California Press, 2003), 165, quoted from Judi Freeman, "Fauves Abroad," 208, 213n39.

18. Ibid., 12–13, quoted from Théophile Gautier, *Salon de 1849*, in *Voyage en Algérie*, 183.

19. Lockspeiser, *Debussy*, 1:230. When asked on a questionnaire in February 1889 where he would like to live, Debussy replied, "N'importe où hors du monde" (Anywhere outside the world).

20. Gide, *If It Die*, 246.

21. Gide, *Immoralist*, 42.

22. Ibid., 119.

23. Ibid., 36.

24. Ibid., 98.

25. Julie McQuinn, "Exploring the Erotic in Debussy's Music," in *The Cambridge Companion to Debussy*, ed. Simon Trezise (Cambridge: Cambridge University Press, 2003), 127, quoted from unpublished letter, July 31, 1894, in Jean-Paul Goujon, *Pierre Louÿs*, 131. See this article for a fascinating, in-depth discussion of Debussy and the erotic.

26. Gide, *Immoralist*, 36.

27. Claude Debussy, letter to Pierre Louÿs, January 15, 1901, in McQuinn, "Exploring the Erotic," 128, quoted from Debussy and Louÿs, *Correspondance*, 156.

28. Ralph Locke, *Musical Exoticism: Images and Reflections* (New York: Cambridge University Press, 2009), 219.

29. Debussy, letter to Pierre Louÿs, February 9, 1897, in *Debussy Letters*, 88–89.

30. Debussy, letter to Jacques Durand, July 8, 1910, in *Debussy Letters*, 220.

31. Ibid.

32. Quoted in *Matisse and the Alhambra, 1910–2010* (Granada, Spain: Patronato de la Alhambra y Generalife, 2010), 74, exhibition catalog, Alhambra, Palace of Charles V, October 15, 2010–February 28, 2011.

33. Questionnaire of February 1889, in Lockspeiser, *Debussy*, 1:230. Debussy listed his other favorite prose-writer as Edgar Allan Poe.

34. Gustave Flaubert, *Salammbô*, 1862 (Lexington, KY: Made in the USA, 2013), 106.

35. See, for example, the earlier quote from Gide, who delighted in "the sounds of a child playing the flute." The painter, Philippe Zilcken, quoted in Hilary Spurling, *The Unknown Matisse: A Life of Henri Matisse, the Early Years, 1869–1908* (New York: Knopf, 2005), reports also on "an Arab boy who plays a few sweet repetitive notes on his reed flute." Spurling notes that "flute-playing was a specialty with the men of the desert tribe" (359).

36. Claude Debussy, *Debussy on Music*, collected and introduced by François Lesure, trans. and ed. Richard Langham Smith (New York: Knopf, 1977), 48, quoted from "Conversation with M. Croche," *La Revue Blanche*, July 1, 1901.

CHAPTER 6

1. Quoted in Julie McQuinn, "Exploring the Erotic in Debussy's Music," in *The Cambridge Companion to Debussy*, ed. Simon Trezise (Cambridge: Cambridge University Press, 2003), 120.

2. Paul Verlaine, "C'est l'extase," set by Debussy as the first of the *Ariettes oubliées*.

3. André Gide, *If It Die*, trans. Dorothy Bussy from first edition of *Si le grain ne muert*, 1920 (Harmondsworth, UK: Penguin, 1982), 240.

4. Jann Pasler, *Composing the Citizen: Music as Public Utility in Third Republic France* (Berkeley: University of California Press, 2009), 565.

5. For a lengthy and fascinating discussion of the musical implications of the 1889 World Exposition, see Annegret Fauser, *Musical Encounters at the 1889 Paris World's Fair* (Rochester, NY: University of Rochester Press, 2005).

6. Claude Debussy, letter to Prince [André] Poniatowski, February 1893, in Edward Lockspeiser, *Debussy: His Life and Mind*, vol. 1 (New York: Macmillan, 1962), 119.

7. Gabriel Pierné, quoted in Roger Nichols, *The Life of Debussy* (Cambridge: Cambridge University Press, 1998), 34.

8. Edmund White, *The Flâneur* (New York: Bloomsbury, 2001), 126–27.

9. Nichols, *Life of Debussy*, 33.

10. Joris-Karl Huysmans, *Against Nature*, trans. Robert Baldick (London: Penguin, 2003), 11.

11. Ibid., 198.

12. See the discussion in *Art Nouveau in Fin-de-Siècle France* by Devora L. Silverman of the "redefinition of the interior from an accretion of material objects to an arena of self-discovery" (Berkeley: University of California Press, 1989), 77.

13. Debussy, letter to André Caplet, July 24, 1909, in Lockspeiser, *Debussy*, 2:191.

14. Charles Baudelaire, "Le flacon" (The flask), in *The Flowers of Evil*, trans. James McGowan (Oxford: Oxford University Press, 1993), 97.

15. Huysmans, *Against Nature*, 52.

16. Claude Debussy, letter to André Caplet, February 25, 1910, in *Debussy Letters*, selected and edited by François Lesure and Roger Nichols, trans. Roger Nichols (Cambridge, MA: Harvard University Press, 1987), 217.

17. Debussy, letter to Jacques Durand, March 1908, in *Debussy Letters*, 188.

18. Alfred Cortot, *French Piano Music*, trans. Hilda Andrews (New York: Da Capo, 1977), 16.

19. Quoted in Paul Roberts, *Images: The Piano Music of Claude Debussy* (Portland, OR: Amadeus, 1996), 169.

20. Roy Howat refers to the "organum-like opening phrase." Howat, *The Art of French Piano Music* (New Haven, CT: Yale University Press, 2009), 13.

21. Ibid., 116. Howat refers here to a work by Elisabeth de Jong-Keesing, *Inayat Khan: A Biography*, 121, which describes *Et la Lune* as written in "authentic Indian style."

22. Ibid., 116, quoted from *Claude Debussy: Monsieur Croche et autres écrits*, 229.

23. In fact, Debussy is far from the only composer to turn to the piano as a gamelan substitute. Following the 1889 World Exposition, for instance, Louis Benedictus transcribed what he had heard at the various booths in a composition tellingly entitled *Les musiques bizarres à l'exposition*. Decades later—and with more lasting success—Francis Poulenc incorporated the sounds of a gamelan into his *Concerto for Two Pianos* (1932), having himself encountered the gamelan at a 1931 exposition.

24. Quoted in Nichols, *Life of Debussy*, 133.

25. Milan Kundera, *The Book of Laughter and Forgetting* (New York: Penguin, 1986), 178.

26. Susan McClary, *Feminine Endings* (Minneapolis: University of Minnesota Press, 1991), 127–30. For example, "[T]he point of recapitulation in the first movement of Beethoven's Ninth Symphony unleashes one of the most horrifyingly violent episodes in the history of music" (128).

27. Barbara L. Kelly, "Debussy and the Making of a *musicien français*," in *French Music, Culture, and National Identity, 1870–1939*, ed. Barbara L. Kelly (Rochester, NY: University of Rochester Press, 2008), 64, quoted from Raphaël Cor, "M. Claude Debussy et le snobisme contemporain." The view of Debussy as "feminine" has, in fact, not entirely vanished. In 2014, the eminent Finnish musician Jorma Panula announced that though women conductors were, in general, doomed to failure, they might possibly have some small success with Debussy, since the feminine nature of his music was biologically matched to their abilities. Michael Cooper, "Using a Baton to Crack a Glass Ceiling," *New York Times*, September 1, 2016, 7, and Norman

Lebrecht, "Women Conductors? It's Not Getting Any Better, Only Worse," Slipped Disc, March 31, 2014, http://slippedisc.com/.

28. Quoted in Chad Twedt, "Sergei Prokofiev, 1891–1953: Mystery and Contradiction," Chad Twedt, accessed December 2016, http://www.twedt.com/prokofiev.html.

29. See m. 1, 27, 43, 83, 112, 136–57.

30. See m. 75, 90, 128, 140, 151.

31. See Roberts, *Images*, 275–77, for a discussion of numerous interesting associations with this prelude.

32. Pierre Loti, *L'Inde sans les Anglais* (Paris: Calmann-Lévy, 1963), 318.

33. E. M. Forster, *A Passage to India* (New York: Modern Library, 1939), 70.

34. René Puaux, *Le beau voyage* (Paris: Librairie Payot et Cie, 1917), 20–21, 144–45. "[L]es Arabes, gros maquignons enturbanés de soie et d'or, se pavanant en calèches superbement attelées, les serviteurs venus des présides portugais, les charmeurs de serpents se pressant devant les hôtels pour montrer un cobra abruti et une mangouste édentée . . . tous ces êtres bronzés dont les pieds nus font peu de bruit . . . sont parfaitement pittoresques. On voudrait en arrêter certains, comme ces deux femmes rencontrées tout à l'heure et qui portaient sur leur tête un gros bambou sur lequel quatre paons encapuchonnés se trouvaient perchés. . . . / Savent-ils tous qu'ils sont les sujets de Sa Majesté George V.? Ont-ils une notion précise de l'honneur extraordinaire que leur fait le roi d'Angleterre de quitter pour eux son royaume? . . . / Et quand le 'tiwana' a, dans un suprême effort de sa voix déchirée, vociféré l'ultime 'Dieu sauve le roi!' les trompettes d'argent résonnent, l'orchestre gigantesque attaque l'air national, et l'amphithéâtre entier, se levant, fait songer à une brise de printemps, agitant les millions de pétales du plus extraordinaire jardin du monde. / Ce fut la minute historique, celle dont le symbolism frappe l'imagination et demeurera profondément sensible aux coeurs anglais."

35. I would surely have missed this had not a colleague and also Paul Roberts pointed it out. *Images*, 276–77.

36. The prelude is available in a version completed by Robert Orledge that makes abundant use of materials found in *La boîte à joujoux* (SOUNDkiosk Piano Edition, SKPE 14, 2010). According to the introduction to that edition, when Debussy discarded the prelude, he used many of its materials in *La boîte*. See chapter 8, "Fairies and Fairy Tales," for more on *Toomai of the Elephants*.

37. André Gide, *The Immoralist*, trans. David Watson (Harmondsworth, UK: Penguin, 2000), 117.

38. Forster, *Passage to India*, 289.

39. Charles Baudelaire, "A Girl from Malabar," in *Flowers of Evil*, 319–21.

CHAPTER 7

1. Claude Debussy, letter to Jacques Durand, August 30, 1913, in *Debussy Letters*, selected and edited by François Lesure and Roger Nichols, trans. Roger Nichols (Cambridge, MA: Harvard University Press, 1987), 277.

2. Debussy, letter to Chouchou, December 2, 1910, in *Debussy Letters*, 229. Editors Lesure and Nichols explain in a footnote that this was "a series of six postcards showing Austrian soldiers in a variety of humorous situations. The fourth card is missing." The signature translates into "the papa of Chouchou." The heading, Lesure and Nichols explain, is "a reference to Debussy's alter ego, Monsieur Croche, and to *Mémoires d'outre-tombe*, the autobiography of the writer and statesman François-René, Vicomte de Chateaubriand, 1768–1848."

3. Maggie Teyte, the famous soprano, played Mélisande in Debussy's opera *Pelléas et Mélisande* and Debussy accompanied her in several song performances. His opinions on her singing ranged from the virulently dismissive: "Miss M. Teyte continues to exhibit about as much emotion as a prison door" to the politely upbeat: she "possess[es] a charming voice and a very accurate idea of Mélisande's character," the latter judgment rendered a few short weeks earlier than the preceding declaration, in the same year, 1908. Edward Lockspeiser, *Debussy: His Life and Mind*, vol. 2 (New York: Macmillan, 1962), 192.

4. Debussy, letter to Chouchou, December 11, 1913, in *Debussy Letters*, 283.

5. Lockspeiser, *Debussy*, 1:9, drawn from a biography by Jean Lepine published in 1930 and based on the testimony of Debussy's sister, Adèle.

6. Jean-Jacques Rousseau, *Emile, or On Education* (1762), Hanover College History Department, accessed December 2016, https://history.hanover.edu/courses/excerpts/165rouss-em.html.

7. Jules Michelet, *Le peuple*, part 2, chap. 4, quoted in Isabelle Jan and Wyley L. Powell, "Children's Literature and Bourgeois Society in France since 1860," *Yale French Studies*, no. 43 (1969): 62.

8. Ibid., 67.

9. Claude Debussy, *Debussy on Music*, collected and introduced by François Lesure, trans. and ed. Richard Langham Smith (New York: Knopf, 1977), 243 (December 1910 statement to an Austrian journalist).

10. Debussy, letter to Robert Godet, December 18, 1911, in *Debussy Letters*, 250.

11. Quoted in Sima Godfrey, "'Ce père nourricier': Revisiting Baudelaire's Family Romance," *Nineteenth-Century French Studies* 38, nos. 1 and 2 (Fall–Winter 2009–2010): 39, quoted from "Un mangeur d'opium," OC 1:497. "C'est dans les notes relatives à l'enfance que nous trouverons le germe des étranges rêveries de l'homme adulte, et, disons mieux, de son génie . . . tel petit chagrin, telle petite jouissance de l'enfant, démesurément grossis par une exquise sensibilité deviennent plus tard dans l'homme adulte, même à son insu, le principe d'une oeuvre d'art." Psychologists have suggested that Debussy's own deprived childhood may have contributed to a certain childishness in his adult behavior, particularly as regards money. He was constantly running out of it and, despite decent earnings, spending far more than he could afford. This put him always in a dependent relationship with others, asking for money and needing support, just as a child does with his parents. The theory is impossible to prove or disprove, but if accepted, it helps to explain the adult Debussy's inclination to frequently re-create that childish world in music as well as in empty bank accounts.

12. Léon Vallas, *Claude Debussy: His Life and Works*, trans. Máire O'Brien and Grace O'Brien (London: Oxford University Press, 1933), 226. Also found at "Claude

Debussy," Wikipedia, last updated November 20, 2016, accessed December 2016, http://en.wikiquote.org/.

13. Debussy, letter to Robert Godet, January 18, 1913, in *Debussy Letters*, 269.

14. Debussy, letter to Paul-Jean Toulet, January 18, 1913, in *Debussy Letters*, 268.

15. Debussy, letter to André Caplet, n.d., quoted in Lockspeiser, *Debussy*, 2:198.

16. Debussy, letter to Jacques Durand, September 27, 1913, in *Debussy Letters*, 278.

17. Debussy, letter to Robert Godet, December 18, 1911, in *Debussy Letters*, 249.

18. Debussy, letter to Vittorio Gui, February 25, 1912, in *Debussy Letters*, 256.

19. "Images by André Hellé for Claude Debussy's *La boîte à joujoux*," IMSLP [International Music Score Library Project], accessed March 15, 2017, http://imslp.org/, 12. The entire score to *La boîte à joujoux* (Paris: Durand & Fils, 1913) is available online at IMSLP.org.

20. I learned about this French equivalent from Mark DeVoto's excellent book *Debussy and the Veil of Tonality: Essays on His Music* (Hillsdale, NY: Pendragon, 2004), 31. In the same passage DeVoto takes issue with the view that Debussy is intentionally quoting from *Tristan* in *Golliwogg*. I've been trained to hear the quote, but we have no definitive answer either way. Even if not conscious here, we do know that Debussy intentionally quoted the chord elsewhere, so his eagerness to subtly confront Wagner is apparent.

21. From the score of *La boîte à joujoux*:

"Vieux chant hindou qui sert, de nos jours encore, à apprivoiser les elephants," p. 7
"*Les fées sont d'exquises danseuses*," p. 8
Le petit nègre, p. 9
Fanfare, p. 11, reminding us of *Golliwogg*, mm. 24–25 and *Minstrels*, mm. 28–31
Serenade of the Doll, p. 13
"Soldier's Chorus" of Gounod's *Faust*, p. 28
"Dance of the Adolescents" from Stravinsky's *Rite of Spring*, p. 29
Feux d'artifice (Fireworks), p. 29
Il pleut, bergère (It Is Raining, Shepherdess), p. 39
The Little Shepherd from *Children's Corner*, p. 38
Bruyères, p. 41
Mendelssohn's "Wedding March" from *A Midsummer Night's Dream*, p. 44
"Polichinelle" or "Pop Goes the Weasel," p. 45
"Fan-fan la tulipe," p. 46

22. Debussy, letter to Jacques Durand, January 16, 1914, in *Debussy Letters*, 285.

CHAPTER 8

1. Bruno Bettelheim, *The Uses of Enchantment: The Meaning and Importance of Fairy Tales*," 1975, Goodreads, accessed December 2016, http://www.goodreads.

com/quotes/212155-the-child-intuitively-comprehends-that-although-these-stories-are-unreal/.

2. The French translation is mentioned in *Oeuvres Complètes de Debussy*, Série 1, Volume 5. Préludes, Livre I, Livre II. Edition de Roy Howat avec la collaboration de Claude Helffer. (Paris: Durand-Costellat, 1985), Foreword, XVI. All quotes used here come from Hans Christian Andersen, *Andersen's Fairy Tales*, trans. Mrs. E. V. Lucas and Mrs. H. B. Paull (New York: Grosset & Dunlap, n.d.).

3. Also mentioned in Debussy, *Préludes*.

4. Claude Debussy, letter to Eugene Vasnier, October 19, 1885, in *Debussy Letters*, selected and edited by François Lesure and Roger Nichols, trans. Roger Nichols (Cambridge, MA: Harvard University Press, 1987), 13.

5. J. M. Barrie, with drawings by Arthur Rackham, *Peter Pan in Kensington Gardens* (Mattituck, NY: Amereon House, n.d.). Also available online at Project Gutenberg, http://www.gutenberg.org.

6. See m. 79–83 of the prelude for the Brahms waltz.

7. See m. 58–64, m. 67–72, m. 117–20. The reference is suggested by Siglind Bruhn, *Images and Ideas in Modern French Piano Music* (Stuyvesant, NY: Pendragon, 1997), 151. See also Claude Debussy, *Debussy on Music*, collected and introduced by François Lesure, trans. and ed. Richard Langham Smith (New York: Knopf, 1977), 100–110, where Debussy enthusiastically praises Weber and his opera.

8. Rudyard Kipling, *The Jungle Book* (Garden City, NY: Doubleday, 1932). All quotes from *The Jungle Book* come from this source. Also available online at Project Gutenberg, http://www.gutenberg.org.

9. William Shakespeare, *A Midsummer Night's Dream* (London: Penguin, 1967). All quotes from *A Midsummer Night's Dream* come from this source.

10. See Bruhn, *Images and Ideas*, 146.

11. Claude Debussy, *Monsieur Croche the Dilettante Hater* (as published by Noel Douglas in 1927, trans. B. N. Langdon Davies, Viking Press, 1928), in *Three Classics in the Aesthetic of Music* (New York: Dover, 1962), 91.

CHAPTER 9

1. Friedrich de la Motte Fouqué, *Undine*, trans. Paul Turner, in *German Romantic Stories*, ed. Frank G. Ryder (New York: Continuum, 1988). Also available online at Project Gutenberg, http://www.gutenberg.org/ in a different translation. All quotes used here come from the Turner.

2. Translation from Claude Debussy, *43 Songs*, ed. Sergius Kagen, trans. Edith Braun, Waldo Lyman, and Kathleen Maunsbach (New York: International Music Company, 1951), x. Other songs quoted in this chapter are also in this volume, but I have used my own translations.

3. Richard Specht, *Der Merker*, November 1910, quoted in Edward Lockspeiser, *Debussy: His Life and Mind*, vol. 2 (New York: Macmillan, 1962), 129–30.

4. *Le Courrier français* 17, no. 14, April 8, 1900, 9.

5. Sigmund Freud, "Dora," 1905, in *Standard Edition*, translated under the general editorship of James Strachey, in collaboration with Anna Freud, assisted by Alix Strachey and Alan Tyson (London: Hogarth, 1956–1974), 7:109.

6. Redon and Debussy were in the same circle of Parisian artists, a circle that included Mallarmé, Huysmans, Moreau, Verlaine, and numerous other luminaries. Artists frequently met up at the bookshop run by Edmond Bailly, at Mallarmé's famous Mardi soirées, and at the Chat Noir. Redon even sent Debussy a work of his as a gesture of gratitude for a performance of *La damoiselle élue*.

7. "Odilon Redon: Prince of Dreams," Escape into Life, accessed March 16, 2017, http://www.escapeintolife.com/.

8. Quoted in Rosemary Lloyd, "Debussy, Mallarmé, and 'Les Mardis,'" in *Debussy and His World*, ed. Jane Fulcher (Princeton, NJ: Princeton University Press, 2001), 260, quoted from Debussy, *Lettres*, 12.

9. Though fauns and satyrs had separate mythological roots, those distinctions had little relevance to most composers or poets.

10. Stéphane Mallarmé, "The Afternoon of a Faun," trans. Roger Fry, Angelfire, accessed December 2016, http://www.angelfire.com/art/doit/mallarme.html.

11. *Le Courrier français* 18, no. 40, October 6, 1901, 6–7.

CHAPTER 10

1. Claude Debussy, letter to Jacques Durand, Pourville, July 14, 1915, in *Debussy Letters*, selected and edited by François Lesure and Roger Nichols, trans. Roger Nichols (Cambridge, MA: Harvard University Press, 1987), 297.

2. Debussy, letter to André Messager, September 12, 1903, in *Debussy Letters*, 141.

3. Debussy, letter to Jacques Durand, August 9, 1912, in *Debussy Letters*, 261.

4. This phrase is drawn from the title of a Library of Congress exhibit of Japanese prints (September 27, 2001–January 19, 2002). The full title of the exhibit was *The Floating World of Ukiyo-E: Shadows, Dreams and Substance*.

5. Claude Debussy, *43 Songs*, ed. Sergius Kagen, trans. Edith Braun, Waldo Lyman, and Kathleen Maunsbach (New York: International Music Company, 1951), XI. The line reads, "L'espoir a fui, vaincu, vers le ciel noir."

6. Claude Debussy, *Monsieur Croche the Dilettante Hater* (as published by Noel Douglas in 1927, trans. B. N. Langdon Davies, Viking Press, 1928), in *Three Classics in the Aesthetic of Music* (New York: Dover, 1962), 33.

7. Claude Debussy, *Pelléas et Mélisande*, act 5, scene 1.

8. Ernest Renan, *Souvenirs d'enfance et de jeunesse* (Paris: Bibliothèque de Cluny, Librairie Armand Colin A Paris, 1959), 1.

9. Debussy, letter to Jacques Durand, March 1908, in *Debussy Letters*, 188.

10. Roy Howat, *The Art of French Piano Music* (New Haven, CT: Yale University Press, 2009), 52.

11. Ibid., 53. See pages 51–60 for a detailed discussion of the golden section in *Reflets dans l'eau* and a number of other Debussy piano works including *Hommage à Rameau, Poissons d'or, Mouvement, Cloches à travers les feuilles, L'isle joyeuse*, and *Masques*, which also make use of it.

12. Gabrielle L. Caffee, *The Breton and His World: Requiem for a Culture* (Mobile, AL: Madaloni, 1985), 105–7.

13. Ibid., 107–8.

14. Claude Debussy, letter to Henri Lerolle, August 28, 1895, discussing *Pelléas et Mélisande*, quoted in Edward Lockspeiser, *Debussy: His Life and Mind*, vol. 1 (New York: Macmillan, 1962), 193.

15. Claude Debussy, letter to J. Durand, September 1904, quoted in E. Robert Schmitz, *The Piano Works of Claude Debussy* (New York: Dover, 1966), 94.

16. Paul Roberts tells us that the painting appeared "[o]n the front cover of the United Music Publishers' popular and attractive edition of 'L'isle joyeuse' (a reprint of the original Durand edition)," which would explain the assumed link. See *Images: The Piano Music of Claude Debussy* (Portland, OR: Amadeus, 1996), 87–88, 101–6, for a superb discussion of the relationship between the music and the painting.

17. Debussy, *43 Songs*. Translation is original.

18. *Oeuvres Complètes de Debussy*, Série 1, Volume 5. Préludes, Livre I, Livre II. Edition de Roy Howat avec la collaboration de Claude Helffer. (Paris: Durand-Costellat, 1985), Foreword, XVI.

19. Alex Munthe, *Letters from a Mourning City*, trans. Maude Valérie White (1884; London: John Murray, 1887).

CHAPTER 11

1. Claude Debussy questionnaire, February 15, 1889, in Edward Lockspeiser, *Debussy: His Life and Mind*, vol. 1 (New York: Macmillan, 1962), appendix G, 229.

2. Claude Debussy, letter to Georges Hartmann, July 3, 1899, in *Debussy Letters*, selected and edited by François Lesure and Roger Nichols, trans. Roger Nichols (Cambridge, MA: Harvard University Press, 1987), 105.

3. Charles Baudelaire, "La chevelure," in *The Flowers of Evil*, trans. James McGowan (Oxford: Oxford University Press, 1993), 50.

4. Lockspeiser, *Debussy*, 2:97–98. Lockspeiser reports that Debussy was not enamored of Strauss at this time; Debussy complained that Strauss "grates until blood is drawn."

5. Debussy, letter to Henri Lerolle, August 28, 1894, in *Debussy Letters*, 73.

6. *Pelléas et Mélisande* libretto, act 3, scene 1, in *Collection of Opera-Librettos*, by G. Schirmer (New York: E. Fromont, 1902; A. Durand & Fils, 1907), 24–28, International Music Score Library Project, http://imslp.org/.

7. Claude Debussy, *43 Songs*, ed. Sergius Kagen, trans. Edith Braun, Waldo Lyman, and Kathleen Maunsbach (New York: International Music Company, 1951).

8. Paul Verlaine, "C'est l'extase," set by Debussy in *Ariettes oubliées.*

9. The warning was fastened to the frame of his picture *Lady Lilith.*

10. From Charles-Marie Leconte de Lisle's poem "La fille aux cheveux de lin."

11. From Baudelaire's *Flowers of Evil.*

12. Charles Baudelaire, "Un hémisphère dans une chevelure" (A Hemisphere in Tresses), in *The Parisian Prowler/Le spleen de Paris,* trans. Edward K. Kaplan (1862; Athens: University of Georgia Press, 1989), 35.

13. Claude Debussy, *Debussy on Music,* collected and introduced by François Lesure, trans. and ed. Richard Langham Smith (New York: Knopf, 1977), 85. "Art is the most beautiful deception of all! And although people try to incorporate the everyday events of life in it, we must hope that it will remain a deception lest it become a utilitarian thing, sad as a factory. Ordinary people, as well as the élite, come to music to seek oblivion, is that not also a form of deception? The Mona Lisa's smile probably never existed in real life, yet her charm is eternal. Let us not disillusion anyone by bringing too much reality into the dream."

14. Baudelaire, "Un hémisphère dans une chevelure."

15. Think here about the tale of Rapunzel, published by the Brothers Grimm in 1812 but known in France as *Persinette* since 1698. In this tale, Rapunzel is imprisoned in a tower by a wicked witch; she can only be accessed by way of her hair. A handsome prince learns to climb the ladder of hair, only to be betrayed. Eventually the two escape to safety, and in certain versions of the story, Rapunzel's hair, cut off by the witch, is restored by the touch of the prince.

16. Baudelaire, "La chevelure."

17. Bruno Mantovani, quoted by Zachary Woolfe, "Missing from Podiums: Women," *New York Times,* December 20, 2013. "Sometimes women are discouraged by the very physical aspect: conducting, taking a plane, taking another plane, conducting again." www.nytimes.com/2013/12/22/arts/music/female-conductors-search-for-equality-at-highest-level.html.

CHAPTER 12

1. Edgar Allan Poe, "MS. [Manuscript] Found in a Bottle" (1833), in *Selected Tales* (London: Penguin, 1994), 32.

2. Debussy questionnaire, February 15, 1889, in Edward Lockspeiser, *Debussy: His Life and Mind,* vol. 1 (New York: Macmillan, 1962), appendix G, 230.

3. T. S. Eliot, "From Poe to Valéry," *Hudson Review* 2, no. 3 (Autumn 1949): 335, http://www.jstor.org/stable/3847788, quoted in the *New York Times,* October 3, 2013, C29.

4. Lockspeiser, *Debussy,* 2:140n1.

5. Edgar Allan Poe, "The Philosophy of Composition," *Graham's Magazine* 28, no. 4 (April 1846): 163–67, http://www.eapoe.org/.

6. Eliot, "From Poe to Valéry," 337.

7. Baudelaire on Poe, quoted in ibid., 340.

8. Quoted in Anthony Tommasini, "Debussy's Homage to Poe, with the Blanks Filled In," *New York Times*, November 25, 2009, www.nytimes.com/2009/11/26/arts/music/26debussy.html.

9. Claude Debussy, *Debussy on Music*, collected and introduced by François Lesure, trans. and ed. Richard Langham Smith (New York: Knopf, 1977), 85.

10. Eliot, "From Poe to Valéry," 331.

11. Note, as examples, the pantoum structure (lines 2 and 4 of one verse repeated as lines 1 and 3 of the next) in "Harmonie du soir," which was the inspiration for Debussy's "*Les sons et les parfums tournent dans l'air du soir*," and the sonnet structure of Mallarmé's "Le tombeau d'Edgar Poe," both of which feature strict rhyme schemes (in the original French) as well.

12. See Denis Herlin's introduction to his edition of the piece "*Les soirs illuminés par l'ardeur du charbon*" (Paris: Durand, 2003) for more detail on its origins.

13. Poe, "Philosophy of Composition," para. 14.

14. Charles Baudelaire, "Spleen" (IV), in *The Flowers of Evil*, trans. James McGowan (Oxford: Oxford University Press, 1993), 149.

15. Ibid., "Spleen" II, 147.

16. Ibid., "Le vin de l'assassin," 219–21.

17. Roger Nichols, *The Life of Debussy* (Cambridge: Cambridge University Press, 1998), 58.

18. *Pelléas et Mélisande*, act 3, scene 3, 29, International Music Score Library Project, accessed March 19, 2017, http://imslp.org/.

19. A description, based on his knowledge of Debussy, given by André Suarès in a letter to Romain Rolland of January 14, 1890. Quoted in Lockspeiser, *Debussy*, 1:196, 213.

20. Claude Debussy, letter to André Caplet, August 25, 1909, in *Debussy Letters*, selected and edited by François Lesure and Roger Nichols, trans. Roger Nichols (Cambridge, MA: Harvard University Press, 1987), 212. The ellipses are in the original letter.

21. Lockspeiser, *Debussy*, 1:213.

22. Debussy, letter to Ernest Chausson, September 3, 1893, in *Debussy Letters*, 51.

23. Edgar Allan Poe, "The Imp of the Perverse," in *Selected Tales*, 358.

24. Debussy, letter to Robert Godet, June 7, 1917, in *Debussy Letters*, 327.

25. Debussy, letter to André Caplet, July 24, 1909, quoted in Lockspeiser, *Debussy*, 2:191.

26. Edgar Allan Poe, "The Black Cat," in *Selected Tales*, 313.

27. Quoted in *Modern Critical Interpretations: The Tales of Poe*, ed. Harold Bloom (New York: Chelsea House, 1987), 84.

28. Quoted in ibid., 18.

29. Debussy, letter to André Caplet, August 25, 1909, in *Debussy Letters*, 212.

30. Edgar Allan Poe, "The Domain of Arnheim," in *Selected Tales*, 385.

31. Ibid., 394.

32. Ibid., 397.

33. Edgar Allan Poe, "The Devil in the Belfry," in *Complete Tales and Poems* (New York: Fall River Press, 2012), 290.

34. William Shakespeare, *A Midsummer Night's Dream*, act 3, scene 2, 353 (London: Penguin, 1967), 93.

35. Charles Dickens, *The Pickwick Papers* (New York: Washington Square Press, 1964). All quotes from *The Pickwick Papers* come from this source.

36. Lockspeiser, *Debussy*, 2:247. Lockspeiser quotes Debussy's friend Paul-Jean Toulet on Dickens.

37. Edgar Allan Poe, "The Fall of the House of Usher," in *Selected Tales*, 78. The title of this prelude is already associated with the work of Gabriel Mourey, who had also translated all of Poe's poetry.

38. Edgar Allan Poe, *The Narrative of Arthur Gordon Pym of Nantucket* (Mineola, NY: Dover, 2005), 95.

39. Ibid., 147.

40. Edgar Allan Poe, "Annabel Lee" lines 25 and 26, https://www.poetryfoundation.org/poems-and-poets/detail/44885. Accessed May 8, 2017.

41. Some of the following description quotes from my own article entitled "Debussy: His Preludes and Their Poets," *International Piano* (January/February 2005): 58–62. When I wrote the article many years ago, I knew nothing of the relationships between Debussy, Mourey, and Poe. Returning to it now, I was struck by the quotes I had unknowingly chosen by Mourey and their obvious relevance to Poe.

42. Gabriel Mourey, *Voix éparses* (Paris: Librairie des bibliophiles, 1883), poem 7, lines 2–3 ("mélancholique et froid"), lines 7–8 ("arbres défeuillés / Tremblaient"; "dans le bois solitaire . . . d'indécises pâleurs").

43. Ibid., poem 1, lines 7–8 ("sent gemir sans cesse, avec tous leurs murmures, / Les espoirs, les soupirs et les sanglots humains").

44. Ibid., poem 4, line 6 ("la nuit mystérieuse").

45. Ibid., poem 4, line 11 ("mourir tout espoir de retours").

46. Ibid., poem 6, lines 2 and 7 ("le soir indécisant"; "ces tristes échoes").

47. Debussy, letter to Jacques Durand, July 8, 1910, in *Debussy Letters*, 220.

48. Charles Baudelaire, *Notes nouvelles sur Edgar Poe*, 1857, 7, Feedbooks, http://www.feedbooks.com/.

49. Ibid.; Stéphane Mallarmé, "Le tombeau d'Edgar Poe," Les grands classiques, accessed December 2016, http://poesie.webnet.fr/ ("Aux noirs vols du Blasphème"; "la mort triomphait").

CHAPTER 13

1. Claude Debussy, letter to Louis Laloy, September 10, 1906, in *Debussy Letters*, selected and edited by François Lesure and Roger Nichols, trans. Roger Nichols (Cambridge, MA: Harvard University Press, 1987), 172.

2. Debussy, letter to Robert Godet, February 6, 1911, in *Debussy Letters*, 234.

3. Quoted in "An Open Letter to the Chevalier Gluck," 1905, in *Three Classics in the Aesthetic of Music* (New York: Dover, 1962), 67.

4. Émile Vuillermoz, "Une tasse de thé," *Le mercure musical* (Paris) 1 (November 15, 1905): 505–20, Blue Mountain Project, accessed December 2016, http://bluemountain.princeton.edu/. Also quoted in Edward Lockspeiser, *Debussy: His Life and Mind*, vol. 2 (New York: Macmillan, 1962), 75. "Votre Debussy est le plus encombrant de nos contemporains. . . . Achille Debussy et Alfred Dreyfus ont les deux mêmes initiales. . . . Il n'en faudra peut-être pas davantage pour créer des confusions irréparables dans l'esprit de nos descendants."

5. Raphaël Cor, "M. Claude Debussy et le snobisme contemporain," from *Le cas Debussy*, ed. C. Francis Caillard and José de Bérys (Paris: Bibliothèque du temps présent, 1910), reprinted in Brian Hart, "Le cas Debussy," in *Debussy and His World*, ed. Jane Fulcher (Princeton, NJ: Princeton University Press, 2001), 370.

6. Quoted in Georg Predota, "Bring in the Clowns! Poulenc Sonata for Clarinet and Piano," *Interlude*, January 14, 2013, http://www.interlude.hk/front/bring-in-the-clowns.

7. Debussy, letter to Jacques Durand, August 5, 1915, in *Debussy Letters*, 298; Debussy, letter to Robert Godet, October 14, 1915, in *Debussy Letters*, 305.

8. Claude Debussy, letter to Igor Stravinsky, October 24, 1915, quoted in Glenn Watkins, *Proof through the Night: Music and the Great War* (Berkeley: University of California Press, 2003), 90, from Debussy, *Correspondance*, 361–63. Translated in Igor Stravinsky and Robert Craft, *Conversations with Igor Stravinsky* (Garden City, NY: Doubleday, 1959), 57–59.

9. Claude Debussy, "Rameau," in *Monsieur Croche the Dilettante Hater* (as published by Noel Douglas in 1927, trans. B. N. Langdon Davies, Viking Press, 1928), in *Three Classics in the Aesthetic of Music* (New York: Dover, 1962), 36–37.

10. Erik Satie, in conversation with Debussy in 1891, quoted in Richard Greenan, "Debussy's Nationalism," 4, Academia, accessed March 7, 2017, http://www.academia.edu/, 4.

11. Debussy, letter to Émile Vuillermoz, January 25, 1916, in *Debussy Letters*, 313.

12. Debussy, letter to Nicolas Coronio, [September 1914], in *Debussy Letters*, 293.

13. Ibid.

14. Debussy, letter to Jacques Durand, August 8, 1914, in *Debussy Letters*, 291.

15. See Mary McAuliffe, *Twilight of the Belle Epoque* (Lanham, MD: Rowman & Littlefield, 2014), 315–16, for a more detailed discussion of the casualty list.

16. Debussy, letter to Robert Godet, October 14, 1915, in *Debussy Letters*, 305.

17. Quotes found at "About This Recording: Claude Debussy (1862–1918), Orchestral Works Vol. 6," Naxos, accessed December 2016, https://www.naxos.com/.

18. Debussy, letter, July 22, 1915, quoted in Watkins, *Proof through the Night*, 92. Watkins also points out helpfully that the national anthem is so camouflaged as to be virtually undetectable by the untutored listener.

19. Claude Debussy, letter, July 22, 1915, quoted in Marianne Wheeldon, *Debussy's Late Style* (Bloomington: Indiana University Press, 2009), 52.

20. Claude Debussy, "Preface in the Form of a Letter to *Pour la musique française: Douze causeries*," December 1916, in *Debussy on Music*, collected and introduced by François Lesure, trans. and ed. Richard Langham Smith (New York: Knopf, 1977), 325.

21. See McAuliffe, "Dark Days (1917)," 321–33, in *Twilight of the Belle Epoque*, for descriptions of life in Paris toward the end of the war.

22. Claude Debussy, letter to Gabriel Fauré, February 9, 1917, quoted in the foreword to "*Les soirs illuminés par l'ardeur du charbon*," by Denis Herlin (Paris: Durand, 2003). "Le froid, la course au charbon, toute cette vie de misères domestiques et autres me désemparent tous les jours davantage."

23. The song, "Le balcon," is part of the set *Cinq poèmes de Baudelaire*, written in 1887–1889.

24. Roy Howat, "Rare Debussy Pieces of 1915–17," Roy Howat, accessed December 2016, http://www.royhowat.com/.

25. Debussy, letter to Robert Godet, October 14, 1915, in *Debussy Letters*, 306.

AFTERWORD

1. Marcel Proust, *Swann's Way, Remembrance of Things Past*, trans. C. K. Scott Moncrieff and Terence Klimartin (New York: Knopf Doubleday, 2015), 380. Also available at Google Books, https://books.google.com/. Quotes are taken from the Scott translation.

2. Oscar Wilde, "Intentions," quoted in *The Artist as Critic*, ed. Richard Ellman (New York: Vintage Books, 1968), 389.

3. Charles Baudelaire, *Artificial Paradises*, trans. Stacy Diamond (New York: Carol Publishing, 1996), 50–51.

4. Alex Ross, "Imaginary Concerts," *The New Yorker*, August 24, 2009.

5. Claude Debussy, letter to Jacques Durand, July 8, 1910, in *Debussy Letters*, selected and edited by François Lesure and Roger Nichols, trans. Roger Nichols (Cambridge, MA: Harvard University Press, 1987), 220.

6. Proust, *Swann's Way*, 200.

7. Ibid., 199.

8. Ibid., 201.

9. Ibid.

10. It cannot be a coincidence that these artists were French. Since Louis XIV and before, the French had been identified with a world of sensuality. Taken on the most superficial level, France, still today, is a nation heavily identified with perfumes, wines, delicious food, and fashion. A walk down the streets of central Paris, with the omnipresent displays of beautiful foods, pastries, and high couture leaves one in no doubt as to the provenance of its reputation.

11. Proust, *Swann's Way*, 195.

12. Ibid., 196.

13. Ibid., 309.

14. Ibid., 381.

15. Ibid., 379–80.

16. Ibid., 382.

17. No one has definitively identified the musical origin of Proust's "little phrase," but Lockspeiser makes a case for Debussy's *Quartet*, which Proust found impressive, as an inspiration, if not the actual source. Edward Lockspeiser, *Debussy: His Life and Mind*, vol. 2 (New York: Macmillan, 1962), 93–94. Other, more recent scholarship, has pointed toward Franck, Fauré, and probably most persuasively, Saint-Saëns.

18. Debussy, letter to Ernest Chausson, [early 1894?], in *Debussy Letters*, 62.

19. E. T. A. Hoffmann, "Beethoven's Instrumental Music," in *Musical Writings: Kreisleriana; The Poet and the Composer; Music Criticism*, ed. David Charlton, trans. Martyn Clarke (Cambridge: Cambridge University Press, 1989), 97.

20. Debussy, letter to Henri Gauthier-Villars, October 10, 1896, in *Debussy Letters*, 84.

21. Iris Murdoch, *The Sovereignty of Good* (London: Routledge, 1970). "The most obvious thing in our surroundings which is an occasion for 'unselfing' is what is popularly called beauty." Philosophy for Life, accessed March 20, 2017, http://philosophyforlife.org/.

22. Proust, *Swann's Way*, 383.

Selected Bibliography

Acocella, Joan. "The Love That Kills." *The New Yorker*, September 2, 2013.

Albright, Ann Cooper. *Traces of Light: Absence and Presence in the Work of Loie Fuller*. Middletown, CT: Wesleyan University Press, 2007.

Andersen, Hans Christian. *Andersen's Fairy Tales*. Translated by Mrs. E. V. Lucas and Mrs. H. B. Paull. New York: Grosset & Dunlap, n.d.

Antokoletz, Elliott, and Marianne Wheeldon, eds. *Rethinking Debussy*. New York: Oxford University Press, 2011. https://books.google.com/

Barrie, J. M. *Peter Pan in Kensington Gardens*. Mattituck, NY: Amereon House, n.d.

Baudelaire, Charles. *Artificial Paradises*. 1860. Translated by Stacy Diamond. New York: Carol Publishing, 1996.

———. *The Flowers of Evil*. 1860. Translated by James McGowan. Oxford: Oxford University Press, 1993.

———. *Journaux intimes: Fusées* (1855–1862). Wikisource. Last updated February 7, 2017. Accessed December 2016. https://fr.wikisource.org/.

———. *Notes nouvelles sur Edgar Poe*. 1857. Feedbooks. http://www.feedbooks.com/.

———. *The Painter of Modern Life*. Translated and edited by Jonathan Mayne. London: Phaidon, 1995.

———. *The Parisian Prowler/Le Spleen de Paris: Petits Poems en Prose*. 1862. Translated by Edward K. Kaplan. Athens: University of Georgia Press, 1989.

———. *Paris Spleen: Little Poems in Prose*. Translated by Keith Waldrop. Middletown, CT: Wesleyan University Press, 2009.

———. *Twenty Prose Poems*. Translated by Michael Hamburger. San Francisco: City Lights Books, 1988.

Bellman, Jonathan, ed. *The Exotic in Western Music*. Boston: Northeastern University Press, 1997.

Benjamin, Roger. *Orientalist Aesthetics: Art, Colonialism, and French North Africa, 1880–1930*. Berkeley: University of California Press, 2003.

———. *Renoir and Algeria*. New Haven, CT: Yale University Press (along with Sterling and Francine Clark Art Institute, Williamstown, MA), 2003.

Benjamin, Walter. *The Writer of Modern Life: Essays on Charles Baudelaire*. Edited by Michael W. Jennings. Translated by Howard Eiland, Edmund Jephcott, Rodney Livingston, and Harry Zohn. Cambridge, MA: Belknap Press of Harvard University Press, 2006.

Bloom, Harold, ed. *Modern Critical Interpretations: The Tales of Poe*. New York: Chelsea House, 1987.

Bruhn, Siglind. *Images and Ideas in Modern French Piano Music*. Stuyvesant, NY: Pendragon, 1997.

Brune Blonde: La Chevelure Féminine dans l'Art et le Cinema. Paris: Skira-Flammarion, 2010. Exhibition catalog for *Cinématèque Française*, Paris, October 6, 2010, to January 16, 2011.

Caddy, Davinia. "Parisian Cake Walks." *19th Century Music* 30, no. 3 (Spring 2007): 288–317.

Caffee, Gabrielle L. *The Breton and His World: Requiem for a Culture*. Mobile, AL: Madaloni, 1985.

Clark, T. J. *The Painting of Modern Life: Paris in the Art of Manet and His Followers*. New York: Knopf, 1985.

Cockrell, Dale. *Demons of Disorder: Early Blackface Minstrels and Their World*. Cambridge: Cambridge University Press, 1997.

Cocteau, Jean. *Paris Album, 1900–1914*. Translated by Margaret Crossland. London: W. H. Allen, 1956.

Cortot, Alfred. *French Piano Music*. Translated by Hilda Andrews. New York: Da Capo, 1977.

Debussy, Claude. *Debussy Letters*. Selected and edited by François Lesure and Roger Nichols. Translated by Roger Nichols. Cambridge, MA: Harvard University Press, 1987.

———. *Debussy on Music: The Critical Writings of the Great French Composer Claude Debussy*. Collected and introduced by François Lesure. Translated and edited by Richard Langham Smith. New York: Knopf, 1977.

———. *43 Songs*. Edited by Sergius Kagen. Translated by Edith Braun, Waldo Lyman, and Kathleen Maunsbach. New York: International Music Company, 1951.

———. *La boîte à joujoux*. Paris: Durand & Fils, 1913. International Music Score Library Project. http://imslp.org/.

———. *Lettres, 1884–1918*. Edited by François Lesure. Paris: Hermann, 1980.

———. *Monsieur Croche the Dilettante Hater* (as published by Noel Douglas in 1927, translated by B. N. Langdon Davies, Viking Press, 1928). In *Three Classics in the Aesthetic of Music*. New York: Dover, 1962.

———. *Oeuvres Complètes de Debussy*, Série 1, Volume 5. Préludes, Livre I, Livre II. Edition de Roy Howat avec la collaboration de Claude Helffer. (Paris: Durand-Costellat, 1985).

———. *Pelléas et Mélisande* libretto. Act 3, scene 1. In *Collection of Opera-Librettos*, by G. Schirmer. New York: E. Fromont, 1902; A. Durand & Fils, 1907. International Music Score Library Project. http://imslp.org/.

Debussy: La Musique et les Arts. Paris: Skira-Flammarion, 2012. Exhibition catalog, Musée de l'Orangerie, Paris, February 22–June 11, 2012.

Debussy's Paris: Art, Music, and Sounds of the City. Exhibition catalog, Smith College Museum of Art, February 3–June 10, 2012.

de la Motte Fouqué, Friedrich. *Undine*. Translated by Paul Turner. In *German Romantic Stories*, edited by Frank G. Ryder. New York: Continuum, 1988.

DeVoto, Mark. *Debussy and the Veil of Tonality: Essays on His Music*. Hillsdale, NY: Pendragon, 2004.

Dickens, Charles. *The Pickwick Papers*. New York: Washington Square Press, 1964.

Eliot, T. S. "From Poe to Valéry." *Hudson Review* 2, no. 3 (Autumn 1949): 327–42. http://www.jstor.org/stable/3847788.

Fauser, Annegret. *Musical Encounters at the 1889 Paris World's Fair*. Rochester, NY: University of Rochester Press, 2005.

Field, Geoffrey. *The Evangelist of Race: The Germanic Vision of Houston Stewart Chamberlain*. New York: Columbia University Press, 1981.

Flaubert, Gustave. *Salammbô*. 1862. Lexington, KY: Made in the USA, 2013.

Forster, E. M. *A Passage to India*. 1924. New York: Modern Library, 1939.

Frankenstein, Alfred. "A Curious Literary Progress from Man to Mechanism." *San Francisco Chronicle*, March 11, 1945.

Freud, Sigmund. *The Uncanny*. Translated by David McLintock. London: Penguin, 2003.

Fulcher, Jane F., ed. *Debussy and His World*. Princeton, NJ: Princeton University Press, 2001.

———. *French Cultural Politics and Music: From the Dreyfus Affair to the First World War*. New York: Oxford University Press, 1999.

Fuller, Loie. *Fifteen Years of a Dancer's Life*. London: Herbert Jenkins, 1913. http://archive.org/.

Gide, André. *If It Die*. Translated by Dorothy Bussy from first edition of *Si le grain ne muert*, 1920. Harmondsworth, UK: Penguin, 1982.

———. *The Immoralist*. 1902. Translated by David Watson. Harmondsworth, UK: Penguin, 2000.

Godfrey, Sima. "'Ce père nourricier': Revisiting Baudelaire's Family Romance." *Nineteenth-Century French Studies* 38, nos. 1 and 2 (Fall–Winter 2009–2010): 39–51.

Gold, Arthur, and Robert Fizdale. *Misia: The Life of Misia Sert*. New York: Morrow Quill Paperbacks, 1981.

Goncourt, Edmond de. *The Zemganno Brothers*. 1879. Translated by Leonard Clark and Iris Allam. London: Alvin Redman, 1957.

Gordon, Rae Beth. *Dances with Darwin, 1875–1910: Vernacular Modernity in France*. Aldershot, UK: Ashgate, 2009.

———. "Natural Rhythm: La Parisienne Dances with Darwin, 1875–1910." *Modernism/Modernity* 10, no. 4 (November 2003): 617–56. doi:10.1353/mod.2003.0077.

The Great Parade. New Haven, CT: Yale University Press, 2004. Exhibition catalog, Pierre Théberge, National Gallery of Canada, Ottawa, 2004.

Green, Martin, and John Swan. *The Triumph of Pierrot: The Commedia dell'Arte and the Modern Imagination*. New York: Macmillan, 1986.

Greenan, Richard. "Debussy's Nationalism." Academia. Accessed March 7, 2017. http://www.academia.edu/.

Herlin, Denis. Introduction to "*Les soirs illuminés par l'ardeur du charbon*" by Claude Debussy. Paris: Durand, 2003.

Hoffmann, E. T. A. *Musical Writings: Kreisleriana; The Poet and the Composer; Music Criticism*. Edited by David Charlton. Translated by Martyn Clarke. Cambridge: Cambridge University Press, 1989.

Howat, Roy. *The Art of French Piano Music*. New Haven, CT: Yale University Press, 2009.

Hussey, Andrew. *The French Intifada: The Long War between France and Its Arabs*. London: Macmillan, 2014. Google Books, https://books.google.com/.

Huysmans, Joris-Karl. *Against Nature*. 1884. Translated by Robert Baldick. London: Penguin, 2003.

Jan, Isabelle, and Wyley L. Powell. "Children's Literature and Bourgeois Society in France since 1860." *Yale French Studies*, no. 43 (1969): 57–72.

Jordan, Matthew F. *Le Jazz*. Urbana: University of Illinois Press, 2010.

Kautsky, Catherine. "Debussy: His Preludes and Their Poets." *International Piano* (January–February 2005): 58–62.

Kelly, Barbara L. "Debussy and the Making of a *musicien français: Pelléas*, the Press, and World War I." In *French Music, Culture, and National Identity, 1870–1939*, edited by Barbara L. Kelly. Rochester, NY: University of Rochester Press, 2008.

Kipling, Rudyard. *The Jungle Book*. 1894. Garden City, NY: Doubleday, 1932.

Kundera, Milan. *The Book of Laughter and Forgetting*. New York: Penguin, 1986.

Laforgue, Jules. *Essential Poems and Prose of Jules Laforgue*. Translated and introduced by Patricia Terry. Boston: Black Widow Press, 2010.

———. *Poems*. Translated and introduced by Peter Dale. London: Anvil Press, 2001.

Lehmann, A. G. "Pierrot and Fin de Siècle." In *Romantic Mythologies*, edited by Ian Fletcher. New York: Barnes & Noble, 1967.

Lesure, François. *Debussy*. Geneva: Minkoff & Lattès; New York: Congdon/Lattès, 1980.

Locke, Ralph. *Musical Exoticism: Images and Reflections*. New York: Cambridge University Press, 2009.

Lockspeiser, Edward. *Debussy: His Life and Mind*. Vols. 1 and 2. New York: Macmillan, 1962 and 1965.

Loie Fuller Danseuse de L'art Nouveau. Paris: Éditions de la Réunion des musées nationaux, 2002. Exhibition catalog for exhibition organized by the Musée de l'École de Nancy, May 17–August 19, 2002.

Loti, Pierre. *L'Inde sans les Anglais*. 1903. Paris: Calmann-Lévy, 1903.

Mallarmé, Stéphane. *Collected Poems*. Translated and with a commentary by Henry Weinfield. Berkeley: University of California Press, 1994.

Matisse and the Alhambra, 1910–2010. Granada, Spain: Patronato de la Alhambra y Generalife, 2010. Exhibition catalog. Alhambra, Palace of Charles V, October 15, 2010–February 28, 2011.

McAuliffe, Mary. *Dawn of the Belle Epoque*. Lanham, MD: Rowman & Littlefield, 2011.

———. *Twilight of the Belle Epoque*. Lanham, MD: Rowman & Littlefield, 2014.

McClary, Susan. *Feminine Endings: Music, Gender and Sexuality*. Minneapolis: University of Minnesota Press, 1991.
McQuinn, Julie. "Exploring the erotic in Debussy's Music." In *The Cambridge Companion to Debussy*, edited by Simon Trezise. Cambridge: Cambridge University Press, 2003.
Menand, Louis. "Silence, Exile, Punning: James Joyce's Chance Encounters." *The New Yorker*, July 2, 2012.
Mourey, Gabriel. *Voix éparses*. Paris: Librairie des bibliophiles, 1883.
Munthe, Alex. *Letters from a Mourning City*. 1884. Translated by Maude Valérie White. London: John Murray, 1887.
Murdoch, Iris. *The Sovereignty of Good*. London: Routledge, 1991. Philosophy for Life. Accessed March 20, 2017. http://philosophyforlife.org/.
Nectoux, Jean-Michel. *Harmonie en bleu et or, Debussy, la musique et les arts*. 1898. Paris: Fayard, 2005.
Nichols, Roger. *Debussy Remembered*. London: Faber & Faber, 1992.
———. *The Life of Debussy*. Cambridge: Cambridge University Press, 1998.
Orledge, Robert. *Debussy and the Theatre*. Cambridge: Cambridge University Press, 1982.
Pasler, Jann. *Composing the Citizen: Music as Public Utility in Third Republic France*. Berkeley: University of California Press, 2009.
Peabody, Sue. *"There Are No Slaves in France": The Political Culture of Race and Slavery in the Ancien Régime*. Oxford: Oxford University Press, 1996. Google Books, http://books.google.com/.
Peter, René. *Debussy*. 2nd ed. Paris: Gallimard, 1944.
Picasso et le cirque. Martigny, Switzerland: Fondation Pierre Gianadda, 2006. Exhibition catalog, Museu Picasso, November 15, 2006–February 18, 2007; Fondation Pierre Gianadda, March 9–June 10, 2007.
Poe, Edgar Allan. *Complete Tales and Poems*. New York: Fall River Press, 2012.
———. *The Narrative of Arthur Gordon Pym of Nantucket*. 1838. Mineola, NY: Dover, 2005.
———. "The Philosophy of Composition." *Graham's Magazine* 28, no. 4 (April 1846): 163–67. http://www.eapoe.org/.
———. *Selected Tales*. London: Penguin, 1994.
Proust, Marcel. *Swann's Way, Remembrance of Things Past*. Translated by C. K. Scott Moncrieff and Terence Kilmartin. New York: Vintage Books, 1989.
Puaux, René. *Le beau voyage*. Paris: Librairie Payot et Cie, 1917.
Rackham, Arthur. *Once upon a Time: The Fairy-Tale World of Arthur Rackham*. Edited by Margery Darrell. London: Book Club Associates, 1978.
Renan, Ernest. *Souvenirs d'enfance et de jeunesse*. Paris: Bibliothèque de Cluny, Librairie Armand Colin a Paris, 1959.
Roberts, Paul. *Images: The Piano Music of Claude Debussy*. Portland, OR: Amadeus, 1996.
Rosenthal, David. *The Near East in French Painting*. Rochester, NY: University of Rochester Press, 1982.

Ross, Alex. "Imaginary Concerts: The Music of Fictional Composers." *The New Yorker*, August 24, 2009.

Said, Edward W. *Orientalism*. New York: Random House, 1978.

Sand, Maurice. *Masques et Bouffons (Comédie Italienne)*. Paris: Michel Levy Freres, 1860.

Schmitz, E. Robert. *The Piano Works of Claude Debussy*. New York: Dover, 1966.

Schwartz, Vanessa R. *Spectacular Realities: Early Mass Culture in Fin-de-Siècle Paris*. Berkeley: University of California Press, 1998.

Shakespeare, William. *A Midsummer Night's Dream*. London: Penguin, 1967.

Silverman, Devora L. *Art Nouveau in Fin-de-Siècle France*. Berkeley: University of California Press, 1989.

Sinsky, Carolyn. "Loie Fuller." Modernism Lab at Yale University. Accessed December 2016. http://modernism.research.yale.edu/.

Storey, Robert F. *Pierrot: A Critical History of a Mask*. Princeton, NJ: Princeton University Press, 1978.

———. *Pierrots on the Stage of Desire*. Princeton, NJ: Princeton University Press, 1985.

Three Classics in the Aesthetic of Music: Monsieur Croche the Dilettante Hater by Claude Debussy; *Sketch of a New Esthetic of Music* by Ferruccio Busoni; *Essays before a Sonata* by Charles E. Ives. New York: Dover Publications, 1962.

Toutonghi, Pauls. "App for the Ancients." *New York Times Book Review*, August 12, 2012.

Vallas, Léon. *Claude Debussy: His Life and Works*. Translated by Máire O'Brien and Grace O'Brien. London: Oxford University Press, 1933.

Verlaine, Paul. "Pierrot" (1868). In *Paul Verlaine: Seventy-Three Poems*. Translated by A. S. Kline. Poetry in Translation, 2010. Accessed March 12, 2017. http://www.poetryintranslation.com/.

Vuillermoz, Émile. "Une tasse de thé." *Le Mercure musical* (Paris) 1 (November 15, 1905): 505–20. Blue Mountain Project. Accessed December 2016. http://bluemountain.princeton.edu/.

Watkins, Glenn. *Proof through the Night: Music and the Great War*. Berkeley: University of California Press, 2003.

———. *Pyramids at the Louvre: Music, Cultures, and Collage From Stravinsky to the Postmodernists*. Cambridge, MA: Harvard University Press, 1994.

Wheeldon, Marianne. *Debussy's Late Style*. Bloomington: Indiana University Press, 2009.

White, Edmund. *The Flâneur*. New York: Bloomsbury, 2001.

Wilde, Oscar. *The Picture of Dorian Gray*. 1891. New York: Dover, 1993.

———. *Salomé*. 1891. In *Penguin Plays*. Baltimore: Penguin, 1967.

Zola, Émile. *L'Assommoir*. Translated by Margaret Mauldon. Oxford: Oxford University Press, 2009.

———. *Nana*. Translated by George Holden. London: Penguin, 1972.

General Index

Page references in italics indicate illustrations or musical examples.

Index of Debussy's Works

About the Author

Catherine Kautsky is an active performer lauded by the *New York Times* as a pianist whose "music spoke directly to the listener, with neither obfuscation nor pretense." She is chair of the keyboard department at Lawrence University in Appleton, Wisconsin, and previously chaired the keyboard department at the University of Wisconsin–Madison, winning honors at both institutions for research, performance, and teaching. She has played and taught across the United States, as well as in Asia, Africa, South America, and Europe, and is known for the lively commentary that accompanies her music. A sabbatical year spent in Paris stimulated her interest in all things French, and thus this book was born. Its musical counterpart is a CD of the complete Debussy *Preludes* recently issued by Centaur.

She lives in Wisconsin with her husband, Daniel Hausman, a professor of philosophy, and their beautiful German shepherd/collie, Itzhak. She's the proud mom of two grown sons, both social scientists like almost everyone else in her family. Her great-grandfather, Karl Kautsky, was a famous German Social-Democrat who worked with Marx, Engels, and Rosa Luxemburg; his genetic legacy no doubt drew her toward the gnarly social issues addressed in this volume.